HOW TO OVERCOME ANXIETY & EFFECTIVELY COMMUNICATE IN RELATIONSHIPS (4 IN 1)

SKILLS, ACTIVITIES, QUESTIONS & TEACHINGS TO HELP YOU BEAT JEALOUSY & INSECURITY & DEEPEN YOUR CONNECTION & INTIMACY

FAYE PALMER

DEVON HOUSE
PRESS

CONTENTS

HOW TO OVERCOME ANXIETY & INSECURITIES IN RELATIONSHIPS (2 IN 1)

EFFECTIVE COMMUNICATION IN RELATIONSHIPS & COUPLE SKILLS (2 IN 1)

HOW TO OVERCOME ANXIETY & INSECURITIES IN RELATIONSHIPS (2 IN 1)

IMPROVE YOUR COMMUNICATION SKILLS, CONTROL JEALOUSY & CONQUER NEGATIVE THINKING & BEHAVIOR PATTERNS

INTRODUCTION

Money, a big house, a good job... Are these the "things" that make our life good? Ask many people and you will find that this might well be what they *believe.* But then, even if you just dig a bit deeper, you will find that most people know what sociologists and psychologists have been saying for ages: *your quality of life depends primarily on your relationships!*

Think about it. You can have money, a big house, and even a super job... But if you don't have anyone to share your life with... The consequence is obvious: they become worthless. On the other hand, with good relationships, even a less affluent life, a smaller house, and a humbler job can become pleasant.

I personally look back at the many jobs I have had (from working in a factory to pay for my studies to academic positions) and, you know what? The ones I remember with most fondness are not necessarily the well-paid ones. No! Do the same... Think about your past jobs... Or even schools... What do you remember most vividly about them? Your school mates and your work colleagues! And my favorite jobs in the past are those where relationships were good.

But here is a question for you. How many relationships (of all kinds) have you had in your life? Don't tell me; I am not a nosey person... I just wish you to think about them. And how many have you "saved till now"? Very few, I'd expect. And you are no exception.

There is a number being bandied about (also in Hellen Chen's *Love Seminar*) saying that 85% of "dates" ends up in failure. I can't confirm that it is true (we'll get to why later...), but for sure many, if not most, of our relationships fails.

And there is more... *Even successful relationships are not without stress, anxiety, and problems.* In fact, we can quite safely say that the percentage of relationships that have never had a problem must be very close to 0.000 something percent...

And now let's think about our lives. *How impactful are relationship problems in our lives?* Again, we don't need to go far to state that a *good part of our day is spent thinking (or worrying) about our social and personal relationships.*

There are psychological and sociological studies that show how *social relationships impact:*

- *Work and school performance*

- *Our response to stress and disease (even our immune system)*
- *Our mental state (including the ability to deal with dementia in our old age).*

All in all, they can affect most areas of our life. And we all know it, we have tried it on our skin. After a breakup, you just can't function. Going to work is a nightmare as is going to school. You often lose your appetite, you lose vitality, everything turns gray, cold and negative...

Oomph, what a chilling thought... So, let's push it away now... *Is there a solution to all these relationship problems?*

Suspense...

Yes! But hold on – I am not going to give you a magic wand in this book. Like with all personal and interpersonal problems, there are tried and tested solutions to problems, but they do require application, skills, and even time to work.

You will have to put in the time, but this book will teach you all the rest.

We will use *psychology, sociology* but also other fields like *linguistics* to give you two things:

- *A deep and thorough understanding of how relationships work (or fail)*
- *A toolkit of strategies and "tricks" to improve your relationships.*

I am actually excited because there is so much I want to show you in this book… Did you know that there are simple concepts that can turn sour relationships into fruitful ones? Did you know that you can actually change a relationship simply by looking at it with a different (and more experienced) eye?

Then again, how many times have you had the feeling that "this is not what s/he actually means" but you have been able to do something about it? After reading this book, you will! And those little daily "glitches" that feel like "wearing out" of your relationships… How can you stop them? You are about to see!

And so much more…

But there are *practical tips* too I can't wait to give you… You see, like all us professionals, I read sociology and psychology, and even linguistics in my academic studies… But it was only once I became a mentor for young people (some with very serious problems too) that I developed all those little strategies that I could just give as a quick solution to some problems.

Don't get me wrong. A quick solution can be temporary, but sometimes you do need it just to de-escalate a situation. Sometimes it can be as simple as the choice of words you use… And if you had seen the distress on the faces of these young people… And then the smile when they came back to the next session and said, "You know what? It did work!"

This then allowed me to move to the next step, which is to repair the deeper wounds in a relationship. It's like trying to reach the heart when we are still wearing an armor... Better start "peeling off" the problems like an onion...

There are (sometimes small and simple) changes in behavior, language, even body language, and life patterns that you can use to transform a relationship from negative to positive. Did I tell you that I studied *positive psychology* with arguably the greatest authority in the world, Dr. Ilona Boniwell? It is a huge field, but the key concept is simple, and we will use it in this book too. No, sorry – *you will use it* to change not only your relationships, but also to improve how you feel about yourself.

You see, our personal history gives us a lot of "personal insecurities"... These then reflect in our relationships... But if you want to have long term effects, we need to address these insecurities as well. Then, even at the next relationship, you will start with a better footing already...

Most of us cannot even see how *our insecurities have effects on others...* Like Sheila (the name is false for privacy reasons) ... She is one of the young people I told you about. She was basically scared of being judged for her family background... And that meant that she kept others "at a distance". She wasn't actually aware that she was doing it though...

I must say that she was very receptive when I pointed out to her that her approach was a bit aggressive to start with... Well, she did change it, and so did her life... Last time I saw her... She did look like a happy woman (she had grown up); her insecurities gone, she now showed her strength of character through an amazing appearance, very artistic and colorful. It was a bit like watching Cinderella dressed for the ball…

Ok, I can't get into the heat of it all now. But I can hardly hold myself.

This is going to be the journey of a lifetime for many people. From understanding the basics of psychology and sociology to learning how to cope with very specific situations, this book follows a complete path to improving personal but also social relationships. And all of them: love relationships, family relationships, friends, colleagues and working relationships, occasional relationships… All of them follow similar patterns, though personal relationships and romantic ones especially are the most influential in our lives.

Yes, it will take some time to learn all this. In the end this book compresses years of study and practice into a few hundred pages… But all will be presented clearly, and you will remember this book as "a good and pleasant read".

Now, count the days from this moment to the end of this book… Every day is a day away from having all the tools you need to make your relationships shine! And now count every day you can have *without all these problems, anxiety, and insecurities about your relationships...*

My question to you is this: is it worth wasting any more time? Shouldn't you start to improve your life right now? Is it really worth it to delay your life changing journey for another day? I don't think so… The sooner you read this book, the more smiles you will have in your life – to give and to receive…

And we go back to the beginning: *your quality of life...* Read this book now and your quality of life will *very soon* start improving. I promise you that you will see the first results in weeks or even days. So... shall we start?

1

WHAT ARE RELATIONSHIPS? UNDERSTANDING THE BASICS

A house is made of walls. A table is made of wood (plastic etc.) and it has legs and a flat surface… Easy. But when it comes to an abstract concept like "love" or "happiness" or – related – "relationships" it becomes harder to pinpoint the meaning.

This is not because the meaning is imprecise, or the definitions lacking. It's because an abstract concept has some discretion in the way we apply it. Let me explain… Is romantic love, in fact "love"? Surely yes. But "love of Nature" for example, may mean a lot to a tree hugger (term which I don't use as derogatory – on the contrary!) and something very different to a game hunter… And how about when we say, "I love these shoes"?

Similarly, if you have a partner, for sure you have a relationship with him or her. Surely with your family members… But most of us already find it uncomfortable to use the term "relationship" with work colleagues. Yet we have relationships with objects, like our vehicles, even, as we said, our shoes (not all of us, to be fair).

So, what are we really talking about here?

What Is a Relationship?

You will be surprised to know that "relationship" can be defined in many ways, but maybe the one with most "potential" for meaning is this:

A relationship is ***the way*** *in which two or more people, animals, or things are connected.*

So we cannot look at relationships as "things" but as:

- Ways
- States
- Processes

Going to an extreme example (from our perspective), relationships are states: "green and red are complementary". "Good and evil are opposites". We use relationships to describe the state of things. But even if we say, "Carole and Mohammed are wife and husband," we talk about the relative states of the two people.

I know that it looks like I have gone to the other "pole" of the meaning of the word, but bear with me... hold on to this because we will come back to it. (And no, "pole and bear" were not meant to be a pun...)

But a relationship, for most of our personal lives, is mainly a *process*. It is the *way in which we interact with people (and how we feel about it) in our daily lives.*

So, if the word "relationship" is abstract, it actually describes a form of practice. With no practical "living of the relationship" the relationship does not exist. Oddly enough this is why we sooner or later disconnect from old relationships...

I don't want to bring up negative thoughts, so I will ask you to recall your oldest friend. Not the oldest one you have now... that smiling face from your early years... Surely you still have an emotional attachment to that experience – when you recall it!

But because it's been years (decades) since you last saw your friend, you are no longer in a steady relationship with him or her... *The practical side of the relationship, the "living it" has gone.*

Looking at your relationships as "processes" already gives you a different perspective, doesn't it? We need to pause on this point, because it is a life changing concept.

Relationships as States and Relationships as Processes

John and Greta got married 25 years ago today. Today, in fact, they decided to celebrate their silver wedding anniversary re-enacting their wedding, with vows and all...

And this is the text of their wedding vows:

"I Greta take thee John as my wedded husband, to have and to hold you from this day forward, for better or for worse, for rich for poor,

in sickness and in health etc." (No, "etc." is not actually in the vows) ...

These are the classical vows people take when they get married. And I put some verbs in italics: "take, have, hold" for a reason: the first expresses the starting of a state, the other two the preservation of a state.

Brenda and Joshua too are celebrating their silver anniversary and they read their vows too. But they wrote their own and they include phrases like "I will *love* you forever", "I promise to *help* you" etc... You can see from the verbs that they see their relationship more as a process, not just a state.

And we have come to the source of many relationship problems!

Looking back, many people recalling their wedding vows will also think, "It was not what I had expected it to be". But we live in a world where fairy tales and romantic comedies end with the sentence, "And they lived happily ever after". What matters is that Cinderella married the Prince Charming. That's it. The bond is formed, it is an immutable state, and the story is over.

Can you see the problem? Society fools us into believing that relationships are "states" that cannot (or should not) change. Imagine a child (especially girls, but society is structurally sexist) ... She grows up reading Cinderella, Snow White, Sleeping Beauty, the Beauty and the Beast...

You see, these stories (as do *Pride and Prejudice, Bridget Jones's Diaries* and all romantic movies) tell an *archetype* (a basic story, a basic concept, a basic version of reality): *"the process is in finding the relationship but once you establish it it will be a state, it will always be the same and never change".*

This is so true of romantic relationships for so many people. People walk into them with expectations, they imagine themselves twenty years from now – yes, with children – but with exactly *the same relationship as now!* We know it is impossible... But this is the story we are told to believe, or at least to pursue.

So, when things change, what happens?

In most cases, *people find it hard to admit that the reality is not the same as the "dream" (or myth,* should we say?) You see, it is hard to accept that a "state may change". And if our wedding is a state, when it changes, we are out of our depth, we don't know what to do about it, and, very often, *we end up in denial.*

Oddly enough this experience is more common with women. Boys are not so much exposed to the same archetype as women. Stories for boys, studies show, are full of "action", "processes" and "performative verbs". Stories for girls are full of "adjectives", "states" and "passive verbs".

You can never stress enough the influence that what we experience (read, see, hear, feel etc.) as children and adolescents has on our adult life. And this is really at the core of much psychology, as you will know. They are *not* "just children's stories" ... They shape how we see and interpret the world and, above all, what we expect from our lives...

Now to the *"empowerment"* side of it... if you stop seeing your relationship as a "fixed state" and you start seeing it as a "process" then you are *free to build it and improve it.*

Now, let's look at these two statements:

1. *A relationship is a blank canvas to paint together.*
2. *A relationship is a fixed bond that needs to be preserved at all costs.*

Now...

1. Which of these do you agree with more?
2. To what degree?
3. What do your relationships look like, a) or b)? Note, each relationship is different.
4. Which one has more potential?
5. Which one do you feel more comfortable with?
6. Can you turn a) into b) and the other way round?

Get a cup of tea, relax, mull over the questions at your time and then we'll meet again right here, ok?

...

How was your cup of tea? Let's go through these points calmly together...

To start with, question i). *Do not feel embarrassed if you chose b).* I know it is by now clear that this is not *what relationships ought to be*. But for most of us this is what relationships look like "on the ground". And for many of us, this is all relationships have ever been. We'll come to that when we look at relationships and culture...

What matters is that by now you know that a relationship should be more similar to a blank canvas than a bond. Even if you understand it purely on an "ideal" basis, that's absolutely fine and nothing more is expected of you.

ii.) You may imagine your ideal relationship as very much like a canvas or "more like a canvas but with a bond in it". You don't need to eliminate the "state" or "bond" understanding of relationships. It can coexist with the "canvas" or "journey" concept.

Problems arise when the "canvas" concept disappears completely. In *any successful relationship there needs to be flexibility, open doors, and the potential to improve – and that means changing!*

We will see in detail that *many of us are scared of change in relationships.* But this is often *the reason why relationships fail.* For the time being, we will not develop this point much further, but we'll come to it in a lot of detail very, very soon. Just hold onto the key concept for now.

iii.) You will most likely have some relationships that are more like a canvas and others more like bonds, and many degrees in between. This is to show that the two elements often coexist in many relationships.

But it is also good for you to *learn to put the relationships you have on this scale, on this line...* That will be very useful because it is *much easier to change, improve, or repair a "canvas" relationship than a "bond" relationship.*

On the whole, *friendships are more "canvas" while family relationships are more "bond"*. This may not be everybody's case, but it's a very common tendency, or pattern. As to relationships with partners, well... Some are more "canvas" (especially at the beginning), some are more "bond" and very often when they turn "bond" they also start to deteriorate. The "marriage" thing is more than a comedy troupe...

This also answers point iv.) *All relationships have potential.* This potential depends on many factors (individual potential, affinity, cultural context, life events etc....). However, *it is easier to express the potential of "canvas" relationships.*

If you see your relationship as a "bond", it is already everything it is going to be. You may put things in it, like you do with a container... It will hold memories, other bonds (those with children, e.g.) and property and the family pet. But by definition it won't be easy to change the very relationship itself.

Fortunately, very, very few relationships are 100% bond (business partnerships are, but we are not primarily concerned with them here). If you are thinking about improving a relationship and it is "very much bond", my advice to you is to *start looking for canvas elements with it now, or as soon as possible.*

Those will be the elements you will use to correct, improve, change, or reshape the relationship.

You see that even if we have to "talk theory" we have moved straight into it?

Knowing which sides, aspects, elements, and patterns of a relationship you can successfully change is the first step you need to take.

The next point, v.), or "Which do you feel more comfortable with?" is actually a critical one. I fully understand if you said, "Actually, I am more comfortable with "bond" relationships." However, if this is the case, try to find it in you to *be comfortable with **some change**, with **some "canvas"**.*

There is no other solution. But I'll give you some very good news: *you will always change a relationship by degrees.* And another piece of great news: *you can change your relationship also by very small, manageable steps that make your progress easy to accept, actually seamless.*

The same applies to changes you need to bring to ***your own role, attitude, habits, communication etc. within the relationship***.

This is in fact a very important rule. If you go to counseling, even couples counseling, you will never get home one day and say, "Wow, the whole of my life just changed in 50 minutes!" No, that's not how it works. Your perspective on life can change in matter of minutes; that's why we have epiphanies. But the actual daily grind... No...

Good non traumatic and permanent change happens slowly. In fact, the softer and more seamless the change is (especially in relationships), the more it sticks and the more efficient the counsellor has been.

If you are not confident with change, therefore, don't worry! You will work at your own pace, not just with this book, but with the relationship you want to change. Actually, my *absolute advice is to avoid drastic and traumatic changes at all costs.*

There are many reasons for this:

- You don't want your relationship to become a "bumpy" one.
- You have a responsibility towards your partner, or the other person/people. You risk upsetting them with sudden big changes.
- You want to have room to step back in case something does not work.
- You need to reduce the unforeseen consequences to a minimum.

So, if you are, understandably, wary of change, I hope you feel a bit reassured and more comfortable with it now.

What is more, *we often fear change because we don't feel in control of it.* We don't know what the end result will be. But this is by *no means* what we are going to do with this book. *What you will achieve is* ***controlled change.*** This is change that goes:

- *In the direction you want.*
- *Where you want.*
- *At the pace you want.*

And finally, we get to point vi.) – yes, you can turn a canvas into a bond and a bond into a canvas. But this point and the point before, which deal with "changing relationships" deserve more detailed discussion.

Changing Your Relationship from "Canvas" to "Bond" and Vice Versa

Philip and Adele have been married for 40 years now. When they got married they dreamed of setting up their own homestead, but then, life was not too kind on them. Lack of money, lack of opportunities and even the fact that decades ago you could not research your project on the Internet… well, all these combined mean that they now live in a flat in a big town.

In the evenings, they mostly spend time in front of the television, and they bicker over small things most of the time… They still like animals and plants but all they do is look after their three cats…

Let's look at their story (which of course is an example) – actually, at the story of their relationship. You see the canvas that never was? The homestead was a working dream, a lifestyle dream… But it was also a *relationship dream. Because it did not work out financially, their relationship's potential was never fulfilled.*

Instead, the television "stepped in" and took that "space", that "time" that was set aside for the potential of their relationship. It is now the TV (society) that is painting their relationship (gray) instead of them.

How many people like Philip and Adele do you know personally yourself? I bet loads. I bet most of your neighbors are in that situation. I bet most people past 35-40 you know now have their private time controlled by the television.

In the case of Philip and Adele, a "canvas" has turned into a "bond", made of routine actions, controlled by some media company, but still a bond, static relationship. Also note that *the television is now in control of part of their communication.* It both dictates what they talk about, prompts them, and filters their communication times.

What could they do to change this? In this particular case, you would need them to realize that they can still "paint their relationship" even outside their lifestyle dream. The "third person" or element of their relationship was Nature, so... Leaving Nature outside has left a gap, and that gap was filled by society.

In fact, *it is very easy and common to turn a "canvas" into a "bond" relationship.* This is for many reasons, or better *forces at play over our relationships:*

- *Society tends to turn all relationships into bonds through financial, social, cultural forces.* Just the fact that your life becomes a routine means that you are stuck in a pattern, and your relationship will adapt to that daily, repetitive pattern... That alone becomes a "bond" and produces a static relationship.
- *We naturally adapt to new situations, including relationships.*
- *We naturally tend to preserve what we have (so we turn our relationships into static).*

- *Sometimes it's just easier to leave things as they are, or we do not know how to change them.*

In some couples, then, the idea of "changing the relationship" in itself is embarrassing. There is a social taboo... Imagine an old couple who suddenly decides to change all their ways, rediscover their passion etc. ... I am sure we privately would feel *proud of them.* But in many places, neighbors would start gossiping, the idea of "not aging gracefully" still means a lot to many people etc....

So, people may be embarrassed, also with the partner. And even saying, "Listen, we need to change our relationship," needs some courage. Going to couples or relationship counseling is still seen as "having problems" rather than "finding solutions" by many people. Many of us, for social and cultural reasons, are *so afraid of admitting the problem that they cannot even consider finding a solution.*

But if changes from "canvas" to "bond" (*dynamic to static*) are common and driven by society, how about the other way round? *Changing a relationship from static to dynamic takes effort and conscious steps.* And this has two sides of it:

- On the one hand, *you need to work at it, invest time, energy, resources etc.*
- On the other hand, *you can control this process and lead it where you want it to go!*

You see that we have come full circle? *Changing your relationship from static to dynamic is also a way of taking control of your life.*

In fact, *relationships that are too static or too rigid often end up being a burden on one or all of the members.* People who complain about the "strict father" when they are not just adults, in most cases such relationships have impacts that keep us "going back to them" even when we are old and retired... The examples are really many...

But now you know that I'm asking for a bit of effort, let's relax for a second... Let's go back to our example of Philip and Adele... What would you do to help them?

I would say that to start with, they need to identify the reason why their relationship has fossilized. And that's because their working life didn't work out as they wanted.

This, to start with, will free them up. You see, in many cases *we feel guilty about the state of our relationship and that prevents us from improving it.* But it is no one's fault if their lifestyle dream did not come true...

Removing any sense of guilt from the partner opens the most beautiful doors in a relationship. I hope you will treasure this, and I will remind you of this.

Next, well, we need to reinsert the third element! Ok, they won't have a homestead, but their relationship's potential still needs to express itself. And it still can, but it will need an alternative route, an alternative place, an alternative project...

Maybe they can go and help at the local city farm? Ok, it's not like having your own homestead, but it has similar *opportunities for their relationship.* The TV certainly does not.

And here is another little point I would wish you to take with you. *When a shared project fails, the members of the relationship should not attach the future of their relationship to it. Instead, they should look for a plan B, an alternative project which allows their relationship's potential to flourish.*

In the end, how many times have you had a "practical project", but the "hidden agenda" was the relationship involved? We do it as children when we invite friends to play at our homes. We do it when we invite someone out to a romantic dinner (come on, you didn't actually go for the entrées...)

The problem with long term relationships is that we then end up forgetting the "hidden agenda" and it becomes hidden to ourselves. This is what happen to Philip and Adele... They now need to rediscover their own original plan, which was for themselves and their relationship, not just a working plan...

Anxiety, Insecurities, Static and Dynamic Relationships

Let's tie these concepts together. You see, I did not introduce these two concepts of relationships just because they are fundamental archetypes... No, *these perspectives are also at the roots of how you feel about your relationship.*

So far, in fact, we have used the practical, the actual "living the relationship" aspect as the starting ground of our conversation (ok, I know, I talk more than you do... But in your mind, I am sure you converse with this book...) Now, we need to *start looking at the emotional dimension of relationships.*

Do you remember when I asked you to recall your school friend? Fine, the actual relationship does not have physical realization. You don't meet, you may not even know what's happened to him or her... (assuming you did not get married in the meantime, but you get my point...) But *one aspect of the relationship lasts much longer than its daily realization: the emotional one.*

Think about a great friendship from your past and you won't materialize the person in front of your eyes, no, but *the feeling will still be present and as real as back in the days.* Maybe it is less strong, but the feeling persists.

We enter the field of philosophy when we say that *feelings have an extemporal dimension.* What do we mean? We mean that they are not tied to time. If you stub your toe, the physical pain will last for as long as it needs then disappear. But *feelings exist even in the absence of what causes them: once you have felt them, they are forever yours.*

And, of all feelings, shall we talk about love? How many types of love have you felt in your life? The Greeks had *four words for love... "Eros"* is passionate and romantic love; *"storge"* is the love you have for family members; *"phileo"* is brotherly love, the idea is that of "friendship love"; finally, *"agape",* difficult to define, but similar to "disinterested love" or "unconditional love"...

This tells us one thing at a basic level: the Greeks attributed more importance to love than we do. Where languages have many words for one concept, it is because that concept is important to them (Inuits have more than 50 words for "snow" – well, of course, they are surrounded by it, their homes are made of ice and snow, they use it to drink etc....)

It is telling that in English we have one word that you can use quite generally to say a wide range of things, from, "You are my friend," to "I am passionately in love with you" ... But I wonder how many people actually feel confident in using the word "love" at the height of intimacy and passion...

Oddly enough most of us are more at ease using this word with someone who is just a bit more than an acquaintance than with our partner. Not all of us, by any means. But if you do feel embarrassed with using that word, *don't blame yourself.* It is society which teaches us that expressing feelings is "unmanly", "childish", "not appropriate", "a sign of weakness" and so forth...

Now we are on this point... ***Never blame yourself or your partner(s) for the responsibilities of culture and society***. These are such powerful influences on your life that freeing yourself from them is almost impossible, especially on your own. ***Society and culture are often the source of anxiety in relationships.***

So, we were saying... Even within the same type of love, you will have different "shades", or "flavors" or "tones" etc. You may love your brother and your mother equally in degree, but the exact "taste of the feeling" is different. With your past partners, if you have had more than one, you will know that *each love tastes, or feels, different.*

Having said this, however, ***society and culture promote static, even "off the peg" relationship patterns.*** This has a deep functional purpose. When you board a plane, for example, you already know how to behave. We meet many people every day and if we didn't have a "ready-made rule book" to go by, we would not know how to behave.

So, we have a simple "how to behave with the Vicar" set of rules but also "how to behave with the shop assistant", "how to behave with the teacher", "bus driver" ... the list goes on! You can see the practicality of all this in a society like ours...

But... The fact is that this societal "ready-made relationships" often affect or border into *our personal and private relationships.* In the past (and in many countries) the relationship between husband and wife was dictated by strict social rules. To many of us, this is quite striking, but even in the USA or Europe, our parents and grandparents took it for granted. *Entering a formal wedding meant accepting rules that society put on the couple!*

There were even laws that said what you could and could not do with your husband or wife (adultery was a crime not long ago; and it is still unacceptable to many cultural groups). ***This of course puts pressure on people who enter a relationship. All the expectations that society puts on a relationship are a source of anxiety.***

And here we come to the key point: ***both the static and the dynamic sides of relationships can be causes of anxiety and/or insecurity.***

This very much depends on how you relate you relate to these aspects. Yes, it means "how you relate to your relationship" ... It's not a tongue twister...

- *You may feel anxious and insecure because the* ***balance of static and dynamic*** *in your relationship does not suit you.*
- *In a* ***very static relationship,*** *you will feel the burden of the expectations it carries. Many people feel they are not up to them, which is a major source of anxiety and insecurity.*
- *In a* ***very dynamic relationship,*** *you may feel that you do not have those clear guidelines (rules), those parameters and reassurances (that it will last, for example) you need. This can be a cause of anxiety and insecurity.*

So, before you jump the gun and decide idealistically, ***you need to strike the right balance between static and dynamic in your relationship between you and your partner(s).*** If ideally you would like a "free love" super-dynamic relationship, for example... Well, for many people that is as disappointing as the Cinderella story, in fact. It is not easy to achieve. It is idealistically fantastic, but maybe your partner is not so keen, maybe you too will suffer from a relationship that has so few steady points, if any at all...

Like with all things in life, it is not a matter of "black and white". It is a matter of delicate shades and hues of all the colors of the rainbow.

Even the canvas... It's not easy, but what you need to do is ***strike a balance in your relationship keeping in mind:***

- ***What you wish for.***
- ***What you need.***
- ***What you can achieve.***
- ***What your partner wishes for.***
- ***What your partner needs.***
- ***What your partner can achieve.***

This is along all the lines of static/dynamic, but also open/closed, intensive/relaxed, mutually dependent/mutually independent etc.... All things we will see very soon.

Remember in a relationship, everything you do affects your partner, as researchers and psychologists Zeider, Heimberh and Iida say in 'Anxiety Disorders in Intimate Relationships: A Study of Daily Processes in Couples' appeared in the peer reviewed *Journal of Abnormal Psychology* in February 2010, there is a:

... "cross-partner effect, such that on days when wives experienced increased anxiety, their husbands were more likely to report a reduction in positive qualities of the relationship."

This, in a way, confirms that relationships work as processes. What you do within it has an impact on the other people involved and on the relationship itself. At the same time, it is easier to understand the cause and consequence dynamics of relationships if we look at them from this perspective and not as states.

Then of course, ***changing your relationship may include changing yourself too,*** *and in most cases, it is necessary.* ***But now that you know that your anxieties and insecurities mostly come from the "structure" (dynamics) of the relationship itself, however, you can start putting some insecurities and anxiety aside!***

This is an important first step.

Now, don't you feel that things are starting to change already? Can you see how fast your perspective of relationships has changed? I am sure that you have seen doors open in your mind and in your life when reading this chapter. If you came to this book with the idea that "certain things cannot be changed," now for sure you see that there is a way, but it involves changing how we understand relationships.

I promised you this was the case, and now I am sure you feel much more positive and confident.

But we are at the beginning of a long journey, and next, well, let's say we need to start reading "road signs", or distinguishing different types of relationships.

2

TYPES OF RELATIONSHIPS AND ANXIETY

Sheila wakes up and her partner Stephen is already out of bed, making her breakfast (back to Cinderella and fairy tales!) She wakes up their child, Tom, who needs to go to school. She then spends some time chatting on a famous social network, before she sets off to work. While Stephen does the school run, Sheila goes for a quick coffee at a local café, then she gets the train with the usual fellow travelers and has a few words with them. She finally walks into the office and greets her colleagues, but today is a very special day... She strides into her boss's office, because she has something important to tell him...

A typical day... Actually, a typical hour or two in the morning... How many relationships have you spotted in this story? Ok, I'll help you. It's seven different groups of relationships and an unspecified number of actual relationships. We do not know how many her colleagues and her fellow travelers are...

We can see how *relationships are all pervasive in most people's lives.* But there is more: ***there is a wide range of types of relationships.*** This is true on so many levels! In fact, we may even venture to say that "there are as many types of relationships as there are actual relationships". But this is not very practical, because we'd end up with billions (if not trillions) of groups, categories, or types. It's a bit like when people ask you, "What type of person are you?" If you answer, "Every individual is unique," – well you *are* right, but you are not being helpful, are you?

So, we need a way of putting relationships into groups. And there are many reasons for this... One, which is at the core of our book, follows this question: imagine Sheila talking to her son, Tom, then to the fellow travelers and finally to her boss. Will she use the same language?

The answer is no. It's still English, but the choice of words, the tone, the register (formal and informal) and many other things will change. In fact, we can say that ***each (type of) relationship has its own language.***

We have a special way of relating to and talking to different people... Even the online chat Sheila had before going out has its language, doesn't it? The way you speak to children, to a bus driver rather than a friend, to your parents etc. is always different, sometimes in a very marked way.

Relationships and Understanding Anxiety

What is more, ***each type of relationship has its anxieties and its insecurities.*** Now, there is not a precise list for each type of relationship. This is not physics... But *some types of relationships are more likely to cause anxiety and insecurities in certain ways, situations and because of specific reasons.*

An example will make it clearer... Let's go back to Sheila... Her son, Tom, has some learning difficulties. What do you think will be Sheila's anxieties and insecurities? Of course, what springs to mind is that she is worried about his academic career, what he will do in the future. Maybe she hoped he would become a doctor, and that is unlikely. Also, pupils with academic problems often become naughty and so forth...

I forgot to tell you about Sheila's boss. You see, he is a big, tall, and strong man. He smokes the cigar in his office, and he treats women with disrespect. You see, there is nothing technically improper, but if you are a woman in his office, or even a "non-macho" man, you can feel a bit intimidated, or even just not at ease with him... Again, what sort of anxiety or insecurity do you think Sheila may have about her relationship with her boss?

While anxiety is always the same emotion (at different levels), it manifests itself in different ways in our lives. It can have different "objects" and "reasons", or "subjects" and "triggers". Different relationships will trigger anxiety for different reasons and about different objects and "subjects".

In Sheila and Tom's case, for example:

- The *object* of Sheila's anxiety is Tom.
- The *subject* (topic) of Sheila's anxiety is his performance at school.
- The *reason or cause* of Sheila's anxiety is the fact that Tom has educational problems.
- The *triggers* may be many: a school report, Tom coming back to school, or Tom going to school etc.

The trigger is what sparks each "bout of anxiety" which can be a small event, a memory, a physical object or situation, and it is not the same as the reason or cause. That is the deep source, the origin of this really horrible emotion, not what switches it on...

Now, do you fancy finding the object, subject, reason, or cause and trigger of Sheila's anxiety in her boss's case? If so, I'll go for a coffee and we'll meet back here in five, ok?

...

Here we are! Let's compare notes then... Our words don't need to match. What matters is the overall concept. What is more, an analysis based on a few words, on little data, is always generic and at risk of mistakes. This is only a little training exercise. In real life, you will have many more details to go by.

- The *object* of Sheila's relationship can be her career, her life at work, her own sense of safety and ease at work...
- The *subject* of Sheila's relationship is her boss's personality and behavior.

- The *reason or cause* is that her boss makes her feel uneasy or threatened.
- The triggers can be many, from entering the office, to having to speak with her boss, even just thinking about him.

What you need to take away from this is that ***anxiety has a complex realization, or manifestation in real life.*** Because of the ***triggers,*** people often feel anxiety even in the absence of the actual reason or cause.

For example, if people are anxious about exams, they can feel it even when preparing for them, or talking about them etc. But this process starts a vicious cycle... *The more anxiety is triggered in the absence of the cause, the more it roots itself in the person's personality.*

Put simply, if you are anxious about your first impression when you first meet a date, and you keep thinking about it (triggering it), the more your anxiety grows. But the answer is not "to ignore it". It is to trigger it in a controlled way, so that you can *decrease the anxiety that is triggered.*

For example, instead of looking at yourself in the mirror first thing in the morning when even Marilyn Monroe would have "bummed herself in the mirror", you can do it when you look better. This way, you do not trigger the same *level of anxiety.*

Things in small quantities are manageable. Even anxiety. But you can even tell yourself, "Hey, I look good," and, why not... eat some chocolate before it... it makes you feel good and the *serotonin* it produces actually fights anxiety on a chemical and neurological level.

We will meet serotonin again, because it is our main "natural chemical friend" to fight off anxiety... By the way mushrooms are very rich in it...

You can see that things happen with knowledge, analysis, but also with small steps, which in itself is very encouraging and offers you a sense of security... And we do have many unexpected friends around us (like chocolate and mushrooms).

On the other hand, if you associate a negative trigger to another negative factor (you don't feel good, you have headache, whatever...) you *worsen your anxiety.* Unfortunately, we tend to think about negative things when we are not well (physically, mentally or emotionally).

So, the very first thing you need to do is this: ***when you feel bad (physically, emotionally, and/or mentally) force yourself to think about something positive.***

You may now say, "Yes, it is easy to say, but not that easy in practice, is it?" Ok, I see your point. But if you suffer from anxiety, there are some little tricks you can use. For example carry something that brings back *good memories* on you, like a holiday photograph, the picture of someone you love, keep your favorite uplifting song on your phone (iPod, or whatever you use) ...

Focus on positive and soothing colors when you feel the trigger coming. Green and blue especially help you counter anxiety (avoid colors like red, shocking pink and yellow, and absolutely no gray or black). Red, yellow and shocking pink are very energetic, but in a state of worry, they may heighten it instead of soothing it.

Use lavender, sandal, hawthorn etc. These have a soothing effect, and they are very good to fend off anxiety...

We will see many more. But as I promised, there are many "friends" around us to deal with anxiety.

This, in general, about anxiety and relationships... But there is more... How anxious are you on average? Some people have an average low level of anxiety in their daily lives; others have a very high one, with or without relationships involved. What we would normally define as "being (or not) an anxious person".

Remember *never to be ashamed if you have a problem, an issue or, in this case, if you are "naturally" anxious.* I put "naturally" in inverted commas because this is how people usually say it. From a psychological point of view, that is wrong, and saying it like this makes it worse. The fact is that you are not "naturally" anxious... It is society that, working especially on your early years, has made you anxious. You are "societally" anxious... Once again, it is society's fault. *Not yours!*

If you are often anxious, you are more likely to be anxious about your relationship as well. And this has many consequences:

- Your perspective on your relationship will be less objective.
- You may end up spoiling moments and chances (this happens quite frequently, and, again, it is not your fault, but you may end up being blamed for it).
- The overall quality of the relationship will suffer.
- Your partner(s) will feel the anxiety.

- Your partner(s) may become anxious as well.

The reverse will happen to you if your partner has an anxious personality… Therefore:

If any of the partners in a relationship has an anxious personality, that needs to be addressed; that level of "background" anxiety must be lowered, or the relationship will suffer.

But we still haven't seen how many types of relationships there are. And then you may have another valid question: *does the type of relationship affect anxiety and insecurities?*

Types of Relationship

What would you use to put a relationship in one or the other type? I mean, you can describe relationships in many ways… Shall we try to come up with a list? You go first…

…

You may have come up with words like "happy and unhappy", "long term and short term", "old fashioned and modern" and to be honest, even colors can be used, how about "red and green"?

The point is, which parameters, standards, or descriptors are actually useful… Talking to a friend you can describe your relationship as "A slightly spiced journey in an old world rose garden on a late summer day." Fine, but we can't really use this as a scientific standard.

Even "good and bad", "happy and unhappy" are tricky for psychologists. You see, on the one hand they are fundamental, on the other they are subjective. If you read psychological and sociological studies, you will find them as "people who *think* their relationship is good/bad/happy/unhappy." It does matter. But we need to keep in mind that maybe the partner does not even agree...

The first thing you need is to *have clear categories to identify and analyze your relationship.* Once again, these are "qualities within the relationship" and there are a huge range of levels, but they are specific, not vague. So... here we go...

Equal and unequal relationships

This is a huge point. Are the two partners equal in the relationship? You can see business and work relationships are hardly ever equal. Parent – child relationships are not equal. Some may be "more equal" others less (and in the past they were more unequal, on average, than today). But a fully equal parent – child relationship is unworkable and irresponsible.

Many of the relationships and exchanges we have every day are not equal. And this, again, is often due to the ***social roles*** involved in them. For example, when you board a train or bus, the conductor has a position of power over you. When a traffic warden gives you a ticket... guess? When you have a medical examination, the doctor has a position of power too.

Commercial relationships are interesting, meaning when you go shopping. There are so many different approaches... Good shoppers are those who put themselves in control, and they don't allow storekeepers to do so. But if you go to a fruit and vegetable open air market when it's near closing time, for example, you will find that you are in a position of power, and the merchants will want to sell off everything they have left over cheap.

Ok, you get the idea that there can be, and often are ***power games within relationships.*** But how about emotional, romantic relationships? That too varies a lot! In some cultures, the man is always "dominant" in the relationship. This is dictated by the society they live in.

Here, we go back to that point we made in the previous chapter. *Society often dictates rules on personal and even intimate relationships.* While it is actually an invasion of your own private life. Ethically it is hard to accept. But many people not only accept it; they actually expect it, encourage it, perpetrate it, and enforce it. And the couple's family (or local society) is often the strongest agent of this enforcement.

Put simply, it is often the parents and the in-laws of the couple (aunts, grandparents and even siblings) that encourage the couple to use structures, patterns, dynamics, and power relationships that society accepts. Put even more simply, these people often want the young couple to copy the same relationship structure as the old ones. And if women had less authority in their relationship, they expect their children etc. to do the same.

This is not always successful. Lots depends on the values and beliefs of the couple, and lots on the influence that parents etc. have on them, as on their determination or open-mindedness...

But here we go... ***Some romantic relationships are egalitarian,***

others are not. In Western cultures, the relationships are often "nominally egalitarian". The female partner is officially recognized as an equal to the man, even by law and *overt social rules*. But then we have *covert social dynamics* that push in the opposite direction.

Men still earn more than women; they have more career prospects; they have many social advantages over women that can end up affecting the relationship itself. Even when the male partner is super egalitarian and the most open-minded person on earth, *the very fact that the female partner earns less can be a serious cause of anxiety, insecurity, and frustration*. And vice versa, though it is less common.

The point I would like you to take home is that ***there are power structures and dynamics even within romantic relationships and that these are often the cause of anxiety, insecurity and frustration.***

And these are often hard (but not impossible) to address. In some cases, the very hard ones, *the inequality is rooted in the romantic imagination itself of one of the two partners*, usually the male one. And I am not here talking about sexuality, which can be seen as a "consensual game of sublimation between the partners". Translated: it is actually part of the solution to express these fantasies in the sexual act instead of expressing it in the social relationships of the couple...

Translated... A couple that has an equal relationship during their daily life, when they work, cook, go out, watch TV etc. then "play games" during their intimate moments will usually be a happy one. The social side of their relationship is equal. On the contrary, when this inequality happens during the "social time" one of the partners will usually suffer.

What is the solution? It depends a lot, but certainly it starts with ***communicating and expressing the problem, the frustration, and the anxiety with the partner***. But don't jump the gun if this is your case... Most times this ends up becoming a row that leads nowhere. But we will soon see how you can do this in the right way. It is actually a matter of ***communication and language***.

Open and Closed Relationships and Inclusive and Exclusive Relationships

You will have heard of "open relationships" meaning that two (or more) romantic partners do not see "adultery" or relationships with external partners as a problem. But an open relationship does not need to be a romantic and intimate one. Friendships are usually open, or fairly open.

However, you will see that adolescents (most commonly girls) experiment with open and closed relationships on a friendship level. The "best best friend" relationship is not actually very open, is it? And it is often a source of jealousy, frustration, anxiety, and conflict. While it is simply a friendly relationship, in fact, it becomes *exclusive and formalized, almost institutionalized...*

And in fact, it would be better to use the terms ***exclusive and inclusive relationships.*** And this works on a very wide range of levels when we talk about romantic relationships. It does not just mean "having other occasional or regular romantic partners".

While this is a very high level of openness, ***open and closed, or inclusive and exclusive relationships have a social dimension too.*** Let me tell you about two couples I know...

Patricia is now married to Robert; Maya is married to Carl. They come from the exact same circle of friends. They used to go out together etc.... You know, typical life of a group of young friends...

The problem is that since Patricia and Robert got married, they "locked themselves up" at home... They hardly ever meet other people and they have become partly isolated... they basically *do not invite other people into the social space of their relationship.* Very few dinners with friends and a glass of wine with Patricia and Robert.

On the contrary, Maya and Carl have a different approach to their shared social space. They often invite friends round but they also have an active social life... They go jogging with friends, they have "girls' nights out" and "boys' nights out" with their old friends etc....

Surely you can see that the two couples have a completely different lifestyle. There is no intrinsic problem with either. If the couple is happy like that, fine... Problems start when one of the two partners is not happy with how open or how closed their relationship is to others.

Both can be frustrating. With an inclusive relationship you may end up wishing for more intimate time with your partner. What is more, sometimes keeping a busy social life can be tiring, especially if people work, commute, have children and live in urban areas...

The opposite can be true too. If it's only "you and me" it may become tedious, boring and, what is more, frustrating. Here the frustration comes from the fact that every day may look like a copy of the previous one. You may start feeling that your life is not rewarding, even that you have failed etc....

This often becomes a problem when one of the partners works and the other does not. The one who works has a social life outside the couple, but s/he will also be tired and unwilling to meet people after work or at the weekend. The non-working partner, on the other hand, will feel bored, as their life will be isolated and lacking perspectives as well as a rewarding social dimension.

This is not unusual at all. Actually, this situation is one of the most common sources of frustration, anxiety, and insecurity, and a common cause of split ups, divorces, and relationship failures.

With a little empathetic note... The industrial world has cost the frustration and suffering of a huge number of women. Now more women go to work, but the post war society of "working husband and housewife" (rather than husband and wife) has weighed on the shoulders of millions frustrated and unhappy women...

The importance of friends and significant others in the happiness of romantic relationships is explored by Susan Sprecher and Diane Felmlee in a study entitled 'The Influence of Parents and Friends on the Quality and Stability of Romantic Relationships: A Three-Wave Longitudinal Investigation' (in *Journal of Marriage and Family,* 1992) and it says that:

"...the positive effect of network support [...] increased the stability of the relationship."

So, while one of the partners may be unwilling to meet friends and family and have a wider social life with his/her partner, this is short sighted. Relationships that "breathe" in their social dimension are, in fact, more stable than those that close onto themselves.

And this could be the starting point or even the winning argument if you wish to open up your relationship. But, once again, don't go ahead until we have talked about *how to express yourself.*

As usual, this has varying degrees too. But things can become chronic and even extreme at times... The overall pattern that sociologists have discovered is that we tend to go through phases with our ***circle of friends:***

- It is fairly small as children, mainly made up of parents' friends' children at first.
- As we grow up, we widen this circle.
- During adolescence, we vastly widen the circle.
- The circle stays wide till our early adulthood (our 20s).
- As we form a stable relationship with a romantic partner, this circle starts shrinking.
- The circle will shrink after marriage and especially during most of our working life and especially after the birth of our child or children.

As you can see, all the period from roughly our 30s to our 60s and beyond, the circle of friends shrinks... At the same time, responsibilities and work-related anxiety grows... This is very unhealthy.

But then when we retire, some couples suddenly manage to widen their circle of friends, and this is usually one of the causes of a "second spring" or "Indian summer" of their relationship. Those who cannot do this, on the other hand, usually face dissatisfaction and frustration.

What do we learn from all this? Once again, *lifestyle, society, our working life etc. are often the reason why relationships close up onto themselves and shrink their social circle.*

But at the same time, we learn that *romantic relationships that manage to counter this shrinking are usually more stable and more rewarding.*

Keep the door open to your friends!

We will come back into "open relationships" in the common sense; these are, be aware, quite hard to manage but not impossible and often they can be rewarding. However, you will need to learn some important points about how you can have a successful one. This, of course, requires a whole detailed section.

One-Way and Two-Way Relationships

How much do you get out of your relationship? How much does your partner get? Again, no need to answer me... But this is a chat you may want to have some time first with yourself and then with your partner(s).

In a healthy relationship, there needs to be mutual satisfaction. This can be a problem with inequality, but not necessarily. It can just be that one partner gets more satisfaction than the other. The reasons and the dynamics can be quite varied for this. Paying attention that your partner is happy too with your relationship is fundamental to its success.

The relationship itself should be the source of satisfaction for all partners or members. This applies to romantic relationships but also family ones, friendships, and even work relationships.

When a relationship is mutually satisfactory, there is a virtuous cycle of satisfaction that goes around the partners. Or, if you want, it *goes back and forth, making this a two-way relationship.*

But this back and forth is not just for happiness and satisfaction; it applies to:

- Satisfaction
- Problems
- Projects
- Ideas
- Responsibility

On the other hand, if this does not happen or it stops, *one of the partners becomes a receiver and the other a taker: this forms a one-way relationship.* And this applies to the same elements: satisfaction, problems, projects, ideas, and responsibility. Maybe only one of them, maybe more, and maybe all.

But it can also happen that one element goes one way, and another goes the other way. For example, one partner may be getting most of the satisfaction while the other gets most of the problems…

You can look at these as “ingredients” of your relationship. What you want to have is a “balanced meal to share equally” – or as equally as possible in any case. Every day the meal will be different, of course, but you should always try to have a balanced diet over any period of time.

Even here, ***part of the solution is communication.*** But if you feel your relationship is “going a bit one way” there is something you can start doing now, even before we look at how to talk about these issues.

For sure, if you suspect your partner is not “receiving his or her due”, you can start changing things to make him or her happy. But “due” also means responsibilities etc.… It also happens that when a relationship goes one way in one element, it happens that it goes the other way for another element.

For the time being, check if this is the case. Check which elements go one way, which go the other way, and which go both ways… Ok, take some time over this.

…

Now, well done! What do you suggest doing? Maybe you thought this is a “bargaining situation” … You know what? You are not far off the mark! Indeed, what you can do, at least this is one of your “bargaining tools” is to propose to change things round so that the distribution and direction of elements becomes even and two directional.

But for the time being, just mull over it. You have part of the solution in your hands but to implement it, you will need the communication skills we are going to start learning soon.

Intensive and Light Relationships

How often do you meet with your partner? How long do you spend with him or her? How often are you alone? Do you also work together? Let's look at two extremes...

Aida and Frank wake up in the morning; they are a newly wed couple who have decided to get away from it all and now they live alone in the middle of nowhere. They don't have "proper jobs"; they work on a farm they have bought, so, after breakfast, they start working together. They spend the day together and then, at night, they seldom go out... They spend their evenings together playing board games as they do not watch TV. Ah, by the way, they have no children.

That is an *intensive relationship.* By "intensity" here we do not mean the depth or passion of feelings... No, we are being technical. We mean that *the people in the relationship are in close, frequent and repeated contact.*

Did you know that Aida has a sister, and her name is Celia...? She too has a partner. Her name is Matilda. But Aida has decoded to work as a volunteer helping orphans in a very poor village in Africa, while Matilda is a teacher in Ottawa. They think about each other a lot, but they can only text each other every now and then, because there is no line where Aida works, and she needs to go to the nearest town even to send a message. They do meet, but that is only once every few months, and for a week or so...

Ok, that is a *light (or mild) relationship.* By this, again, we mean that they may love each other more than anybody in the world, but their actual time together is limited. In this case, they are having a distant relationship.

In between, you can have different levels and stages: you may live near each other or further away. You may live together and have different jobs. Even the size of your home can be a factor in this.

And now I'm asking you to use your analytical skills. Look at the lives of Aida and Frank on one hand and Celia and Matilda on the other. Which do you think could be the sources of anxiety, problems, insecurities, and frustration in the two cases?

Take your time and I'll be waiting for you – here. I'm not going anywhere...

...

I told you that I'd be waiting... Here I am! Do you want to go first? Did you find lots of problematic areas? Potential for anxiety? I bet you did, in both cases.

Maybe you too thought that Aida and Frank risk getting on each other's nerves? Then I would agree. Such an intensive relationship needs exquisite affinity and fine tuning of personalities. But even so, over the years, this very closeness all the time may end up damaging their relationship.

And how about Celia and Matilda? We all know that these relationships are very hard indeed. The more people are independent, the more they are likely to succeed. But then of course some little jealous thoughts are more than likely to creep in. You see, when one partner feels the need for intimacy, say Celia, then she would start thinking that Matilda too feels the same. And as Celia may find it hard to resist, so she may suspect that Matilda has the same problem... and we know where we are heading with this.

Then again, when long distance relationships are also long in time one or both of the partners may actually change, in terms of personality, attitudes, values, but also physically over time. Coming back after a long time and finding a changed person... You know what that may entail...

In both an intensive and a very mild relationship, communication is essential. And here by "communication" we must include nonverbal communication too. If you talk too much in an intensive relationship you can cause a negative reaction. While texting or writing letters is not the same as face-to-face communication. Then again, if Celia comes back and Matilda has changed the way she dresses, her hair color etc., Celia may become very insecure about their relationship...

However, ***relationships that are extreme at both ends often need changing in order to survive.*** Long distance relationships work well only in Victorian romantic novels. I mean, they work with family members, less with friends, but romantic relationships of this kind have a time limit.

When they are too close, there are many factors at play...

Some young couples think that because they are so passionate about each other they can live together all the time. And sometimes it does work. There is no actual "rule" that says this is not possible. This, however, works better in the countryside. Why? Because they have more open spaces, and because Nature is actually a "friend", a "significant other" that you can relate to, thus making the relationship less intense and even more open. You can even invite her to dinner, though normally she *is* the dinner...

Anyway, yes, sometimes it may work. But in many cases, there are problems. Passion may be a good start, but it is no guarantee that a very intensive relationship will work. You need that *mutual respect* which you find in old, tried, and tested relationships. That sort of relationship grandparents have. People who know each other perfectly and above all, respect each other perfectly.

More than passion, you may need wisdom to succeed in a very intensive relationship.

A World of Relationships

Then again, you can distinguish relationships according to the people (animals) involved. You can have friendly relationships rather than passionate relationships even within a love relationship... And we will see them in a separate chapter. But first I want to give you the basics of how to use *language* to address problems, anxiety, insecurity etc. in your relationship.

And I want to do it right now!

3

THE LANGUAGE OF HEALING AND RELATIONSHIPS

I know that you are eager to get going, so, even before we look at all the many facets of relationships, I would like to give you some tools to start working on yours. As I said, before you put your foot in it, or you put your foot wrong, you should learn how to talk about your anxieties, problems, insecurities, and frustration. ***Using the wrong language can have the opposite effect of what you desired***.

This point is so important that I need to stress it. How many couples do you know where both partners keep saying the same thing and nothing changes? Especially in long and mature relationships this is very common. Tom keeps telling Sandra not to interrupt people and all he obtains is that Sandra keeps interrupting. Sandra is always telling Tom not to moan all the time and all she gets is that he moans even more.

This is an example that I am super sure everybody finds familiar. And you don't want to end up like that, do you? But isn't it weird that looking at these relationships from the outside it would seem that the very fact that one partner says, "Don't do this," makes the other actually do it? And in a way, this is true...

The fact is that no one wants to accept their own flaws. And hearing their partner bring them up is *seen as a challenge*, an insult, an excuse to bicker, a put down... And instead of becoming a solution, *stating the problem becomes the trigger to "misbehave"* like naughty kids who do the opposite of what the teacher asks...

So, this, however, is a process that starts early on and it takes years or even decades to become so ingrained in the relationship that in many cases you would need a professional to help. In some cases, these attitudes can become even aggressive, and what is a chronic problem can become both acute and pathological.

I have seen a case of an old woman who attacks her husband with such vehemence over the smallest matters and with such sudden impetus that it's actually shocking to witness. And this is a long story, but this woman is attacking the husband on minor matters because the husband for decades has been trying to show that he is right on other points... She feels treated as inferior for those points and finds any excuse to "score a point" and prove to herself and her husband that she is not stupid.

And do you know what he does in return? He tells her that she is wrong and the whole downward spiral starts over again... This is a pathological case I have had to deal with recently.

But it is good to show two things:

- ***The frustration, anxiety, insecurity or problem was not presented, expressed correctly the first time.*** So, it was received as a challenge, not as a solution. And this has triggered a chain of counter challenges that can literally go on for decades in a relationship.
- ***These chains need to be broken. And sometimes, the best form of communication is silence...*** Here, the husband should stop trying to establish who is right and just let her score some points.

Silence

We need to understand the importance of silence in a relationship. The example you have just seen is extreme. But using silence correctly can make a huge difference to the communication within your relationship.

How many people talk over their partner when s/he is trying to express him/herself?

Especially when we disagree, we tend to talk over each other. This is often because we are eager to bring forth our point, which "we know will debunk their point". Yes, but it does not... because then our partner brings out another point (even on a slightly or not so slightly different topic) so *we end up jumping from point to point never agreeing on any of them.*

And while we leave the discussion convinced that we are right, we also leave *frustrated because we have not reached a clear, well stated agreement on anything* at all.

It is ***better to deal with one point at a time, and give each other time to express it fully. And this means being silent when our partner (friend etc.) is speaking.***

Good teachers listen to students, good parents listen to children, good doctors listen to patients and good politicians – don't exist! Joking, of course, or am I? You get the point… ***Good partners listen to one another respectfully.***

Now, put yourself in your partner's shoes…S/he is trying to get you to see something, to understand him or her… And if you at least *listen respectfully, you show that you care!* Maybe then you don't understand, but what do you think is better? A partner who cares but does not understand or one who does not care? It does not matter if the partner who does not care then understands or not, does it? In most cases it will also be "not", but even if it is "yes" you failed at the *most basic level as a partner... the empathetic, emotional level.*

Now, especially if someone is *trying to express feelings, do listen with care and avoid interrupting.* Imagine it is like you are trying to get a wave out of your chest… If someone interrupts and sends it back, what do you get? A bigger wave inside of you. And big waves are not manageable. This is how ***many discussions escalate into rows***.

Of course, this does not mean that you can't say a word. Asking for further details and clarifications, showing empathy, or the simple "mm" to show that you are listening are fine.

Now, do you remember Aida, Frank and their intense relationship on a farm? Some people are very talkative by nature (I am!) This is fine, but if you are, do try to get some silent spells. Being talkative, you see is great at social gatherings, with strangers, acquaintances, even in the workplace and certainly if you are a salesperson or even a stand-up comedian…

But try to understand that when you are in an intensive situation, hearing the same voice all the time in itself becomes tedious and even annoying. And you don't want to have your voice associated with "being annoying". You see, once we make a link between two things ("voice" and "annoying") it is sometimes hard to get rid of it… especially if the link gets remembered frequently…

Keep in mind that ***being capable of being silent together is a sign of a comfortable relationship.*** You do know that sometimes people "talk to break the silence" and this is because *silence is embarrassing among strangers...* among strangers! Not partners…

So, there are times to talk and there are times to be quiet… be wise.

The Quality of the Conversation

Small talk is fine when you are with acquaintances, and it is also part of our daily life with our partners. However, it should not be *all or most of the conversation we have with our partners.* It is sad, sometimes, when people argue and then they start again with small talk to avoid the topic and pretend nothing has happened. But at the same time, they know that it's a "show" they are both putting on.

This is by all means sometimes necessary; ***if people are not ready to face a topic, never force it on them***.

Having said this, however, try to ***keep the quality of the conversation high within your relationship.*** This has many effects including:

- It makes the relationship more rewarding and meaningful.
- It can be a bonding element.
- It makes addressing serious problems within the relationship easier.

On this last point, imagine that you and your partner only/mostly talk about small irrelevant things like which brand of canned beans you should buy... It looks extreme but there actually are quite a few relationships like that... Now, how comfortable would you feel if/when you have to address a serious problem within your relationship? Very little or not at all.

Keeping the quality of conversation high within the relationship is practice for when you have to tackle relationship problems.

How can you keep it high? Here are a few tips:

- Talk about your hobbies and interests in detail.

- Don't just watch the news! Discuss current affairs, politics etc.
- Talk about what you read.
- Discuss work in detail. Explain what it is like and what you do in detail. It's amazing to find out how many people have only a vague idea of what their partners actually do at work!
- Invite friends with intelligent conversation to dinner.
- Do not be afraid to express your feelings.

And on this point, we need to take a long pause, a long breath and...

Expressing Feelings and Emotions

Welcome to the center of it all. The heart of relationships. The healing room of all relationship problems – the heart indeed!

There are many other things you will need, but ***nothing is more important in a relationship than being able to express feelings and emotions or states of mind.*** That is the all-important factor in any relationship.

And, unfortunately, most of us are very badly equipped for it. I mean, nowadays the "man in touch with his feminine side" is more accepted, for example, and many women nowadays actually find these men very attractive indeed... But wind back a few decades and all men were expected to be masculine, macho, and – above all – never to express feelings...

Thankfully things have changed, and this bodes well for relationships. Nevertheless, we are still poorly equipped. If some men have learned to respect their emotions, we come from school systems, value systems, work environments, social setting etc. that don't value feelings and make it hard for us to express them.

Once again, it is society that causes most of our problems. And then, when new relationships form, there are many factors and variables at play. ***If you don't start expressing your feelings freely early on in the relationship it becomes harder, more embarrassing to do it later on.***

This is also because *we get used to habitual things,* and if in the relationship there is little emotive talk, we feel uneasy about changing this aspect of the relationship. Actually, *we may even feel anxious about it.*

I know that many people are not confident about expressing their feelings and this can actually be a major cause of anxiety within a relationship. And now the value of listening silently becomes even more clear and explicit.

But how can you actually say those very difficult words and make sure that they are understood?

The Language of Feelings and Emotions

Remember how we said that the problem is often that there are "chains of challenges" that started long ago (like feuds) *because the point was not expressed correctly the first time?* Let me show you two examples:

Joseph keeps complaining about everything... Clarissa, his partner, has put up with his grumbling and moaning for years and now she can't take it any more... They are in front of the TV, he grumbles about some stupid ad and she turns to him, and with a brisk and sharp tone she says, "Oh, stop moaning for heaven's sake!"

How do you think that Joseph will react? What do you think is his first thought, feeling?

...

I am sure you would agree that maybe his first thought or feeling is one of surprise, upset, even disbelief? But then, the "feeling personally hurt" will set in, and... well, Clarissa would be very lucky indeed if he took it well. If he goes silent, he may internalize the offense and that can cause all sorts of serious psychological problems later on. From insecurity, to self-deprecation etc.

So, what can he do? You see, Clarissa has put him in *a situation where he must defend himself.* Even if he does not know it consciously, he at least unconsciously knows that if he does not react his own emotional well-being is at stake. So, the most likely response in a situation of (even small) panic and surprise is not rational nor correct... It's to "kick the ball back". Maybe he will deny that he moans, maybe he will say he was not moaning, maybe he will say something along the lines of, "You can't say a word in this house," or maybe he will answer back with, "And you – will you stop talking to your sister when I watch TV?"

The last one is quite common. If a partner says, "You do this," the, "You too," answer is very common and instinctive. We learn it at school. The teacher goes, "George stop picking on Chan," and the "But he..." is expected and quick...

But this also makes a link between Joseph's grumbling and Clarissa's phoning her sister. This link is very emotionally charged, and it is likely to become one of those chains that go on for decades... Twenty years from now, they will still be pitching these two arguments, one against the other at every trigger...

The only worse thing Clarissa could have done is add personal insult, like, "You old fool". And the only way Joseph could have saved the day would have been to collect himself, swallow the pain, and say, "Is that really what bothers you? Can we talk about it calmly?"

But, as you know, these are very difficult words to find when you have just been hurt...

Now I will use a special machine, it is even more advanced than a time machine... This machine can shift you into a parallel dimension... Ready? Here we go! Now, in this dimension Joseph is still a moaner and a grumbler. He still watches TV and gets triggered by silly ads (I do too, don't tell me Joseph is based on me?)

But in this dimension, Clarissa had read this book, and she knows how to communicate emotions... In this dimension the ads are still the same, and the same ad comes on. And Josh grumbles...

Clarissa is really tired of this, and she decides to solve the problem... She leaves the room... She goes to collect her thoughts, and at the same time, *she allows Joseph to get past the grumbling moment.* You see, even if he just grumbles, even if it may look like something very small and superficial, the very fact that he reacts like this may mean that there is something deeper at stake in his mind.

That ad is emotionally charged for him. Maybe it presents society in a way that hurts him. Think about all the ads that show women in the kitchen... they can be emotionally charged for some people...

Ok, so, then she comes back and says, "Joseph, I need to tell you something." This way *she prepares Joseph for what she is about to say, avoiding a surprise, a shock and a gut reaction.*

And finally, when he is ready, the TV is off her "masterpiece":

"Joseph you are a lovely man but when you grumble about these things it makes me feel upset".

She could have said, "It makes me feel sad, tired, old..." whatever expresses her state of mind and heart.

But have you seen the difference? Have you noticed how *she opens her heart to Joseph actually telling him the truth and at the same time she invites him to address the problem in a constructive way?*

And she leaves the talking ground to Joseph, so that he can ask for more details.

And the conversation may go on like this:

"Oh, really, I had not noticed. How exactly do you feel about it?"

But for most couples, these are really stories from another dimension.

Let's look at all the steps in detail.

- ***Do not react immediately.***
- ***Collect your thoughts before you express yourself.***
- ***Allow your partner to get out of the situation that triggered what you wish to criticize or address.***
- ***Prepare your partner for what you are about to tell him/her.***
- ***Make sure you have his/her full attention.***
- ***The sentence you use must have some clear elements.***

1. ***It must have a compliment or an empathetic phrase at the beginning. "I love you to bits but..."***
2. ***It must point to the activity, the action, not the person ("when you do this", not "you are").***
3. ***It must use a verb like "feel" to express the feeling and emotion. This way the partner understands that they are hurting you.***
4. ***It must never ask for immediate action ("stop grumbling"... give him or her time to mend his or her ways).***
5. ***It must then leave space for the partner to reply.***

This is the time to slow down and take stock of what we have learned. This structure is so fundamental to communication within relationships that we need to make sure we know it perfectly well.

Every step and every element of this structure is *necessary.* But you can add parts, for example a final bonding sentence. But you can only add positive statements. You cannot cut bits out. Now, put yourself in the shoes of someone who hears this… How would you feel? Despite the fact that this is put in the gentlest possible way, it does have *emotional consequences.*

For most people hearing a sentence like the one we have seen is:

- *Disarming*; when we hear feelings expressed honestly and calmly, we just try all our defense mechanisms (which are the ones that Sandra activates… and we all do when we accuse someone without presenting our pain…)
- An *epiphany* in many cases; people realize that they had done something wrong of which, most likely they were simply not aware.
- *Cathartic* in many cases; the person can feel their own feelings surging and wanting to "come out" and be expressed.

If you just obtain the first, you have opened a sound path for discussion, a way forward. If you obtain all three, you will most likely move straight into a resolutive moment. The conversation will turn emotional (in the good sense) and the solution in these cases is usually within reach in this very "session".

In other cases, it may take some time before you actually find an agreement. It really depends on the complexity of the problem, on the moment, on how your partner responds to it, and on practical issues. If for example you feel you need a holiday and your partner had not noticed it, it may take some time before you actually put your flip flops on and set off to a sunny beach…

But now you have a very important tool at your disposal, try to learn it by heart and practice it before you actually use it with your partner. And here are some suggestions for you on how to memorize it and "hone it to perfection".

- *Write down a few statements with this format.* Change the content but keep the format and write down a few to familiarize yourself with the structure.
- *Practice it in front of the mirror.* You need to make sure that the delivery is credible, not overstated nor understated, calm and that it sounds natural. Do what actors and ballet dancers do then; look at yourself in the mirror and correct the bits you don't like.
- *Try it out on "less important people".* You can use it (with less personal topics and feelings) with acquaintances, work colleagues, and even customers or clients if you want. One thing is delivering a "line" to yourself; another is delivering it in front of an audience. Start with an audience with "no consequences" so that when you have to face your partner you will feel much more confident. Do you have a dog or a cat? They are the perfect audience to try this out. Yes, even budgies and hamsters...

I cannot stress enough the importance of communicating emotions and feelings correctly. So, practice, practice and then practice again!

But now you really can start changing your relationship at a very deep level. There are so many different sides to a relationship that, of course, this is not the solution to everything. But you need to make an even playing field before you build on your relationship (and even your personality). And these misunderstandings and problems are huge obstacles on the way...

So, start getting rid of what hurts you and then you can improve what pleases you...

Phatic Language

Many of the things we say have no actual practical function. Example? The old fashioned "how do you do?" It does not mean what it says, does it? The answer is meaningless too. In the UK, even "how are you?" is becoming the same. People more and more often answer, "How are you?" without even bothering to give a proper answer...

So, what's all this about? These are ***bonding expressions***; they only serve to *(re-)establish a social and emotional bond, to say, "Our relationship is fine."* And this is what we call *"phatic language".*

Do you say good morning when you wake up and see your partner? Do you say something nice before you leave home? Oddly enough, some people do, and some people don't...

There are many social variables and cultural influences on the use of phatic language, so, let's try to shine a light on this. Some people will take phatic language as "a pure formality" or even "small talk". But while it can be "part of small talk" in some cases, it is not small talk when it is used to bond.

But this means that some people also put phatic language – erroneously – in the category of "things to say at work, with strangers, when I am in suit and tie" and not with their close significant others, partners.

It so happens that in some relationships, phatic language slowly disappears or becomes less regular. Do you still say, "Thank you," and, "welcome," to your partner or do you find yourself using these words more promptly with strangers?

What do you say when you come home? Do you go straight into, "What a horrible day at the office!" or do you take the time to say, "Hello, how has your day been," first?

Things that seem unnecessary, irrelevant, and redundant can make a huge difference to the quality of the relationship. This is so important, in fact, that even social media have had to come to terms with it... People naturally started using letters to express simple bonding concepts, like :-), or ;-), the winking variant or :-D... Companies took the hint and came up with emojis...

There is, in fact, a study by Wang, Tucker and Rihll, entitled 'On Phatic Technologies for Creating and Maintaining Human Relationships' (in *Technology and Society,* vol. 33, 2011) which explores the way that social media users have felt and expressed the need to use phatic language on the web and its platforms as a way "to establish, develop and maintain social relationships."

So, if we feel the need to use phatic language with our Facebook "friends" why is it that we are scared to use it with our partners?

Now, be aware of your use of phatic language. Observe yourself for a day (on and off, of course), and then, at the end of the day, answer these questions:

1. Do you use phatic language all the time or do you omit it sometimes?
2. Who and in what situations do you use it more?
3. Do you use it regularly with your partner?

And you can come back to this after you have answered.

...

If your use of phatic language is regular, homogeneous and evenly spread during the day and with the people you meet, well done! Just make sure you keep it up. This, however, is not the case for most people. Some people use it more in the morning and less when they get tired. Others use it more with people in a position of power (your boss) and less with their peers.

Well, you know that people who use it frequently also have career advantages... But if you only use it with your boss, you may lose on the collaboration of some of your colleagues... Yes, it is sadly true that people in power usually receive more "thank you's" than our peers and colleagues...

How about with your family, friends, and partner? If you think that there is room for improvement, then make it a point to use phatic language more often. Remind yourself of it in the morning and then, in the evening, ask yourself, "Have I used it a bit more?"

Little by little, it will come back into your everyday language as if it had never left.

And now you have the basic tools to improve your communication, you can actually start getting your "hands dirty"...

So, next we can finally have a "rosy chapter" ... You guessed, we are entering the realm of romance, and we will explore all the different hues and shades that romantic relationships can have...

Ready for fifty shades of romantic relationships?

4

FIFTY SHADES OF ROMANTIC RELATIONSHIPS

And they are not fifty... In reality, with all feelings, like with colors, we can find as many shades as we can see, virtually to infinity. But there are some "large areas" that deserve some attention. We said that no romantic relationship is the same as any other romantic relationship, but there are some things that we can say for sure:

- *Romantic relationships are the most intimate of all.*
- *Romantic relationships are among the most important in our lives* (children often become more important, but not necessarily).
- *Romantic relationships tend to be among the most intense we have.*
- *Romantic relationships are very emotionally charged.*
- *Romantic relationships develop over time.*

And it is with the last point that we shall start…

How Romantic Relationships Develop

A romantic relationship is a bit like a day… Maybe you look at the same place, maybe a lovely cottage surrounded by flowers, trees and birds in the countryside. But while the cottage is the same, the sunrises in the morning and the light is bright at first, then at noon, colors become warmer, as the quality of sunlight changes. In the afternoon shadows stretch in the ground and colors become mellower, then darker, till you see a warm, sunset behind the cottage that breaks the sky…

Ok, I wanted to be poetic… But I bet you see the point. At any stage during this day, we cannot see how the scenery will change and, what is more, *we do not believe, or admit that our relationship will ever change, especially at the beginning.* When we are in the arms of passion, we don't believe that one day we may end up being two old bickering "life mates" … But if the relationship lasts, the chances are that is the "evening" awaiting for you...

What is more, *we resist changes in our romantic relationships.* This is not always and not always consciously. We resist changes. For sure consciously, when things are going well. One of the main sources of anxiety in a relationship is the *"fear to grow apart".* The "let's take a little break to think" is a horrible thought for anybody. We never want that moment to come. So, when things go well, any change is a risk…

The problem is that sometimes, actually quite often, we are so scared of changing our relationships that, consciously and even unconsciously, *we resist changes even when they will improve our relationship.*

A typical example is when *a relationship needs to develop.* Maybe from the passionate stage, it needs to move into a more responsible stage... Moving in together, for example, or having a child. This is not an easy step to take... What will happen to all the passion? On the other hand, it may be the only solution, because the passion is burning out and the relationship has no other way of surviving unless it changes.

In some cases, the only option is "stepping down" the intimacy ladder. In the case of two married people splitting up, this is very clear. Both need to give up on the romantic and intimate relationship and move to a friendship type of relationship. If one of the partners cannot accept this, the whole relationship (in general terms) is at risk... and if you are still (very much) in love with your partner this is a very difficult step to take.

So, we need to *understand that relationships evolve and be ready to let it happen and evolve with them, but any change can be a challenge.* Some relationships may in theory stay the same forever, though I don't think we know one yet... But what we can do is look at the different ***stages of a romantic relationship*** *and be prepared for the many changes.*

This alone can *abate anxiety, worry, frustration, and insecurity.*

Now, note that what follows is a list of *all the possible stages, not of the necessary stages...* People have been known fall in love, get married and get divorced over 48 hours, and there's a few stages you need to skip to achieve that… So, be aware that *not all relationships go through the exact same stages.*

One thing though is that *with the different stages of romantic relationships language changes and the partners need to change too.* And we will address this point in detail soon. Some stages here are pre-relationship and others are post-relationship.

Stage 1 – Meeting (usually pre-relationship)

Of course, the first thing you need to do in most relationships is meet your partner. For most of us that is a "magic moment" which we will remember with fondness all our lives. And the way we recall it is always a clue on how we feel about our relationship. A typical comedy troupe is one of the partners cursing that moment creatively. In real life this usually never happens, if not as a shared joke…

So, look at your partner's eyes when you recall that moment and you will see that glint that reassures you that you are still very much in love with each other, even if sometimes it is hard to express it.

But did I say, "for most of us"? Yes, because it has not, and it is not always like that. Many people in arranged marriages only meet their partners *after the engagement,* and this has happened as a norm with royal families all over Europe for centuries.

Stage 2 – Infatuation (usually pre-relationship)

This is that time when the world changes… It feels so strange, doesn't it? The light is different, smells are different, food tastes different, even time seems to have changed pace. But above all, at this stage we can think only about one thing all day round – actually, one person.

But infatuation is a transitional phase: *in most cases, infatuation only lasts a few months.* But a lot depends on the individual and on the situation. Some infatuations can literally last a few days. Then, maybe practical reasons, or even a change of mind (of heart?) put it to an end.

Some people can control infatuations. Some people stop it because the person is already attached, and they can do it. Others stop this phase because the person is a colleague. Yet others stop it because they are "not ready" for a relationship. Or, in some cases, the infatuation just vanishes as fast as it had come.

In any case, *infatuation is for many people fairly easy to control and even end.* Despite being a very powerful feeling, there is not too much at stake, because this is usually something that happens before a relationship actually starts.

Usually, again, because there are the usual exceptions, like, well, even people who fall in love with their wife or husband after years of marriage... Or people who fall in love again etc.... Love is really unpredictable!

In any case, *during infatuation we find it easy to express our feelings, to ourselves, as well as significant others.* This is the time when we keep telling our friend that, "Oh, I am so in love with – "and then we sigh absentmindedly...

This is also the time when *feelings take the upper hand over reason.* True, this seems to be contradictory with the fact that some people can stop infatuation very easily. But the mind is far more complex than people think. When we are irrational, the one rational thought ("this is not the time, this is not the time") stands out very clearly, much more than when our mind is cluttered with other rational, analytical, and logical thoughts...

In any case, infatuation is a great experience.

Phase 3 – Getting to know each other (pre-/during-relationship)

To be honest you never stop getting to know someone, but here we mean "getting to know the bulk of someone's personality" the first key steps. Now, *how you do this really can shape what kind of relationship you are likely to build.*

This is also something on which people often have great preferences, even if subconscious ones. Some of us have in mind that the way they will meet and get to know their partner is, for example, casual. For these people, dating apps, agencies and sites take away all magic of meeting new people.

Other people like sudden intense "getting to know phases". Yet others like friendships to develop into romantic relationships. Then again, there are people who bar firmed from becoming romantic partners and they want this phase to be new with the infatuation.

Can I repeat it? Love is really unpredictable. But *this phase is likely to leave a footprint on the whole relationship.*

If your getting to know phase was a friendship phase, your romantic relationship is likely to have strong characteristics of friendship. We all know that partners you got to know as a child have extremely intimate but also understanding relationships. If you got to know your partner during a summer holiday, your relationship may tend towards that passionate but careless dimension that holidays give. A getting to know phase in the workplace instead may incorporate common interests, even mutual respect in the relationship.

Be aware of the importance of this phase without worrying about it. In a way, *this too is a low-risk phase.* This is the time when *you can still change your mind.* So, without causing useless anxiety, keep in mind that this phase too is very important and that you can always look back at it to gauge out the inner workings and basic structure of your relationship.

Phase 4 – Dating (start of relationship)

This is a very wonderful and romantic phase. Dating may last from one single night or day to... well, as long as you are comfortable with. Some people who love their independent life turn the dating phase into the main part of their romantic relationship. This has also been promoted by many US sitcoms, where the characters date for a whole series (or two, three series) before they actually settle down...

This is a phase when usually, *people are eager to express their emotions, but they can feel anxious or insecure about it.* It is fully understandable. *This is the time when most people say, "I love you," for the first time.* And this is a very difficult, anxiety fraught step to take.

One thing I could suggest at this stage is *never to say those three words unless you actually believe it.* Some people may say it because it opens the door to a stable relationship. But if this is the only reason, it may actually lead to massive frustration, incomprehension and insecurities.

Also, avoid saying those words too early. Well, unless there is a massive chemistry between the two of you, the chances are that you would look a bit "in a hurry" or "a bit too keen" if you say, "I love you," to someone you have only met once or twice. But on this, please use your discretion. You may have loved someone from a distance for example (and in this case, oddly enough, you will usually want to delay saying those words...)

And choose a great time to say it... Kissed by the moonlight is always better, or in front of a fantastic sunset... Make that moment special for both of you...

And if your dating partner says it first, *don't feel obliged to reciprocate unless you love him or her for real.* Saying, "I love you," out of politeness may cause more damage in the long term than you can imagine. Don't get yourself into a relationship you are not ready to start. Ok, love is not necessary for a relationship (for many people). But if your partner starts a relationship with you thinking you love him/her and you don't.... They may have higher expectations while you just want a light relationship. Or you may develop an unbalanced and unequal relationship.

Don't use dating as "a mean to an end" only. It needs to be a phase you actually enjoy. And *don't use dating to secure a stable relationship.* Even if this may be the ultimate end of a dating phase, it should come naturally and not because you have forced the events.

Also keep in mind that dating needs, especially at the beginning, to be *open ended.* Start with the idea that *things may or may not work out during this phase and it's no one's fault.* And if things don't work out for you, well, you may still have had a good time!

Don't load dating with expectations. You would be amazed to know that *your partner may (and likely will) actually "sense it".* People realize when expectations are put on them, even at subconscious level. And if they do, they will think of you as "needy" and in many cases, this in itself will prevent the success of the dating phase.

When it comes to dating, really never try to force things or your dating partner's hand; in a few words, *go with the flow!*

Phase 5 – Experimenting (beginning of the relationship)

The first phase of most relationships has an experimental character. This does not mean only in intimacy, though it does too. It also means in terms of the interpersonal and social shape of the relationship itself. Does it sound a bit abstract?

It is in this period that the *partners work out if they are sexually compatible,* but this is also the period when they *establish their roles within the relationship.* It is also the period when *the couple* (or more, we will get to this) *establishes social patterns with others.*

This has many consequences.

- At this stage, you may develop *habits that will then ossify* in the relationship. And this is very important. At this stage it is usually *more difficult to notice unpleasant traits in the partner or in the relationship.* But if you do, *try to change things now, before they become a habit, a "given", before they are taken for granted.*

At this stage, pay in particular attention to *what type of relationship* you are shaping: equal/unequal, one-way/two-way / open/closed etc. Once more at this stage you are *negotiating what type of relationship you want to build.*

I know that seeing it in terms of negotiation is not a fairy tale romance perspective. And you can (should) keep the romance at all costs. But add this dimension to your relationship. Without worrying *feel free to talk about directions you like and directions you don't like.*

If you do it now, when the relationship is still malleable, you will spare yourself a lot of headaches later on in life.

- Unless you come from the same group of friends, *this is when the two groups of friends become involved.* In some cases, one of the partners abandons his (more often her) friends and starts going out with the friends of the partners. This is very risky indeed. To start with, it requires an extra effort on behalf of a partner. *Having a new partner and new friends at the same time is hard to manage.*

What is more, in most cases, the unlucky partner will always remain "so and so's boyfriend" or "so and so's girlfriend" especially if the friends had known each other for a long time.

This, in turn, means that *if the relationship breaks up, the "partner from outside the friendship circle" will be left without a partner and friends.*

So, ***never stop seeing your old friends.*** Sorry if I repeat it, but I can never stress enough how important friends are for a relationship. There is a wonderful book about it, *Vite Normali,* by sociologists R. Brigati and F. Emiliani. Unfortunately, it is only in Italian, still, it describes how a healthy life needs some meaningful others, and friends are core to the dynamics of happiness and "normality".

Even if you have to see them "on the side" and not as your main social group, always keep a few close friends of yours with you. They are your best haven when things go wrong, and you will also need their perspective, opinions, and advice as your romantic story progresses.

- This is usually also the time when *first encounters with the partner's family* are made. Again, it is not a "100% rule"; you may have known them since childhood, or met them before. Still, this too is a very important moment. Why?

With the family you will meet the past, the social background, and values that have shaped your partner. Then again, it is so hard to establish a collaborative relationship with the in-laws! In most cases, these end up being "conflictual" relationships, but it does depend.

If your partner's family is open minded, you will most likely be welcome as a new member of the family. However, some families see any "addition" as a *potential challenge to their family's identity, history, and values.* This may end up causing strains *within* the relationship.

What can you do if this is the case? *Try not to antagonize your in-laws.* Establish a "sense of complicity" with the in-law of the opposite sex from yours. You may see that the partner of your own sex is the one who is most critical of you. *Don't take it personally;* your in-law is simply defending his or her identity and family role with your partner.

At the same time, however, *do not allow your in-laws or your own parents to dominate your relationship.* Now, *you can only do this if you work together with your partner.* It is the couple that needs to establish itself as an independent and autonomous social unit. Let me explain...

If you allow your patents to have undue sway with what you do with your relationship, your partner will feel entitled to do the same with his parents, your in-laws, and vice versa... You see, if you do this, you end up with *both sets of in laws* intervening in your personal relationship.

Make things clear with your partner, these forces can literally tear a relationship apart. Establish that *all suggestions from parents and in-laws must be discussed by you as a couple (or more) and that the decision must be joint.* There cannot be one of the partners working with his/her parents against the consent, will, plans, or without the full knowledge of the other partner. That is a fracture within the relationship itself.

- This is also the time when *hobbies, interests, sports, outdoor activities, and cultural activities are established within the couple.* At this stage, most people underrate how important it is *to achieve a balance with these and be as comprehensive and inclusive as possible.*

Do you like bird watching? Try to take your partner with you? Does your partner like art galleries? Go along with her or him... You will have to drop *some activities,* but try to keep as many as you can and above all, *share* as many as you can.

This sharing of common activities is like a fresh and continuous source of vitality for your relationship. And imagine your relationship becomes the one you will have for life... *Having a set of shared interests and activities works wonders for the quality of life in mature and even old relationships.*

Having said this, don't be "sticky..." *Keep at least one activity you do without your partner and expect her/him (they?) to do the same.*

"How long does this phase last," you may ask? There is no end-time, to be honest. People will and should experiment with their relationship till it lasts. What really happens is that the experimental side of it progressively decreases and the relationship becomes more fixed and less mutable.

However, in most cases this phase lasts within a year (not necessarily). The first few months are very experimental. Once you have lived a full year as a couple, things start becoming repetitive. An example that shows this well is the holiday together. That is a new situation, and a big one… You plan it together, you go together, you see each other in a new place, with freedom, new challenges etc.… What happens next year? The place may be different, but you have already gone through the experience of planning together etc.

"Can there be more than one experimental phase?" Yes, absolutely! There are events like moving in together, having a child, retiring, setting up an activity together etc. that *trigger a new experimental phase.*

In some cases, people actually choose one of these (well, usually not retiring!) also to "rejuvenate their relationship" or, as they may say to, "rekindle the spark". The reality is that, in fact, the relationship may have become dull, lifeless, and not functional and throwing it into a new experimental phase can be a solution. What these people are looking for is actually *a reason to experiment with their relationship.*

On an ethical note, I would not suggest having a child as a valid reason. It may even be irresponsible. But I have a little tip for you: *find small reasons for small experiments regularly.* Instead of waiting till the relationship as a whole becomes "tight", keep it experimental at a low level. For this, you can, for example:

- Seek new activities to do together.
- Find new interests.
- Get new friends.
- Visit new places.

Even changing restaurant or type of movies you watch can be a good idea. Start going to the theatre if you don't, or poetry readings. Find a nearby beautiful natural park to visit. Take up yoga or painting... Every experience is a small experiment and *relationships are far more likely to manage many small experiments well than a big one, especially when they are already showing signs of tension and/or weakness.*

And to show how important this phase is, many relationships break up at the end of this phase. If you pass the first few months, you have basically "passed the experiment", and if this happens, most people feel ready for a more committal phase: the responsibly phase.

Phase 6 – The responsibility phase (the relationship reaches maturity)

If the experiment goes well, usually *the partners feels the relationship is strong enough to take on new responsibilities.* The most important, of course, is having a baby (by birth or adoption). But this is not the only one. Responsibilities may include *any project you undertake as a couple, from small to big ones.*

From setting up home together, starting a business together rather than designing the patio or changing the bedroom furniture, *this phase is characterized by the relationship taking on more and more responsibilities.* But this has two sides to it:

- On the one hand, *it cements the relationship;* it also adds new dimensions and meaning to the relationship. If successful, this can be a source of great satisfaction.

- On the other hand, *this can put the relationship under strain,* especially if the projects are unsuccessful or if they are too heavy for the couple (or more).

One of the reasons why family planning is good for relationships is that couples who suddenly have the responsibility of a child may really buckle under its weight. Whether you agree or not on a moral basis with family planning, *a couple (or more) who plan when to have children is far more likely to be happy and successful than one who does not.*

Now think how difficult it can be for couples who meet, she remains pregnant during the dating phase, and they skip on all the steps a relationship *needs* to become mature. It is actually a much deeper set of problems than people understand... It means not only that they may not have financial means to grow the child up appropriately. It often means that each partner resents the other for what has happened (a very "toxic" situation). It actually means that they have not even had the chance to check if the "experiment has worked!"

On the whole, a responsible couple should aim to have children only once they have moved safely into this phase. How early or how late may depend on many factors (not last the financial one).

But now that you know that taking on new responsibilities can have a negative effect on the relationship are you sure that the first responsibility you want is a child? I am teasing you, or dropping crumbs towards a solution...

Be experimental and wise even with responsibilities.

Yes, because being experimental does not exclude being wise! The idea is to:

- *Start taking on small responsibilities.* Test how your relationship holds under them.
- *Do not take on more than one responsibility at a time,* if possible. And this is important... Couples (or more) who feel they can do everything with the "strength of their love" – well, sometimes they do succeed – but they do risk overrating the strength and stability of their relationship and may face hard times, even failure and they may actually even lose faith in their own relationship.
- If you can, *take a break between projects and responsibilities.* Ok, you set up your home. Now enjoy it! Take some time off, enjoy life before you move into the next step! Get the point? You need to rest and top up your energy levels...
- *Take responsibilities that are progressively bigger.* It's very tempting to start straight with "the big one", but is it wise? Do you want to set up a homestead? Start with a small garden...
- *Reflect.* To reflect, in education means to *pause, look back, analyze, assess, and decide what you did right and what you need to improve.* It is essential to the *learning process.* Use each experience as *an opportunity to improve and learn.* One thing though, reflection cannot be done in a hurry.

- *Be ready to stop, even give up a project.* Well, this is why you should be careful with children... You can't just give up... But if possible, don't think that if a project fails you have failed. This is a big lie society has been telling us for far too long. Projects fail for a variety of reasons. And they succeed for a variety of reasons. Society, social opportunities, and macroeconomic factors (like a recession) are *far more important factors in the success of a project* than the ability and work of the people involved. The rest is a fairy tale for children (and adults). So...
- *If you fail, don't blame yourself.* Ok, there may be things you need to improve. But sit down and look at all the possible and likely causes of the failure. You will find that what we have just said is likely the case. External factors must be counted. And above all, even if you have made mistakes, *it is fully natural and human.* Do not feel "inadequate"; learn from them and move on.
- *Keep a plan B.* Which, of course, once again you can't with a child. You can't say, "Well, let's replace the child with a gerbil." But in terms of plan B, this suggests one thing; make sure that plan B is lighter, easier, and less demanding than plan A.

This is a very important part of the relationship. ***Unless you move into a "constructive relationship" you will end up feeling dissatisfied with your relationship.*** This is why this phase needs to be managed well, wisely, slowly, and in small steps.

At the same time, ***this phase can and does change the character of***

the relationship. From a passionate and romantic character, your relationship will become more "goal oriented' and responsible.

This can be a major source of anxiety and frustration.

It may happen that both partners move into projects and responsibilities full-heartedly and then they look back and say, "But where has all the passion gone?" and this would be bad. But there is worse...

How about if one of the partners shifts all her or his attention to the "constrictive" side of the relationship and the other would like to focus more on the romantic and passionate side? In this case, you can see very dark clouds forming on the horizon. In fact, ***every time the partners are not in step it can cause serious problems to the relationship.***

But to everything there is a solution. In this case, there are two:

- In this phase, ***make honest and open communication a central part of your relationship.*** You should regularly talk about your projects but also about your relationship.
- In this phase, ***keep the romance and intimacy alive.*** One of the reasons why you should be ***taking breaks*** is to keep the warmth of love, romance, and intimacy alive. It's far too easy to switch focus completely. Don't wait more than a month to tackle a loss of romance and intimacy. Yes, it can be hard, but you will have to *talk to your partner about it as soon as possible.* If you do not, you may fall into that vicious cycle where the more you wait the more it becomes

hard and the more it becomes hard the more you feel uneasy about it and you wait...

Phase 7 – The "harvest" phase

Many relationships end up becoming a "workshop" of activities and projects, and they keep like that till the very end. Others, however, introduce a *new element: the enjoyment of the relationship.*

This is more of an element than a phase, in fact. To start with, *it does not exclude new projects and responsibilities.* But as relationships progress into their late years, people tend to cut down on new responsibilities and replace them with "time together" and, when possible, with "having fun together".

When these become the predominant part of the relationship, we can talk of a "harvest phase".

You see, there is no actual law or rule that says that the productive phase should be all that there is (preserving romance) of a relationship. And when we look at old couples, we can find that those who have found a way of having fun have rekindled their relationship (and often passion, even sexual life can be better later on, especially after retirement).

This phase brings a "second spring" to relationships. Think about when you are old; maybe you just don't have the energy to keep taking on big responsibilities. In some cases, it is even irresponsible to take on responsibilities late in life. It's not a paradox... Just think about adopting a newborn at the age of 70...

And *retirement often marks the beginning of this phase*. But it does not need to be and actually it is better if *this phase is introduced in stages, with planning before retirement.*

In fact, retirement can be a real shock to people's lives. And this is particularly true to people who have not followed my advice so far:

- Those who have not kept friends
- Those who have allowed their intimacy to go cold
- Those who have not shared activities with their partner
- Those who have not shaped an equal, inclusive and two-way relationship.

For these people, retiring can end up meaning, "You are no longer useful, and you have nothing left to do in your life." And that usually results in lowered libido and the whole negative cycle starts, sometimes leading to depression.

If instead the relationship has already started seeing "the fun side of having time on your hands", even such retirements can turn into a great opportunity to enjoy life!

It also gives you a chance to ***see your relationship as a value in its own right***. If you center your relationship around an external focus, like a project, bringing up a child etc., you can end up believing that that very project or activity is the reason why you have a relationship at all. This does not mean that it is bad to have an external focus. Like with all things, it is a *matter of balance.*

If for example you and your partner share a common project, say running a shop, the conversation will mostly be about it. And it can actually take away some stress from the relationship itself.

On the other hand, there are people who think they are "married because they need to bring up children" … Well, that's reductive, isn't it? A healthy approach would be that they bring up children as a married couple who love each other independently from the fact that they have these children.

But slipping into one "mode" is fairly simple… Switching back into the "romantic" and "let's have fun together" mode is much harder indeed. This is why you should always ***preserve this fun and enjoyment dimension of your relationship alive at all times.***

A happy couple (or more) will need ***at least one afternoon or evening every week to enjoy themselves and have fun together.*** Be careful here: *change the activity and keep the "having fun together" constant.* You know, very often people have those nights, but they become routine nights. The "Tuesday night at the neighbors'" sort of thing becomes monotonous and then, again, you will switch the focus from inside the relationship (having fun) to outside (keeping social relationships with the neighbors!)

So, to avoid this, keep a night every week (afternoon or morning) when you are free from all routine engagements and you do something pleasurable, fun, enjoyable with your partner and something that is not fixed. Call it "our wild night" if you wish…

Phase 8 – The post relationship (after the end of the relationship)

This is not a phase that needs to happen. It may happen or not. We all dream of the "happily ever after" ending, but most relationships end... And dealing with past relationships is not easy at all.

The key is to ***try to close the relationship on consensual and friendly terms.*** Sometimes it is hard, especially because your ex-partner won't allow it. If this is the case, you need to make sure that you do not blame yourself for it. Leave a door open for when s/he is ready to accept the new terms of your relationship and move on.

You need to be very firm and calm when you communicate to a (soon to be) ex-partner that you *want a sense of closure and you intend to stay on friendly terms.* Your best chance is to do it when you are:

- Alone (a park is far better than a busy road and even a restaurant).
- Free from other engagements (trying to sort these things out during a lunch break isn't a good idea).
- Relaxed (as far as possible) and not hurried.
- Both prepared (try not to surprise him or her if possible).

Here too, you must ***express empathy and even sadness for the end of the relationship.*** Sentences like, "Finally I can see the back of you," even if sometimes it is very much truthful, it is not the best way to negotiate a deal, and this very much what you want to do.

You want to make sure that *your past relationship won't become a problem for your future life,* and an angry ex-partner is not the best solution. This is a *must* for you. It is your main goal. And this is the reason why ***you should never end a relationship trying to leave the ex-partner with a sense of guilt, of being "the bad one" etc.*** If possible, of course.

If it is not possible, ***at least draw a line; get your ex to understand that, yes, things will be hard to get over, but that you do not want any more problems.***

If it is possible, try also to ***turn your relationship into a good friendship.*** This too is sometimes very hard, and it is easier if your romantic relationship already has strong elements of friendship. It also requires you both to be ok with not being together anymore.

True, you are correct; very often the pain in one or both the partners (or wound, in any case) is so big and strong that this is impossible. But maybe tell him or her that you are willing to restart as friends when you both are ready.

This will give your ex (and yourself) something to look forward to, and a perspective to use in order to reshape the relationship. You can't imagine what a powerful tool this is. Our mind fantasizes a lot, and when we know that something is even remotely possible, we feel comfortable with imagining it.

And if you start imagining something, like a friendship, you *start accepting it.* And that would put your partner (and your friend) on the first step towards turning what used to be a love story into a friendship.

So, as you can see, if you manage your relationships well, and, of course, with a pinch of luck, but above all with the collaboration of your partners, the "happily ever after" ending is not just a thing of fairy tales!

Very soon we will also look at many more shades and colors and flavors that relationships can have. What we have seen is that relationships evolve and change. To have a long life, usually a relationship needs to do this. But with every change, there are new challenges, new insecurities and, often, new problems too.

But we have seen how to manage these, so that your relationship can be a happy one at any stage. Part of the success is due to lifestyle and life choices, but a lot is also a matter of communication, and this is where we are heading next.

5

"THE RELATIONSHIP TALK"

It can be one of the most embarrassing things to do... You think about it for days (even weeks). You fret about it. You worry about it. You try it out in front of the mirror... When the moment comes, though, your knees go weak and you talk about the latest reality TV show instead...

This is a far too common scenario. Mind you, some people are better at it than others, and, in fact, there are many elements involved in the "relationship talk", by which, of course we mean that very difficult chat we sometimes need to have with our partner(s) to save, change, or improve (or sometimes end) our relationship.

So, *the relationship talk itself can be a cause of insecurity, anxiety and, if it does not work, even frustration.* And this is why we need to talk about it...

What NOT to Do in a "Relationship Talk"

I have just shown you what not to do... I guess you got the joke... "This is why we need to talk about it," is not the best start of a conversation talk. It sounds like you have a bone to pick, that you are the one in control of the conversation and in many cases, it may sound like you want to put your partner on the spot.

And there is another thing you should not do: *don't assume that your partner is aware of the problem.* He or she may not be (this is fairly uncommon though), but first start gauging out if s/he is already aware of the problem. That would be the correct, polite and gentle way of going about it.

Do not make it into a trial of strength

Approach the whole process as a "negotiation" or even better as "collaboration" or as "coming together to solve a problem". If you change your perspective to this, already it will make it easier, less anxiety ridden, and more focused at the same time to talk about such an important thing as where your relationship is going.

Do not make your partner's faults and flaws the center of the talk

What's the point in telling someone that you don't appreciate their ways? Unless you have a positive goal and outcome in mind, it only comes across as a personal attack. This is a key point of positive psychology (which I have already mentioned): *if you really must point out something negative, frame it in a positive way and give a positive alternative or solution.*

Keep in mind that *the stakes are high in these talks.* And I am not just talking about your relationship... There are identity, confidence, emotional aspects at stake too... The same reasons that may worry you apply to your partner: *you are both very vulnerable during this talk.*

Think about how embarrassing it is to "lose face". In the end, if you want things to work, think that your partner will have to live with you even *after the talk*, and if s/he is badly hurt by it, your relationship may suffer.

And this is one of the main reasons of anxiety about these chats... "What will my relationship be like after the talk? Will it be the same? Will I feel the same about my partner? Will my partner feel the same about me?" These are all questions at the back of our mind when we need to face a "relationship talk."

The good news is that the answer really depends on you; if *you don't make the conversation about the flaws and faults of your partner, but the solutions, the chances are that your relationship may well improve.* Otherwise, the opposite may be true.

We'll look at how to approach it and structure it soon, don't worry, but I think you can already breathe a sigh of relief... Ok? Shift the focus from your upset to the solution, or it will only become a finger pointing exercise... And this is exactly what you are worrying about...

Don't try to have a "dominant position" during the talk

Sorry if I need to moan about society and the education system... We are taught that "to be powerful, in an advantageous position, in a negotiation means winning". We can see it on TV, it is part and parcel of Western culture etc.

To start with, this is not at all necessarily true. And then it may well work in a predatory transaction, where one wants to "snatch something from the other" (like taking over a business, winning a competition etc.…) but it really does not work when you want to build something together…

And yet many of us approach it like a competition… It isn't. And if that is how you feel about it, then the issue is with you. You need to put it off until you have finally found the actual focus of the "relationship talk".

This also applies to how you talk, when you talk and where you talk… And now, let's turn the hourglass: after having seen what *not to do,* we can turn to the positive side and see *how to manage the "relationship talk".*

How to Manage a Successful "Relationship Talk"

Now you know what to avoid, you should already have a more positive "feeling" about the "relationship talk". Now, step by step, you will see how to manage the whole talk, from when you first think about it to when you have it and then even afterwards…

Find the talk's focus: "What do you want from it?"

Martha needs to have a "relationship talk" this is her fixed idea: "I need to tell Paul how upsetting he has been recently, he goes out with his friends and he is ignoring me!" On the other side of the world, in New Zealand, Ari too has a similar problem with Laura, and he is thinking.

"I need to get Laura to come out with me a bit more, because recently, she has been going out with her friends while I had to stay at home." Who do you think is closer to succeeding?

Of course, it is Ari in New Zealand that has the right approach. And the right approach gives you the right perspective. This is why *you need to* ***find some time when you can put the upset aside and focus on what you want to achieve.***

You see, I understand fully how if you are upset, if you have been hurt, it is very hard to see the positive. But you do have a friend here, time. You cannot wait too long, not certainly long enough till you give up on resolving a problem. But you need to wait long enough for you to have that "moment of lucidity".

Then you can just ***find and state the positive outcome you want from the talk.*** Done? Ok, repeat it to yourself over and over again, do it over a few days every now and then. When you feel that this is a clear focus that you can use. When you feel that if you get drawn into a "you hurt me more" kind of argument, you can recall your real focus and switch back to it… well *then you are ready to call the talk.*

Choose the time and place correctly

Think about the *best possible situation where you can have the talk.* You know by now that it should not be in a hurried and crowded place. Let's play a game… put the following options in order from worst place to best (with you and your partner in mind):

- On the commute to work
- At your place after work

- Walking home after the cinema
- During lunch break in a café
- In a park on a sunny weekend day
- At his place before you go to a friend's birthday party

The exercise is self-explanatory; you need to negotiate different factors:

- *The place,* which needs to be neutral and peaceful.
- *The time,* which needs to be open ended, and not squeezed between other engagements.
- *The personal tastes and needs of your partner and yourself;* if it is spring and your partner has hay fever, maybe the park is not the best solution...

In any case, *choose a place and time which is good for both of you;* you both need to be comfortable with it. And be *willing to negotiate this place and time.* Don't make your partner feel like s/he is under pressure or that you have "imposed the meeting" onto him/her.

If you live together, think about going out for a walk... Talking about problems in the place where they "live", in places full of memories of these problems can bring them back in a negative way. On the other hand, walking out of a place "laden with problems" is already a liberating experience.

Plan and Structure the Talk but Don't Overdo It

Some of us like to ad-lib, and that is fine to a certain extent. I mean, if you really are one of those people who can always keep a level mind, who can always find the right words etc., please if you wish trust yourself.

But for most of us, this is not the case. Especially when there is an emotional involvement, it is hard to remember all we wanted to say. So, we will need some planning. Now, do please note that ***planning itself lowers anxiety and insecurities.***

We can go from the situation of Catherine who thought she would sail through it without planning, met her boyfriend by the riverbank and just went, "Er..." then silent to Matthew who, totally lacking confidence, went to the meeting with his beloved Charlotte with a whole set of notes. Unfortunately, Charlotte didn't like the idea of a "political rally kind of speech," as she put it and it all ended in failure and frustration.

Planning needs to be in general terms and flexible. You cannot predict everything that is going to happen, and you cannot predict how your partner is going to react. ***Keep your plan simple enough so that you can commit it to memory very easily.***

Three to five key points and maybe a few key words are all you need, but in particular, make sure you have ***your goal*** clearly in mind.

Of the key words, ***think carefully about how you can describe how you felt or feel***. Remember that expressing correctly how you feel as we said in Chapter 3 is the key to success. *Follow the structure in Chapter 3, "The language of feelings and emotions".*

Also ***allow your partner to express his or her feelings too after you have (or vice versa).***

That should already make sure that ***you both feel equal and empowered in the talk.***

Divide the talk into three parts:

- ***Expressing the problem.***
- ***Discussing the solution.***
- ***Agreeing on the steps to take next.***

So, after you both have expressed your feelings, you can, if you feel like it, ***forgive each other***. This would be ideal. If you do, do it with a smile and a hug etc. But this should not mean that everything is ok. This should be a first step to make sure things are not repeated.

Next, you can move into the second step: ***negotiating the solution.***

This is a different type of talk altogether. This is the actual negotiation. Don't try to impose your solution, but *present it as practical, show its benefits and argue it.*

But you should also be ready to *adapt it, change it, and incorporate your partner's suggestions.*

And how about if your partner has another solution in mind? Be prepared for this possibility and be very *open to your partner's solution.* This is not a matter of "who wins". It is a matter of *choosing the best solution.* And if you think your partner's is better, so be it.

Make sure *you pause on the solution you have chosen; it needs to be very clear to both of you.* Close with a toast, an ice cream, a small celebration of any kind… That will highlight the positive aspect of the relationship.

You can now ***agree on what steps to take next.*** This is the "implementation" phase of the solution. But I would add a little element which I will tell you at the end…

Try to be quite *specific but relaxed with this step.* If the problem is the same as Ari and Laura's and you wanted your partner to spend more time with you, maybe you should do as follows. On the one hand, choose one specific day (two, three etc.…) which you two will spend alone, together and having fun. On the other hand, you should still allow your partner to meet with his or her friends freely, as long as s/he honors her side of the deal with you.

Also decide *when to start* and, if it is a complex solution, *break up the solution into manageable steps and outline a sequence and timing for them.* This should not, however, become a source of stress. It should become a pleasurable project. Give yourself time; take it easy!

Ah, I was forgetting… The last tip… ***Take some time to bond after the talk.*** You see, making sure that your relationship is as sound and as loving as before is essential at this stage. Even you achieve a lot with the "relationship talk", it is never easy, and you have been through a tough negotiation, you have used logic and reason…

All this distracts you from the emotional and deep value and dimension of your relationship; so, this is time to "re-establish that emotional bond between the partners".

Is Rehearsing the "Relationship Talk" a Good Idea?

Like with all important things, yes. But don't turn it into a 24-episode TV series

Rehearse only bits of it, like the "expressing feelings and emotion" structure or routine. This is to make sure you don't get the wrong words out at the salient moments. Rehearse maybe some key parts and points. Find sentences or concepts you have in mind that you must make sure you say and rehearse only those.

But *only rehearse key bits and only till you feel fairly confident with them.* You *need to avoid that the "perfect delivery" ends up being a "soulless delivery".* If you rehearse too much, you will end up just "saying the words" without expressing the feelings. And that would be bad for the whole talk.

Do you know that one of the main problems with movie actors and actresses is that if they don't get the delivery right in the first few takes; the risk is that even they will fail to "express" the lines?

And have you ever tried to repeat a word over and over again till it has no meaning? This phenomenon is well known, and it is called *"semantic saturation".* On a different level, this happens to "over-rehearsed lines" too.

And *do not rehearse the whole talk; this can be very counterproductive.* To start with, you do not know how it will go. If you rehearse it and your partner leads it in another direction, you will find it harder to adapt, change and in the end get what you want.

What is more, if you rehearse it all, you may end up thinking that if it does not go as you have planned, it is not a success. And it will not go exactly as you planned. Even if it is successful! So, rehearsing the whole talk (like politicians do with speeches and actors with scripts) will end up being a source of frustration...

How to Behave During the Talk

Once you have a good idea of what you want to get from the talk, of what you are going to say (in general terms) and how the talk will be structured, you can "face the music" with much more confidence and a stronger heart.

But like with all "live events" there are always surprises and unforeseen events. What can you do then? Here are a few handy tips for you...

Be flexible

Be ready to change tack and follow your partner. This does not mean "giving up"; it means collaborating. Keep your goal in mind, but don't become too strict with the ways you can follow in order to achieve it.

Be calm

Try to be calm and in control of yourself, rather than in control of the conversation. If you become upset, do take some time off. Five minutes to cool down if necessary, or even more, must be granted to you and to your partner every time they are needed.

Which leads us to the next point...

Take breaks

If you or your partner get tired, upset, nervous, tearful, confused etc., be absolutely ready to take a break. Even if the talk goes on for too long...

You need to *focus on getting things right, with calm and serenity (as far as possible) rather than getting things "done quickly".*

And on this point...

Be ready to adjourn

What an official sounding word... But the point is that if you cannot reach an agreement, and you are feeling tired, frustrated, or in general you feel that you are not moving forward, stop the talk and agree to meet again another time.

But another time does not mean "some time"; decide the time and place and make it as soon as possible. Just give each other enough time to "collect your thoughts and reflect" and then meet again.

A long wait can be frustrating and even induce anxiety. So, "next week" is a bit too late, and if it can be done within a day or two, do it.

Keep to the point – don't start chains or "go down memory lane"

Try to stick to your points, the ones you had planned, as far as possible. Above all, avoid making long lists of "the times when you..." or "things that you..." These can be taken as "insisting on something painful". They can be felt more like an accusation than a chat with a solution in mind.

At the same time, if past memories come up, just pick the positive ones to share with your partner. If negative ones come up, avoid going "down memory lane" with them… it will have the same effect as before: *your partner will feel like s/he is on trial while you are reading the counts of accusations to him/her.*

Fend off eventual "attacks"

This is very important, and we will look into it in more detail next, when we talk about "de-escalating", a skill which is so useful in all relationships of all types and it comes in handy in so many situations…

Understand that your partner – through past experiences, maybe – could have the wrong idea of what the whole exercise is about… We are "programmed" to react to any criticism with "but you" or "how about the time when you?" etc.… We look at these situations as a "match" rather than a collaboration. And this can happen even if you use the most sympathetic, soft and welcoming words…

The best solution is to ignore any "attacks". This can be hard, and we will see how you can be successful at this next, but for now, think that if you fall into that logic of "you against me" the whole talk is going to turn into an argument.

So, *be very aware of any signs of the talk turning into an argument.* When you spot them:

- *Ignore them*
- *Defuse them (even with a joke)*
- *Do not return them*

- *If necessary, walk away and take a break*

If you can, do tell your partner that your intention was not to have an argument, and that this is not the time to bring up all the little disagreements and problems you have...

And this leads us straight into the next chapter. In fact, a very, very important one on de-escalating situations... And even the very, very best and most romantic relationships sometimes have "their moments". Better be prepared then!

6

DEALING WITH ARGUMENTS IN YOUR RELATIONSHIP

"... And they lived happily ever after" – bickering every now and then and with the occasional epic row. Let's face reality, even the most close-knit couple will have the occasional crisis. Of course, there are exceptions, but they are very rare. And we need to be prepared for all eventualities.

In fact, we all have first-hand experience of rows... And here is where we will start. It is an unpleasant thought, I know, but think about a row you remember well. Even one you have seen in a movie if you want to keep some detachment.

Just go through it like a story, just a normal narrative first. Then, try to identify this:

- The phrase or action that *triggered* the argument.
- The *response* to that trigger.

- The *escalation*.
- The *tipping point,* which is when the row actually became "full out".
- If you can, also look at before the row or argument, and see if one of the two people gave any signs of *"being closed to others"*, of not wanting to deal with any challenge, like the way s/he walked, talked, looked, sat etc.…

As usual, take your time… I actually live in a cupboard and come out only when you need me…

…

Out of the cupboard then… Take a deep breath. I fully understand the emotional price of remembering negative episodes… Anyway, have you identified the *trigger, response, escalation,* and *tipping point?*

I bet you have, and you have likely found signs of closure in one of the participants too.

And if you have, you now know…

The Stages of an Argument or Row

There is a huge difference between having a disagreement and having an argument, or a row. A disagreement is simply a matter of having different opinions; in a row, you have *a clash and signs of hostility.*

And rows or arguments have a very specific pattern. We all recognize it, at least subconsciously. In fact, we all *know* when an argument is about to burst between two people because we recognize the stages.

The pre-stage

Even before the row, there are usually elements that can bring about the clash. These may be many, like long term hostility or competition between the people involved, or one of the people having had a bad day (signaled though verbal and nonverbal signs, as we said – signs that are not picked up by the other person, most often).

Now, imagine a child at school, her name is Namina... She is really sulking and refusing to collaborate... She is looking out of the window, and she looks angry. The teacher does not know why Namina is behaving like this. But she is worried and keeps looking at her and she goes to her. She also goes over to her side of the classroom quite often, and then she tries to talk to Namina...

Of course, to no avail... Namina, instead of collaborating, gets even more upset.

Now, can you see what has gone wrong here? Look at this example and see what has happened that has spoiled the teacher's effort?

...

It's full of woodworms in my cupboard, I have just found out... Did you have time to think about it? You may have come up with a few answers like:

- They are in front of other people, so, this is not the place to talk to Namina, as she may want to keep her privacy.

- Maybe the teacher is the cause of Namina's upset and she does not know it?
- The teacher missed to read Namina' "keep off" body language.
- Maybe Namina would like a friend to talk to her?
- Going over to her side repeatedly may have worsened the situation.

All these could be good reasons. The key point is to *identify pre-crisis or pre-argument signs in others.* And by all means ***if you see an argument coming, do not trigger it, step away!***

Really the only solution at this stage is to ***allow the other person time to sort out his or her problems, to stay alone and cool down.***

The trigger

This can be very small. It can be a word, a gesture, even just a look.

The problem is that ***the trigger is not the real cause of the argument, but it often becomes the center of the argument itself.*** This means that *in arguments, people often talk and argue about the wrong point...*

You all know that when couples (especially small ones) argue about small things, in reality they are bickering about "something else". This happens so often, "Eat with your mouth closed," sometimes can mean "We never have quality time together..."

In the short run, the people concerned are trapped in a *topic that will not give any real solution to the real problem.* In serious cases, then, when there is a long history of disagreement and problems, this can become a pure "exercise in hostility". At this stage, the topic is totally irrelevant... That is a pathological stage. But it is far more common than we might imagine.

In the long term, the couple often use this "shift of focus on the trigger" to avoid facing the real problem, which is often more painful, more difficult to approach and solve...

Now, hold onto this information for a few minutes. You will need it when we talk about the solutions.

The response to the trigger

If the trigger goes unnoticed, the argument does not start (and this is a hint...) But if it is picked up with hostility, then the argument is in the making. In this case, the trigger is seen as any or all of these:

- A (personal) challenge
- An act of hostility
- Unfair
- A signal that the other person wants to argue
- A challenge of one's position

The response, then, will be one of *confrontation, rather than reconciliation.*

There are also some typical qualities of this response, like it is quick, it is negative, it is not thoughtful, it is often loud etc.

But while you can see that with a proper analysis of the dynamics of arguments (like this) you can already see possible paths to a solution, I will ask you to wait for few minutes... We will get to it soon.

The escalation

After the trigger it is usually hard to calm things down. The opposition of the two parts becomes bigger and bigger, stronger and stronger... words become louder and louder and *the more the exchange goes on the further apart the people involved become.*

This is a phase called escalation. Do you remember Namina? I didn't tell you what happened after the teacher asked her:

"What's wrong with you, Namina?" (Wrong question – trigger!)

"Nothing, Miss," answers Namina with a grunt and looking away.

"It can't be nothing," replies the teacher.

"I said nothing," insists Namina.

"You are sulking, Namina, why?" the teacher says, her voice louder.

"Why are you hassling me?" Namina's voice too gets louder.

"How dare you talk to me like that!" shouts the teacher.

Namina storms out of the classroom.

Escalation is characterized by:

- None of the participants giving up.
- Increasing intensity.

- Increasing loudness.
- Stronger and stronger words.
- Sometimes, even aggressive gestures.

Escalation pushes one of the participants to take action, in some cases, this is shouting so loud that the other is silenced. In other cases, it can actually get physical. Namina, a child, actually has the best reaction she could have: she storms out, yes, breaking school rules, but she actually stops the argument the only way she can. High five Namina! You are wiser than the teacher! And we'll see why in the solution part of this chapter.

The tipping point

The *escalation forces a tipping point: because none of the participants is willing to give up, one of them needs to take drastic action to put an end to the argument.* This is also the most dangerous point in an argument. It is usually at this stage that, if one person has aggressive tendencies, things become physical.

Even in arguments among thugs the dynamics are the same and there is little expectation of violence till the tipping point. Looking at them (even how their arguments are portrayed realistically in films) you can see all the stages leading up to what is often a physical reaction.

Then, of course, in movies there are friends who split them up or things become really nasty.

But a violent end to arguments is comparatively rare. In most cases, there is a *total breakdown of communication, accompanied by loud and angry words and a breakup of some sort.* I don't mean a breaking up of a relationship – not necessarily, though there are relationships that break up after arguments, quite a few indeed! In case one of the partners has the cool head Namina has, the breakup can just be one of the partners walking away.

Now you know how the teacher felt… She felt Namina's walking away is a challenge to her role and authority, even an insult… And when the relationship is personal and even more intimate, the walking away can be even tougher, often followed by tears etc.

But some people have this as their exist strategy, like Namina. They are people who, for whatever reason (it can be a very personal reason, like, in some cases children who often witnessed their parents arguing) cannot stand an argument. Their gut reaction is to walk away.

If your partner is one of these people, *respect his or her "strategy".* It is actually a good and wise one. But the key thing is that *you should not take it as a personal insult or challenge or disrespect. Nor should you necessarily think your partner does not want to face the problem you have. It may just be that your partner will not face the problem during an argument.*

If you notice this attitude in your partner, try to discuss the actual problem (not the trigger) with serenity, a bit like we said in the "relationship talk" chapter. If you notice that your partner is more open to talking there, then you are onto a solution.

And talking about solutions…

How to Avoid a Bad Argument

We have already seen some solutions, and there are quite a few we are going to see right now. Before we do, however, we need to look at some general points.

You need to understand the stages of arguments to apply the right solution. And you have just seen them all… so, we are at a good point.

At each stage, you have a way out. So, don't worry if the argument has been triggered, you still have a way of getting out of it, maybe even with a smile!

Your aim to avoid the tipping point at all costs. You see, if you look at a bad argument from its "climax", from its final point, you realize that all that goes on before, while bad, is far less painful. So, whenever an argument starts, please understand that it is going to become more and more painful the longer it goes on, so, as a consequence…

…*Try to stop the argument at as early a stage as possible.* Put your ego and your immediate goals (that may be "getting it off your chest" or "venting your anger" or "this time I'm not letting him/her off the hook"). Instead, *focus on your long-term goal, which is to have a happy relationship with as little tension as possible and to solve problems...*

If you argue often, you will notice that at first you will manage to stop the tipping just before it happens or to "soften it" while it still happens. Then, after some time, you will usually stop the arguments at increasingly earlier stages. Habits, even arguing habits, are hard to break and progress is usually gradual... But keep at it and in the meantime focus on how more relaxed, and happier your relationship is gradually becoming.

Avoiding the Bad Argument

We have already touched on it. The best way out and the earliest way out is to *understand when your partner is "closed" and avoid nagging or teasing her or him.* The best thing the teacher should have done is what Namina was asking with her body language and attitude: leave her alone. You will be amazed at how common Namina's story is in classrooms... And how some teachers still don't get the key strategy point: if a student is angry, it may not be about you, and don't take it personally. Leave the pupil alone and if you don't, then it may become about you...

The same often applies to partners. How many times have partners quarreled because one of them was tired and the other didn't understand it? You get home from work and you are knackered. That's really not the time to have a trigger thrown your way, like, "Once more you have forgotten to put out the garbage!"

You understand how you feel when these things happen to you, right? You think, "I am exhausted, can't s/he see it?" Then, as things happen again and again, the odd thought like, "S/he's done it again," or even, "Now s/he is doing it on purpose," sneak in and make things even worse.

Then again, we can even take things personally, with thoughts along the lines of, "If s/he has not seen how exhausted I am, it means s/he has not even looked at me!" And this is quite a sad thought, really. But maybe s/he has not been able to read your nonverbal cues, like you slumping into the sofa... Maybe s/he is tired too and sees you on the sofa while s/he is cooking...

Now, I'm not taking sides (and this is the wisest thing to do when you see people arguing...), but I am trying to make you think from your partner's perspective. Surely you have been in both roles, have you not?

So, the first trick is to ***understand when your partner is "closed" and that at this stage, even things that may have a very innocent intention can be seen as "triggers".***

Defuse the Trigger

"But how about if my partner gets triggered when I had not meant to?" is your very good question. There is a simple answer. Do not follow on from his or her response. Instead, *step back and explain that you had not meant it like that.*

Imagine an argument being like two boats that keep bumping into each other... You trigger (involuntarily) and that's the first bump, then your partner responds, if you start from their response and keep going in that direction, you are in for a bumpy ride. If you step back, you are in for some smooth sailing.

Example?

Tom: "Hey, Mary, you have not posted the letter yet."

Mary: "I have been working all day, what have you been doing?"

Tom: "I have been looking for a job, why do you make me feel guilty about it?"

...Bumpy ride for the next 30 minutes.

You see, Tom triggered and then replied to Mary's response "what have you been doing?" But that question really did not want an answer, did it? The real function was to vent Mary's frustration...

Let's wind it back then:

Tom: "Hey Mary, you have not posted the letter yet."

Mary: "I have been working all day, what have you been doing?"

Tom: "No, Mary, I didn't mean to accuse you. Just noticed and I was asking if you wanted me to post it..."

Mary: "Sorry I misunderstood, thanks, if you can..."

...Smooth sailing and candlelit dinner in 30 minutes then...

The only issue with this example is that people don't use paper mail anymore, but sure you can see that if you catch things at this early stage, you can literally turn a potentially painful situation into a nice experience.

But what happens when the trigger comes to you? What happens if it is actually meant? The best way is to *defuse the trigger*. There are three ways you can do this:

1. *Ignore the trigger,* walking away pretending not to have heard it is quite good but if you do it repeatedly it may get on

your partner's nerves, depending on her/his personality and if s/he has a bone to pick with you.

2. *Take it as a joke*, this may be risky. If it is involuntary, then usually things get sorted immediately, but if it isn't your partner may take it as a challenge, like, "S/he doesn't even take me seriously!" It also depends on the importance of the topic...
3. *Explain expressing your feelings,* which is the hardest but best and safest response. Something similar to what we have learned already, like, "I understand you are annoyed but please understand that I am very tired too now," and then add a suggestion or an "action point" as businesspeople like to call them: "Shall we talk about it after dinner when we are more relaxed?"

This usually gives the other partner the chance to think about the *real issue* (not the trigger, remember?) and you can turn what would be a useless and unpleasant row into a chance to talk something over constructively.

However, if you say, "Let's talk about it later," then do... Do not use it as a "get out trick" – even if the temptation is big...

In conclusion, ***if you need to respond to a trigger, defuse it, if you give a trigger by mistake, explain that you did not mean it.*** This will do the trick in most cases.

Try, if you can, and especially as you become more experienced at managing these situations, to stop the argument at this stage. At this stage, in fact arguments are mainly a matter of "getting on each other's nerves", which is unpleasant but manageable. It is in the next stage, however, that things start to become personal...

De-escalating an Argument

Escalation is the longest part of the argument, and it is the one before the tipping point. So, in a way, it is very unpleasant and as we have just said things start to become painful and personal during escalation. On the other hand, the trigger and first response are usually a matter of seconds (even less than one second!) How about if you are caught off guard, or simply you couldn't defuse the trigger?

Then, the good news is that the next phase is longer, and this gives you more time to try to change it. And the way to change it is by *de-escalating.*

First of all, you need to understand that ***to de-escalate an argument you must avoid getting caught in all its twists and turns.*** What do we mean? We have the tendency to answer all the points, all the questions, all the challenges. It's like being on Twitter. And that is useless, tiring, and bad for your relationship. We feel like we are at a football game or basketball game and we need to score as many points as possible.

The reality is that this very fact leads us away from *the real goal which is to avoid a useless argument (or match), avoid pain and hurt and protect your relationship.* Who cares if it was really you who forgot the keys 3 years ago when you got locked out? And if it was? And if it was your partner? What would change? The only thing that changes is that *by bringing unpleasant and conflictual topics up you strain your relationship, and you suffer.*

So, keep the eye on "the big prize" rather than on all the crumbs that lead to the tipping point. Keeping this in mind, here is what you need to do.

Listen to your partner

We tend to interrupt each other in arguments and a clear sign of escalation is increasingly frequent and faster interruptions. This in itself becomes annoying and a cause of frustration etc.…

So, listen till your partner has finished and you will have already reduced the *tension in the argument.*

Agree when possible

Because we have been triggered, we already start every exchange with the "no, you are wrong, and I am right" attitude. Well, that is a recipe for disaster. Instead, try the exact opposite. I know it is hard and our egos get in the way with these things but try to use sentences like these as far and as often as possible:

"I agree…"

"I can see your point."

"I had not seen it from that perspective."

Even

"I am not sure, but I will think about it."

If you feel like doing it just to defuse the argument, please go ahead…

Allow your partner to chill down

Take time before you reply. Who said that you need to answer straight away?

Then again, on some points you may want to give your partner a chance to "ramble on a bit". You see, jumping from point to point is very stressful and tense. Elaborating on a point instead is more relaxing.

Be careful which point you pick; choose one that is not too sensitive, not very confrontational and literally sidetrack your partner saying, "Can you explain this a bit more?" You see, this way you will give your partner a chance to "breathe"…

The best chances are when s/he brings into the argument a third person (not present of course!) like "When I saw Charlie he was still walking back on foot and his car was broken and you told me..." Stop him/her there (not verbally, just ignore the "and you told me and …" and anything after that) and say, "Tell me more about Charlie's accident that night."

This way you show interest, you divert in another person and you also give your partner a chance to cool down, on a less emotional topic.

Express your feelings!

You have already seen the power of expressing feelings… Now, it is hard to do it during an argument, but if you do… This is the most disarming tactic you can have.

Arguments are based on the "being right or wrong" plane... They are structured around rational, not emotional points. Arguments don't start with sentences like, "When you said I was stupid I felt really hurt inside..." (emphasis on feeling) but, "You even told me that I am stupid!" (meaning, "Admit you are wrong, I am not stupid!").

So, if you can, do bring in how you are feeling about the argument. Do it without shouting and try to be as calm but sincere as possible. Also *do not express your feelings like an accusation.* Avoid saying, "you". Use sentences like:

"At this stage the conversation is becoming painful for me."

"These are things that are upsetting me very much."

"I am not ready to talk about painful things in this situation"

Even give warnings like:

"I am not sure if we go on like this that I can bear it much longer."

But at all costs avoid sentences like:

"You are hurting me now!" That's an accusation.

"What you say is very painful."

It does take time to de-escalate an argument. You may end up talking for a while, but keep calming it down rather than "sparking it up."

In most cases, *after a few minutes of de-escalation you will notice your partner has started collaborating with it.* Incredibly enough you only need to "hold the fort" (of peace of course) for a few minutes and your partner will come back to his/her senses.

At that stage, s/he will realize that what was about to happen was too painful and start giving soothing topics, ways out… the first joke is always the best sign ever that the argument is fully and finally over!

Walk away

Yes, Namina was actually right. If everything fails, walk away. When you have no other option, physical distance may be your only one. If your relationship is quite "argumentative" this may well be all you can do to start with. Later on, you will be able to de-escalate or even defuse the trigger. Don't be ashamed if this is all you can do.

High five to you too; it is always wise to avoid the tipping point. In fact, it may send your partner the message that s/he has gone too far. Walking away is a clear boundary setting signal. And in relationships sometimes boundaries are necessary

But if you can, ***try to walk away calmly.*** Explain why, with sentences like:

"Sorry, this is becoming too much, I need to take a break."

"I really can't manage this anymore, I need some fresh air."

If you can, ***stay away for at least 20 minutes.*** That's the time it takes for people to cool down… If you approach him or her earlier, you may re-ignite the argument.

Finally, ***follow up with a friendly chat***. And there is one thing you should not forget in this: tell your partner that your walking away was not personal but because of the tension of the situation. This is your message. The "solving problems" conversation can (and maybe should) happen at a later stage. This is primarily to explain your reaction.

Moving onto Sunnier Beaches

This has been a tough chapter, I apologize. I understand that these are painful topics, but I had to discuss it in full, I hope you understand me… But now we can all breathe a sigh of relief and what makes me happy is that now you can solve even quite problematic situations! You must be quite relieved, as – you know, now you can avoid most arguments, which takes away a lot of insecurities and anxiety.

But before we move on, two little tips…

In any follow up to the (hopefully missed) argument don't be afraid to say "sorry." This beautiful word can literally disarm anybody and defuse any sticky situation. It is also very cathartic, very liberating…

After any (hopefully missed) argument have some bonding, some quality time together... Like after any problem you face – ***relationships need constant nourishment...***

But now onto new beaches… And some may well be very new to you indeed! What do I mean? Well, you'll have to read the next chapter to find out…

7

MODELING YOUR RELATIONSHIP

Let me introduce you to some friends of mine. Their names are Lisa and Geoff. They have been together for a long time now. They are not married, but they have been living together for some time. And yes, they live in a flat on the suburbs. Unfortunately, so they say, they have two cars, because he works as a clerk on one side of town while she works as a teacher on the other side of town.

So, as you may expect, they have busy professional lives, but they do spend their weekends together. Their plans? Well, the main one for this year is to have a "proper holiday..." Disappointed? Did you expect the tapping of tiny feet? Er... maybe in the future; it's not off, but you know... it's a big choice.

But did I mention that I also have friends a few miles off in the countryside? They live on a hill and they set up their organic farm there. They have been doing it for some years now. It was hard at first, and it still is. But they are now seeing the fruit of their work. To start with, what used to be barren land is now a forest.

Of course, they live together and work together, and they are in a relationship. Their names? Ah, sorry, I was forgetting, Paul, Miles and Frank...

Can you help me now? I need to know what sort of challenges the two "groups" have, what their relationships may be like, what are the differences etc.... While you are at it, you can even think which you would like best... Don't need to tell me, just for you... I'll be out on the balcony if you need me.

...

It was a bit windy outside. Now have you compared the two relationships? Sure, you can see that one is turning into what we may call a *traditional relationship.* It is heterosexual, it is a couple, they live together, they have a "normal" life and "normal" plans. By "normal" we mean "common". In psychology and sociology normality has a different meaning from what people usually intend. Yes, I *am* teasing you and yes, it is a theme of this chapter.

Looking at my countryside friends, you can't have missed that there are three of them in the relationship, and that is fairly unusual (not that much, really). You will have noticed that it is a homosexual relationship and that is not "canonical".

On to their challenges now... Remember that this is a "mind experiment". I think we will agree that from what we have seen,

Lisa and Geoff are already dealing with pressures from work, social life and urban living. Tom, Miles and Frank on the other hand may be facing a bit of prejudice. They are not the kind of relationship the local villagers are used to seeing at church on Sundays. And of course, living and working together has its disadvantages.

But have you also considered that having a *polyamorous relationship* also means having possible problems and even few role models and past examples to go by? It's actually quite hard...

So, what can we learn from this thought experiment?

- *There are many relationship models, some common and some not.*
- *Each has its internal dynamics but also challenges.*

And this is really what this chapter is all about. We have seen how relationships change with time; now we will see ***archetypal models that you can use to shape your relationship on***.

Having said this, you can be creative, mix models, and take a bit from one and a bit from the other... You don't need to follow each model exactly; relationships are not flatpack furniture with instructions to follow in detail...

Relationships and "Normality"

Today you are going to meet lots of my friends. Martha and Stewart are a couple from the Midwest. He works in a bank and she stays at home, minding the children and doing charitable work. They are not married but they are very happy together. But I made a mistake... They *were* a couple from the Midwest in the 1950s!

You see, what appears "normal" now was totally unacceptable some time ago. A lot depends on where you live, but to take the average US provincial town, even an interracial couple would have been "taboo" just a few decades ago (I suppose it still is in some places)...

What does this tell us? That *"normality as we mean it is a cultural construct".* It does not exist; in fact, it keeps changing. It depends on *the traditions and values of a community.* In fact, what is normal in some northern European countries and has been normal there for decades sounds "outrageous" or "futuristic" (depending on your approach) to most people in the USA nowadays.

So, psychologists and sociologists do not like to use the word "normal". Normal in fact means "adhering to a norm", which is a rule, a law. And the only "norm" that matters to psychologists and sociologists is that people are happy and that they do not do any harm to other people with their behavior.

So, three or even twenty people living a relationship who are happy with it and bother no one else are perfectly "normal" from a psychological or sociological point of view. And here, we use the word "normal" as "acceptable".

No relationship is the same. But this "normality myth" tends to make them all the same. It puts limits that are often a barrier to the partners' own happiness. In the Western World and also some Asian society it is becoming more "permissive". By this we mean that it is more "accepting of people's personal choices".

Therefore, things that were normal and expected just not long ago are now no longer so. For example, a married couple was expected to have children in the first few years of their marriage. Now, because children "cost" and because society in general has become less strict, this is no longer expected.

But it's also true that some rules were (are valid) for some people and not other people. We mentioned polyamory… It's nothing new though… Not if you were a European king… As a poor person you would have been hanged or burned on the stake or whatever if you had an affair. On the other hand, kings were expected to have "concubines" and they actually lived with the King and the Queen, went to their parties and were literally paid for their services from the royal purse.

So, here you see, this "normality" has always had differences… Yet again, while we look at the European aristocracy (noble people like dukes, counts, and barons) as "traditional and conservative" they too have always had a very open and relaxed attitude towards extramarital affairs and even homosexuality. Only among their class though. Apparently, the poor "could not manage such things" and had to be deterred and even convicted for them…

We will see that all the "models" in this chapter are not at all new. We should not see the modern world as being "the most liberal" when it comes to relationship. It is not necessarily so. For example, an Ancient Greek man was expected to have a wife and a male lover. Expected by the age of 9 – the boy lover, I mean.

On the other hand, in the "cradle of democracy", Athens in Ancient Greece only 25% of people were actually considered "humans" or "people" as the other 75% was made up of women and slaves, both regarded and treated as animals and property…

What I am saying is that things are not "linear" in history and "progress" is not one directional. They are multifaceted and complex instead. But we can also find examples of "modern relationship models" in the old days…

Taking the US as an example, statistics show that 64% of people are really happy with their relationships. The worrying data is 19% of people who are in some ways not happy with it, according to a survey by eHarmony. This is quite a lot, in fact.

But there is good news too. In a study by Perelli-Harris, Hoherz, Lappegård and Evans the results show that married people in the UK, Australia, Germany, and Norway are on the whole happier than people who are not in stable relationships. This is based mainly on midlife people, but it shows that relationships on the whole have a positive effect ('Mind the "Happiness" Gap: The Relationship Between Cohabitation, Marriage and Subjective Well-being in the United Kingdom, Australia, Germany, and Norway' published in *Demography,* August 2019).

Being Comfortable with Your Relationship

But we skipped on the most important point ever: ***to be happy in a relationship you need to be comfortable with it.*** That little word, "comfortable" is the key to everything. It is the *foundation of all relationships.* Both partners (or more) need to be comfortable with it.

One of the reasons why many relationships break up is adultery. Now, if the couple is comfortable with one (or both) having an external relationship, a "lover", then it's all fine. The problem arises when one of them is not comfortable with it. Even here, habits are different according to class in the West. Rich entrepreneurs live in a social milieu where having "lovers" is normal. It is quite common for both partners to have extramarital relationships and to be open about it. It is much less accepted in middle- and lower-class couples though.

So, ***it is not up to the sociologist or the psychologist to tell you what you should be comfortable with. It is up to the psychologist and sociologist to help you reach that level of comfort that will make your relationship successful***.

This is very important because we need to understand your role and my role in this chapter.

I will offer you a wide range of models, to consider, play with, tweak etc. But the choice must be yours. I cannot tell you which one is the best relationship model for you. And use this word as your guiding light: "comfortable".

You won't need to tell me. You know I am like the elf you keep locked in a draw... Silent and discreet. But then my job is to help you make those changes to your relationship so that you have a model that you feel comfortable with.

And being comfortable with the structure and dynamics of your relationship is the best way to avoid anxiety and insecurities.

Modeling or Molding Your Relationship: Key Concepts

Even before we look at some models and their issues (and advantages, why not?) we need to see some principles.

Model consensually

You cannot add or change aspects of your relationship without the consent of your partner(s). This is why many extramarital relationships spell the end of the relationship... They are carried out behind the back of the partner...

But even with small changes, you need to make sure that your partner is happy with them. If you want, for example a more "friendly" relationship (wait and see), then you must make sure you both are comfortable with it.

Work together

Collaboration is key to all relationships and it follows from consent. What matters is that any change you want to bring to your relationship is tackled as a collaborative task. Take it as a "shared project". This alone will strengthen the bonds of your relationship.

Pause and reflect

Don't go full steam only to find out that "it wasn't like you had expected" ... Take things slowly and take regular pauses to reflect (together!) on how things are actually working out for both of you.

Be ready to step back and change plan

If things are not working out, fine. Don't feel that "you have to finish what you have started". You should be ready to go back to how things were before. Maybe you can try it another time, later on? Maybe it was just a bad idea! It does not matter. Your key aim is to be – remember? – *comfortable* with the changes!

Archetypal Relationship Models

What follows is not a series of rules or rigid structures. On the contrary. Like being a "mother", "teacher" or "friend" is a general idea with some key qualities, but it allows for a wide range of shades and realization in practice, the same applies to an archetype.

Archetypes are key anthropological concepts. For example, we have the idea of tyranny or democracy in politics, but then there are many different types of tyrannies and democracies. So, read what follows as "general overall types", which is exactly what archetype means.

Some are common nowadays and some less.

The Married Couple

The most widespread "mold" for relationships is the "married couple". Until recently, and still in many countries, this mainly stands for a "heterosexual married couple". However, this very archetype is changing in very liberal countries like Sweden and Denmark.

It is also true that with the introduction of LGBT weddings or civil partnerships in many countries, LGBT couples have embraced the values and dynamics of the “married couple”. In many cases the lifestyle of a gay married couple is very virtually the same as that of a straight married couple. And this is what matters from the point of view of relationships.

There are some great advantages to this model:

- Stability over time
- Legal protection
- Financial protection
- Easy recognition and acceptance by society and the community
- Religious choice (especially if straight)
- Strong legal protection for children

On the other hand, it is quite demanding too. In fact, it requires:

- Long term commitment
- Usually (exceptions can be found!) a faithful and monogamous lifestyle
- Intensive relationship
- Lack of freedom in case you wish to change – a divorce has big legal, and practical consequences and it takes time. In some countries and cultures, divorce is not even accepted.

This gives you a clear idea that when you want to mold your relationship into the "married couple" model, there are big considerations to make. But it is also a good starting point to show you that this modeling of relationships needs consensual partners, collaboration, and some deep thinking.

And this is true even if you do not want to institutionalize your choice.

The Same or Different Culture Relationships

These are two models, one opposite to the other, and we shall see them together. Having a partner from your own culture is usually easier and this is the reason why most people choose this route. Moreover, society makes it very easy.

On the other hand, sharing a life with someone from a different culture can be fascinating and a wonderful experience. This, in successfully well integrated cases, ends up mixing the two cultures. However, the cultural difference usually remains to some extent and it can cause frictions all through the relationship.

A key issue is the language. Usually, people choose the language of the place where they live as their main language. But then there is the challenge of which language(s) to speak with the children, when and why.

It is quite common that the partner who does not live in his/her culture will want to preserve his/her culture with the child or children. This will mean communicating in a language that others do not understand. This can also cause conflictual situations with the partner.

The Friendly Relationship

I have been waiting to talk to you about this for a long time. In most romantic relationships there is also *a strong element of friendship.* We have seen how when this is true, the ex-partners often (not always) find it easier to keep good relations after breaking up.

People who become romantically attached after they have been friends for long usually preserve this friendly element. And this can continue and even grow all through the relationship.

This has some beautiful traits:

- Shared activities
- Shared views
- A sense of complicity
- Playfulness
- Mutual support
- Adaptability and flexibility within and with the relationship

However, not everybody finds the "friendship/intimate" distinction easy to manage. Some people for cultural reason do not see friends as people to have an intimate relationship with. Macho men who see friendship mainly as an "absolute denial of one's own sexuality" kind of bond, where playing darts or talking football are based on the mutual understanding that there cannot even be a sexual thought between them… Well, you get the picture… People with this cultural idea of friendship will find it hard to be friends with their sexual partner.

And this means that if the relationship becomes friendly oriented, these people may find having intimate moments "weird" and "uncomfortable". "Like having sex with my best friend," is the usual sort of phrase they will use to describe how they feel.

On the contrary, there are people who are quite fluid with the sexual/friendly dimensions. If that is your kind of person and your partner is similar, then you will find it easy to introduce more of a friendship into your relationship.

If you choose to add a "friendship element" to your relationship though do it "playing games". This is how friendships naturally develop: through shared activities with a bonding element. Instead of saying, "Now we have to behave like friends," do things that friends usually do together and you will naturally start behaving like friends.

Nice trick, isn't it?

The Polyamorous Relationship

This is quite a complex topic, but polyamory and metrosexuality are becoming more and more popular, or maybe they are just surfacing now after decades if not centuries of repression. We said that these were both expected, not just accepted in Ancient Greece. But of men, not women! That was more than a bit unfair.

Similarly, in some Arabic countries polygamy is perfectly legal. Again, if you are a man and you want more than one wife. Not if you are a woman though.

The dynamics of this sort of relationships however are very, very complex. They are not impossible by any means, but you need a very open attitude towards relationships. There is also the risk of jealousy within the relationship. So, ***absolutely key to polyamorous relationship is excellent, constant, honest, and open communication.***

There are whole books about it now. If this is where you are going, this very book has too wide a scope to deal with polyamorous relationships in detail. It's like bringing up a child... A huge learning curve. So, I would suggest that if this is where you are heading or if you want to experiment with it and you are new to polyamory you should:

- Read specialized books about it (check in the reading list at the end of this book).
- Maybe try with experienced people first.

If you are in a monogamous relationship and to wish to bring a third into it (or another couple etc.; the number is not the point), then make sure your partner is fully happy with it. Also make sure that you two take responsibility for the progress and happiness (and integration) of the third.

You see, in this case, you would be the "majority" to start with. But then again, make sure that the newcomer(s) does not try to split you two up. Unfortunately, there are actually people who derive pleasure from splitting other couples up. Of course, a couple wanting to introduce another partner can be an inviting situation for these people.

But I don't wish to worry you, scare you, or prejudice you. This, as we said, is a very complex and delicate process. You will find yourself navigating very narrow straights, but if this is what makes you happy...

- read a lot about it,
- talk to specialists,
- join groups that share experiences,
- take it slow.

And of course, good luck! It can be an almost magic journey.

The Intermittent Relationship

There is the time factor too to consider. Who said that all relationships need to be continuous? I personally have friends who have a relationship with people they only meet once in a while, usually regularly, but then each goes to his/her home and they meet again maybe a month later.

This is also quite common with young relationships. Sometimes partners only meet at the weekend and they keep separate all week. For people in their teens or in their twenties, this is a very common type of relationship.

It is fairly convenient from many points of view.

- You don't need to share daily stress, often during working days. That, remember, can be a heavy strain on any relationship.

- It is long term but not intensive.
- It suits a wide range of commitment level. This type of relationship where you can be fully committed to each other or just experimenting with each other.
- It gives each partner his or her private space and time.
- It's a good stage in between "dating" and "going steady".
- It can be a good compromise when the relationship is facing trouble instead of "taking a break". It can be that, "we are still together but we also want time on our own individually to think things over".
- It can work to keep the "infatuation" and attraction alive.

However, in many cases, these relationships don't last in this form for too long. I do know some that have gone on for years... But this is also an "in between stages" type of relationship. Also, it often happens that one of the two partners wants to "move to the next stage", which means "having a closer and more committed relationship".

When this happens, the other partner may accept, even enthusiastically. But sometimes s/he won't. Losing that freedom, the time on your own etc. can be deterrents. And any increased commitment can find people unwilling or not ready for it.

In this case, maybe you can try to reach a compromise and propose an experiment. Take it gradually and, for example, if you meet a weekend every month, instead of jumping straight into the "let's move in together" phase, meet twice a month instead... Easing the less willing partner into the new situation is a good strategy and it will also give both partners a chance to become comfortable with each other.

Painting Your Relationship

Thus, we have seen a series of archetypal relationships. There are also others if you wish, in fact we said that every relationship is unique. The fiery relationship for example (those "love-hate/fight – make peace" kind of relationships) or the super passionate one. These, however, are not models you can choose rationally. You are far more likely to choose one of the archetypes we have seen when a "thunder and lightning" relationship is calming down and you may be looking for it to take a more "sustainable" shape...

The fact is that I would invite you to take these archetypes not as "boxes in which you can put your relationship" but as ***"a palette of colors to use to paint your relationship so that you are comfortable with it and it suits your needs and wishes".***

There is no reason why you can't have elements of a friendly relationship with elements of a steady "married couple" relationship working perfectly together. And you can even have the commitment of a married couple kind of relationship and the freedom of an intermittent relationship or even a polyamorous one at that and the cocktail can be perfectly fine.

Whatever you choose, however, remember that ***this is your relationship with your partner, not with society***. As long as you two are consensual and harm no one, society has no authority to tell you what sort of relationship you should have or how to manage it.

The lesson to take home is that ***if you are not comfortable with a relationship you will feel anxious and insecure about it, but there are many models of relationships and you can use them to mix and shape the one you feel most comfortable with.***

And here we close with that beautiful word, "comfort" ... in fact, the next chapter will be about switching comfortably from role to role within your relationship, an art that needs some social but also linguistic skills.

8

LACK AND FEAR OF INTIMACY

Intimacy is so important to relationships that we need to spend a few more words on it.... We looked at the "normal", if you want "general" and even "positive" side of it in the previous chapter... But now we need to enter a more problematic area...

I guess you remember when I mentioned the "chance" of having a relationship with little or no intimacy within it. It was fairly acceptable in the past; kings and queens often had little real intimacy; their relationship in many cases was a "state matter" – nothing to do with love and intimacy.

We come from a long history of "practical needs and solutions in relationships". Even if kings and princes were an extreme case, there was often a good level of practicality even lower down the social hierarchy. Keeping the property together or extending wealth were an important consideration among the rich. But even the poor had to choose a partner that could help in the fields, at home, or with the little activity of the family.

But that in itself does not preclude the opportunity to establish a deeply intimate relationship. It just adds another layer of complexity to the relationship. Nowadays, in most rich countries, economic and practical considerations do have a role in these choices. However, they are not often an impediment.

So, how is it possible that some relationships may lack intimacy? Does it really still happen?

What Causes Lack of Intimacy

There is a huge range of levels of intimacy. So maybe we should first understand what we mean by "lack of it". There is no "prescribed" level of intimacy, but... ***There is lack of intimacy when one or more of the partners feel dissatisfied with the intimacy within the relationship.*** In simple words, it is subjective. If a couple hardly look at each other in the face once a week and they are happy with it... so are we! But if a couple for instance have lots of intimacy but one of the partners would like some more... then we have a problem.

Happiness is the key objective of psychology. But what may cause lack of intimacy? There are many reasons, for example:

- *Stress* on one or more of the partners.
- *Wellbeing issues, including mental issues.* For example, depression may lead to lack of intimacy.

- *Tiredness and lack of time.* When people work too much, for example.
- *Decreased affection and attachment within the relationship.* And this becomes a bigger issue, one which we have dealt with in many chapters of this book.
- *Intimacy avoidance*: this is, I am sorry to say, a psychological condition, and one which is hard to manage.

These may be the causes, and each has a different solution. Lack of intimacy, however, can be serious enough to spell the end itself of a relationship. So, in any case, ***catch it early, at the very first signs.***

Wellbeing Causes and Solutions

We can group together stress, tiredness and other wellbeing problems as "wellbeing causes". We will exclude intimacy avoidance, because that is a specific condition, and we will see it later.

What can you do if this is the case?

First of all, you need to *assess the cause.* If there are sudden and/or big changes in your life patterns, if you know or notice that your partner is very tense, tired, despondent, lacking motivation etc. then you are onto something. This may be accompanied by a *decline in libido,* but not necessarily. Let's remember that intimacy is much wider than just eros.

If you know your partner well, you will find it easier to assess if it's a wellbeing issue. And then? Then you will have to act carefully...

- *Do not blame your partner.* He or she is not responsible, but a victim of some stressful situation. Sometimes we cannot hide the fact that we resent something from our partners. Try to avoid giving any sign of "blaming" him or her. Even the odd cynical word can really hurt in these cases.

- *Your aim is to aid in solving the root problem.* This is why you should avoid making it worse with your behavior.
- *Remember that your partner is vulnerable at this stage.* Be extra kind, therefore. When we are stressed etc., we do not have the same tolerance level as when we are relaxed.
- *Do not force intimacy and yourself onto your partner.* Though you may really want that big strong hug, try not to force it on your partner at this stage.

"Fine," you may say, "lots of things to avoid. But is there something we can actually positively do?" The answer is yes!

- *Boost your partner's confidence.* Double down on encouragements! "Well done!", "You don't know how much I love you…", "You are a pro!" etc. In all areas of life, try to add that extra sign of appreciation.
- *Have trials but choose your timing carefully.* Wait for when your partner is least stressed to try *some intimacy.* And this leads us to the next point.
- *Use "reduced doses".* You understood, maybe start with less intimate acts. Instead of the big hug and passionate kiss, start with holding hands for a short while, for example.
- *Check when your partner wants to stop and indulge him/her.* Don't take it personally if after only a few seconds

s/he wants to let go of your hand. It is not against you, but a personal matter. So, let go…

- *Slowly make your partner comfortable with intimacy again.* With well timed, even "scaled down" acts of intimacy, if necessary, patience and a bit of time, your partner will find intimacy more comfortable as time goes by… Then it will be downhill.

To give you an idea, it's a bit like getting a baby to like new food. If you give a toddler a whole big raw carrot and you insist every day the chances are that your child will hate carrots till the day s/he retires and beyond. If you give him or her a tiny, cooked slice with some sauce on it every now and then… Little by little your child will turn into a little rabbit. But above all…

Deal with the root problem. Of course, this may mean taking a holiday, taking counseling, changing life patterns etc. It really depends on what the root cause is. But while you wait for the big solution to come along (and it may take time), keep in mind the vulnerability of your partner.

It will take some time but *focus on progress,* and treasure any intimate moment you get…

Practical Causes and Solutions

There are practical causes too, like lack of time, distance, even financial worries can lead to a decrease in intimacy. Very often, the practical cause triggers a psychological reaction, and this then results in reduced intimacy.

Typical is work problems and financial insecurity. People lose self-confidence when things don't go well at work. Money worries can be really horrible. I hope you never have any, but if you have (had), you surely know what I mean. That anxiety can be literally debilitating. People with such worries sometimes find it hard to carry out quite common daily chores. Even personal hygiene can get overlooked.

And in fact, a sign that there are very deep issues is the lack of self-care. And this can appear at many levels from the way we dress, to combing our hair to untidiness at home and work. I don't mean people who are usually untidy... I mean unusual and increased untidiness.

Even eating disorders (small or big ones) can be caused by both emotional and practical problems. Binge eating is quite a common way of compensating for lack of confidence or excessive anxiety and worrying. Binge eating can also be a way of compensating lack of intimacy, tangentially. So, if you both end up binge eating, there is something you need to talk about...

The solutions are the same as the ones for psychological and emotional problems (wellbeing), but we can add a few tips...

- *Tackle the emotional and mental side of it first and independently from the practical side.* The practical side of it can take some time... But if you can improve the psychological reaction to them, you will open up doors to intimate moments.
- *Don't make your partner feel responsible for the practical*

problems. Ok, this is the same as with emotional problems, but it is worth reminding.
- *Take some time off,* if possible. This can be hard when there are problems, but even a weekend away from it all can work wonders.

Of course, here too, it is a matter of solving the root problem, in the long run. But the more you manage to have intimacy before that moment, the more your partner (and you) will have strength to wait till everything is sorted. You can even have a clearer mind, a better ability to solve problems if you take breaks from them... And even a stroll hand in hand in the park is a bit like meditating.

But now onto the tough one...

Intimacy Avoidance

Intimacy avoidance is actually a very serious psychological condition. There are, of course, many professional studies on the topic, by psychologists, psychotherapists, sexologists, and psychoanalysts. If you want to have an idea of the complexities of this condition, a fairly thorough explanation is in a chapter by Dr Magdalena Smieja from Jagiellonian University, Krakow, Poland, in the *Encyclopedia of Personality and Individual Differences* aptly entitled 'Intimacy Avoidance'.

This condition has been known and recognized for decades now, with studies going back to the 1980s. It can have ***varying degrees and manifestations in real life***, but on the whole, it can be described as when ***"an individual withdraws from emotional contact from a relationship partner."***

This is of course is a technical, generic, and above all abstract definition. But it means that a person is – to different degrees – uncomfortable with being intimate with the partner. And this is ***not a phase, a temporary attitude, or a development***; it is actually a ***steady psychological behavior.*** If someone suffers from it, they don't do it with "him and not her" with one partner and not the other, at some stages and not others, when they are stressed and not when they are relaxed. They will do it, to some extent, in any intimate situation.

It's like when you have a phobia: you just have it, and you can't avoid it. Having said this, such avoidance can be worsened by stress, illness, practical problems etc. ***Intimacy avoidance is, in fact, a syndrome.***

But how can you find out if someone suffers from intimacy avoidance? The *symptoms are many*, but they include:

- Feeling rejected.
- Feeling socially isolated.
- Feeling emotionally numb.
- Feeling emotionally engulfed.
- Having a constant need for approval.

These are fairly generic symptoms, true, but you may also notice a key behavior: ***the person avoids situations that trigger emotions and feelings.***

This does not just apply to intimacy and intimate situations. Intimacy avoidance syndrome can reflect on everyday life. People who suffer from it are ***very vulnerable individuals.*** Over the years, they develop *strategies to avoid feeling emotionally vulnerable.* And that often translates in "not even getting near intimacy if possible."

Because intimacy and being emotionally engaged, alight or awake are closely linked, people with intimacy avoidance syndrome will try to avoid both.

In fact, *intimacy avoidance affects many areas of life:*

- *Intellectual life:* people with intimacy avoidance can find it hard to share their ideas with others (this can have serious repercussions on their career, academic progress etc.)
- *Emotional life:* as we said, these people avoid emotions, but they also find it hard to express emotions.
- *Sexual life:* this does not mean that they do not have sex, but that they will find it hard to live it as a "sharing experience" or to feel as free and engrossed as others, and especially to feel the full intimacy of the act.
- *Experiential life:* these people may find it hard to express how they experience the world to others.

In the long run, people with intimacy avoidance can *become disconnected with reality.* Especially mature people with this syndrome will have gone through so much frustration that they give up on connecting with reality.

What is more ***people with intimacy avoidance syndrome often end up sabotaging their own relationship***. Sometimes people don't understand why their partner is actively undermining the relationship. It looks and sounds absurd. And yet quite a few people do this. They start off very well, but then suddenly it is *"as if they did it on purpose to ruin everything".*

"Is it me?" the other partner may wonder... "Is there someone else and s/he does not want to tell me?" No, there isn't and sometimes, when there is someone, the "lover" is purely functional to ruining the relationship. You can ask yourself all the questions you want, and you will never get to the truth if you don't know what it is.

The person with this condition *wants intimacy with you,* but *also subconsciously fears intimacy with you.* Very often ***they are too afraid of being abandoned that they cannot bring themselves to running the emotional risk of being intimate.*** So, because they cannot break this psychological barrier, they ruin the relationship as a sad, really sad way out.

When they say, "It's not you; it's me," they actually mean it. But they cannot explain why they can't change or solve "their problem". Because it is too deep and subconscious. Their fear is too big and old for them to overcome. Sometimes they don't even know why they have it. Sometimes only mentioning it is too painful to even think about it. When we say "trauma" in psychology we actually mean a wound so deep and so painful – ok, I am getting tearful myself...

But then, *they also feel deeply guilty for ruining the relationship*, and the downward spiral keeps going deeper. It's really sad. You *need a professional.* Sorry if I stress this.

But it is also true that *some of us are instinctively attracted to vulnerable people.* People with intimacy avoidance syndrome ooze vulnerability. And if you are one of those who want to hug everyone with a sad glint in his/her eyes, the chances are you already have met someone with this syndrome or you likely will.

And *you will want to help. But you won't be able to on your own.* And that too can have consequences on your confidence, well-being, insecurities, present, and future relationship(s).

On one hand, this makes us treasure our emotional and intimate life even more... On the other it is a really serious and sad state of affairs. Lighter versions of the syndrome can be more manageable, of course, but heavier ones can literally ruin relationships and whole lives.

Intimacy avoidance syndrome requires professional help. I think you must have guessed it by now. I know that there is a stigma with these things, but really this is the only solution. Even in lighter cases, it is better to seek counseling on the matter. The condition can worsen later in life in fact.

But even if you will need counseling (even therapy, depending on the case) to get through it, there are ***coping strategies that the partners can adopt.*** And we will see them straight away after a little digression.

The question I have not answered yet is "what causes intimacy avoidance syndrome?" I am sure you may have a few ideas already, and I am also quite confident you got them right...

It is in fact one of those psychological problems that have their root cause in childhood. Now, if you like a bit of psychology you will know the "stereotypical Freudian explanation" ... the causes of adult problems must be sought in the early years of life... It is not always like this! There are many problems, even very common ones, that can pop up later in life; depression is a typical example (though it can have childhood roots too).

But you know one thing, I am sure: ***when psychological problems originate in childhood, they are very serious indeed.*** This is because *the trauma that causes these problems has worked its way into the subconscious.* What does it mean? It means that it provokes our behavior, our actions, reactions, and even feelings without us being aware of what is happening.

Imagine the pain and frustration a person goes through when s/he can't have a normal intimate life and cannot do anything about it. This explains why they may become detached from reality. One more reason to get a professional involved.

But what are these "childhood causes"? Even here, I am confident you guessed: ***it often has to do with family or more generically the carers.*** "This is turning into an episode of *Frasier,*" you must be thinking. And yes, intimacy avoidance syndrome has all the classic "psychology stereotypes you would find in a movie" kind of things...

"Anything more specific," you may wish to ask? Yes, there are some types of relationships with cares that are typically at the basis of this syndrome. Now I will tell you, and your eyes will get wet...

- *Aggressive carers;* yes, in many cases it is verbal or physical violence that cause this.
- *Dismissive carers;* in other cases, the carers do not show enough care and attention to the child.

There can be also other specific causes, like *the loss of one or more carers.* Finally, also *being abandoned by one or more carers* can cause a trauma big enough to cause this syndrome.

Cup of tea, little cry, and then we can resume...

...

Ok, this was not an exercise, but I thought that a little break to reflect would do us good. If it is in your nature to fall in love with vulnerable people, I am repeating myself, but I am doing it for your good – do not think you can do it alone, please. At the same time, do not think less of yourself for having sought professional help.

You see, that is the other side of these relationship... The "helping partner" is at high risk of disappointment or frustration:

- If s/he tries on his/her own and fails, that will be felt like a massive disappointment.

- If s/he seeks help then s/he may think, "I am not good enough."

The second statement could not be further from the truth… And… Now onto the good news!

While you wait for the counseling or therapy to show results, there is still a huge and important, but above all positive role for you in this situation. Do you remember the ***coping strategies,*** yes? Then here we go!

There are in fact, strategies for the helping partner but also strategies for the partner with the syndrome. And they can be – actually should be – approached as teamwork.

Strategies for partners of people with intimacy avoidance syndrome

For the "helping partner" there are a few tips that will help you cope with this very difficult condition.

- *Be patient*; this is very important. Understand that your partner will need time. Putting any pressure on your partner can actually make things worse (it is a source of anxiety).
- *Expect setbacks…* progress will not be perfectly smooth. There will be times when – it's just not working right now… - please be understanding and don't make your partner feel like s/he has failed or done something wrong.
- *Do not take it personally when your partner refuses intimacy.* These relationships have an awful lot of attempts, setbacks etc. But very importantly, when your partner says

"no" remember that it is not "no to you", but "no I can't and it's not your fault nor does it mean that I don't love you."

- *Do not react with anger when your partner refuses intimacy.* This is absolutely important. Any sign of anger will only push the trauma deeper into your partner's subconscious. This will make it more difficult to solve and it can even seriously worsen the condition.
- *Avoid surprises;* I know, you so want to book that trip and tell your beloved one over dinner! But that may make him or her feel "not in control" and that will trigger the syndrome. Instead, well, less like an episode of *Friends* but more realistic and, above all, comfortable for your partner... Plan the trip together.
- *Make small steps and clear, joint decisions;* this follows from the previous point. Discuss choices in detail and make sure that there is agreement on every point...
- *Make your partner feel in control.* Again, following from the previous point but applicable to all life choices together, even small ones like which shop to go to and which type of apples you want to buy.... The more your partner feels in control, the more s/he will be comfortable with intimacy.
- *Keep praising him/her and expressing your positive feelings towards him/her.* The praising is clear, but now imagine someone with intimacy problems living with someone who never expresses feelings... That makes it even harder, doesn't it? Instead, convey the idea that for you it is normal and beautiful to share feelings with him or her... This can be a game changer.

- *Make it clear that this is teamwork.* You will set out on a long journey together and if you live it together, if you manage it together, plan it together, share it etc., this very teamwork will make intimacy easier for your partner.
- *Listen carefully, without judgement and without pushing.* At some stage, your partner will want to open up about his or her traumatic experience. Here you need to be a bit like a professional counselor. Don't go like, "And who was he?" or "What happened next?" That looks and feels like you want to know their business. That's pushing him or her. No, instead! Just let your partner say what s/he wants, as s/he wants and as much as s/he wants. Your role is *to listen without judging and express empathy.* Do, say something along the lines of "I understand you," or "You must have suffered a lot," etc.

Strategies for people with intimacy avoidance syndrome

If it is you who has this problem… Above all, don't blame yourself. Ever! Even when those dark clouds come over your head full of examples of things you did wrong keep this light in mind: *you did not do it because you wanted it. You had to and this "thing" cannot be beaten alone.* No exception. Not even Superman can do it.

This being clear now we can look at a few coping strategies too. Your counselor will likely suggest the same, similar ones and even more, but a few to get you started…

- *Accept uncertainty;* things do go wrong, but then we can always fix them later. Playing sports can actually help you get comfortable with the idea. Especially a sport you are not good at. You know why? You will lose a lot. But you'll also get used to the idea that "losing ain't that bad after all!" It's just the matter of a moment...

- *Focus on day-by-day life.* A bit of planning is fine, but seize the day, live in the moment as far as you can. Too much planning shifts the focus into the future, which is uncertain, and uncertainties bring insecurities, and insecurities bring anxiety... You see where I am going.
- *Take on meditation or yoga*; these can be very good to relax and get in touch with your inner self, with your emotions and even face some of those gremlins we don't like too much.
- *Express self-compassion;* you need to be comfortable with yourself if you wish to become intimate with others. Compassion, however, is not just "pity" ... Do tell yourself "I was very unlucky with it," or even "That really hurt me." Fine, but then don't forget to say, "I felt really good about it," and "Look – what a beautiful person am I?"
- *Talk to yourself, tune into your inner dialogue*; don't be afraid to have long and especially honest conversations with yourself. Anything at all. From frivolous and trivial things to important ones. Above all, try to *tell yourself how you feel.* Some people even end up disagreeing with themselves and you know the good side of it? You can always choose to be on the winning side at the end.
- *Give yourself plenty of time.* Don't hurry, that only causes further pressure. It will take time, and you need to be patient.

But you also should not expect too much too soon from yourself. Take all the time you need.

- *Look at your past but take it slow*! If you are not comfortable with a thought from the past, don't dwell on it. In fact, this is better done during professional sessions. But if you do feel that there are a few episodes that you can recall now without being hurt too much, that you can cope with, and manage to recall, then give it a brief try every now and then. But do it when you have time, when you are calm, and especially when you feel good about yourself.

And we have come to the end of this very intense chapter. It was intense for me, so, I can imagine it was for you too. But this is the biggest, most difficult and complex problem we need to tackle in this book. And we have done it. Now you know that even serious psychological syndromes that can affect relationships very badly have a solution. Even if a professional one. But now you can recognize one, which makes all the difference...

In the next chapter we will change topic ("What a silly thing to say," you may think, but it's a clue, actually...)

So, take a big breath, relax, have a cup, of tea, and see you back when you are ready!

9

THE ART OF SWITCHING

. . . Talking about changing topics, how many times during a single day does your relationship with your partner change? Let's be "imaginary voyeurs" for a second... We now have a camera fixed on the heads of two imaginary friends of mine: Aysha and Chris. At each stage, ask yourself what their relationship is like at that moment, and what has changed from before.

It is Saturday morning and Chris wakes up. Aysha is still in bed. But she needs to prepare breakfast for both. What is their relationship like now? When Aysha wakes up, breakfast is ready on the table and they greet with a kiss before they sit down. What is their relationship like now?

Chris is usually the one who reads the paper and talks about politics and the news, while Aysha tends to listen but she does not join in too much. What's changed in their relationship? Then, however, they need to wake up the children. This is quite a troublesome and often chaotic moment because the kids like to sleep, then they often argue over the bathroom turns... So Aysha takes a lead and deals with them while Chris makes himself scarce in the garden while checking on flowers and vegetables.

As it is Saturday, they then get into the car. Aysha has a driving license, but Chris does not. So Aysha drives to the shopping center, while Chris keeps the children quiet...

I could go on for the whole chapter, but I think it's enough to get the point. When they are in the car, for example, Aysha has a ***leading role***, while at that stage Chris has a ***backing role.*** When Aysha wakes up the children, again she is the ***leading partner*** while he literally "gets temporarily out of the way" but still acts as a ***facilitating partner.***

What we understand from this is that ***roles within the relationship are continuously changing.*** Chris and Aysha are not in the same ***relative positions*** at each change, and these changes can happen very quickly and frequently indeed.

And we have not even got through to lunchtime, let alone till Aysha and Chris go back to bed at night! Can you imagine how many times they need to ***change roles during the day?*** It can literally be hundreds of times. Each day. For a lifetime...

Now you understand why ***being able to change and switch roles in a relationship is fundamental to its survival and happiness.*** And of course, we are going to talk about it now.

Before we move on, however, I want to ask you one thing. If you have a partner, fine. If you don't choose the person you spent most time with during a whole day recently. You do know by now that I mind my business, so, instead of telling me, take a few minutes to think about part of a recent day and count the changes of roles you have had with him or her... The whole day would be far too long to consider. No need to tell me.

...

They were loads, weren't they? Then there is the extra factor that the more activities you undertake together, the more you need to switch roles. This does not happen just with partners. It happens in all sorts of relationships.

You know, once upon a time, people had more socially rigid roles and lives. What is more, especially in rural settings, they had fewer encounters during the day... It so happened that we started identifying people by only one single role in their lives. This was often the job or the provenance...

That's where we got names like Smith, Thatcher, etc.... But in the Twentieth Century we realized that everybody has a "range of roles and personalities". You are not the same person when you are at work or when you go shopping. Your role changes. At work you are a teacher, a builder, a nurse etc.... You have (or are) a boss and you have colleagues. You may even have clients, or patients etc.... But when you go shopping you are no longer a teacher or a nurse... You are the client now!

As you can see, we do this fluidly in many cases, but... There can be a few problems with partners.

Roles Within Relationships

While most roles are dictated by society, the same does not apply to relationships. We believe that we live in a free world... in some ways yes, but it's full of unwritten (or written) social rules.

When you meet a professional, there are rules of engagement... We all have that very respectful attitude towards medical doctors, don't we? When a police person stops you at the traffic lights, you take out your license and hope you don't get a ticket... When you board a plane, you listen to the captain and crew when they give you instructions about taking off etc....

These are all relationships with fairly *strict and pre-determined social rules*. But ***in personal relationships social rules are looser, or sometimes they (almost) do not exist at all.***

This depends a bit on the society you live in. Not long ago in Western countries it was society that dictated which roles men and women had in their own personal relationships. This still lives on in many personal relationships, even if in softer version.

Example? There are still couples where some tasks are the sole domain of the woman, like cooking, doing the washing up, cleaning, and most house chores. That is a social rule, a legacy from times of old when women and men were not equal. This is still very common within couples of old people. It is very uncommon with young urban couples. But it does vary from place to place. While in New York or even more Copenhagen this would be very rare, in some rural areas of both the US and Europe, this type of "settlement" is still fairly common.

And we only looked at the US and the EU. There are countries around the world where these old rules are still written in law! But the reason why we are talking about it is another.

If there are pre-established social rules within a couple, the roles tend to be fairly steady. One partner will have one role most of the time, the other another role. These are usually a *leading role* and a *following role.* I used "following" rather than "subservient", "subdued" etc., because it's more general. But in some cases, we can talk about a *dominant role and a submissive role.* Where these definitions start is hard to say; as usual, it has personal and subjective perspectives too.

But when these fixed roles from the past do not exist, relationships become fluid and the two roles (with varying degrees, including middle ones) pass from one partner to the other... This means a lot of switching...

Ok, I am going to say it in very simple words: ***if you want a modern and free, egalitarian relationship you'd better be good at switching roles.***

You may think, "Fine, I am very good at it!" but the problem is that ***both of you must be good at it and willing to do it.*** In polyamorous relationships all members need to be good at this, and the dynamics can become very complex indeed.

Here is very often where problems come... A lot really depends on the past experiences of the partners. Now, let me tell you a story... Lisa and Paul have been partners for about one year, so they decided to move in together. They didn't want to get married straight away, you know...

Anyway, they moved in together and after a few weeks I got a call from Lisa... We met over a coffee and she told me that, well, things were not going as she had hoped. Why? Paul was totally "modern" when they were dating, "But indoors," she said, "he still expects me to be a "wife" in the old-fashioned way..."

I became curious and a bit worried, so I asked for some more details. They were not huge problems, but annoying enough to put a chink in their relationship. Basically, Paul does not like to cook, and that's fine with her in a way, but also, he does not help with the washing and washing up. They are only two things, but she is upset.

I have to ask for your advice here: why do you think Lisa is so upset? Why do you think that Paul has these "strange" habits?

...

Let's see... You may say that Lisa is worried that Paul will start with two or three things and then start withdrawing from other chores? Possible. Or that Lisa wants a perfect, "fairy tale" relationship, so any spot is incredibly annoying...

One thing though, equality cannot be such if there is just one unequal element... And this may be a matter of principle... You see, Lisa has a clear expectation of "equality across the board" and one or two things are enough to "remind her that she is not actually equal in Paul's eyes". And this can be frustrating, even very painful and it can "gnaw away" at a relationship in the long run.

But now I need your help once more. What about Paul? Why do you think he is behaving like this?

I take my coffee white with brown sugar if you're making it this time.

...

That was "the" perfect cup of coffee, thanks! Joking aside, what did you make of Paul? We may agree that he is not fully conscious of what he is doing. Surely, he does not understand that Lisa is anxious about it...

We may also agree that he has problems switching, doesn't he? And then we can try to guess why he is resisting this fully egalitarian settlement that Lisa is looking for. We may guess that there are some ***cultural and experiential conditioning*** in his behavior? This, in fact, looks very much like one of those "family traits" that come from years, decades even, of seeing your Mum or women in your family of origin doing certain things and not others...

Basically, we can expect that at his parents' home, Paul never saw his father do the washing up or anywhere near the washing machine... And it is *often the male partner who resists such egalitarian relationships.*

Imagine an extreme situation… Imagine a man who comes from a family where the male members have a very dominant position and female members are simply not treated as equals because of their culture and tradition… How easy would it be for this man to switch into an egalitarian relationship? Very hard indeed in most cases…

We will come back to this and give Lisa a helping hand in a minute, but first, something even more difficult…

Intimate Roles and Switching

So far, we talked about the washing up… Now, think how many different roles people can have when they are being intimate? Yes, that *includes sex…* Here the world of possibilities is huge. Depending of course on the tastes and preferences of the partners, but really there can be a lot of switching in these moments.

And maybe ***the most "exciting" but also "frightful" switch is the one from "out of intimacy" to "into intimacy"***. You get my point…

This is in itself one of those moments when you get butterflies in your stomach and a flutter to your heart etc.… Very often there are ***key signals, like gestures or words that indicate the willingness to switch into an intimate or sexual moment.*** In the *Adams Family,* remember, it was when Morticia Adams spoke French… Ok, this is a funny take on it, but it does have an educational point; each couple has its own ***"switching signals"****, and these often come from the history of the couple itself.*

In many cases these signals go back to the very "first time" of the couple, or at least to the very early stages of the relationship.

When these signals are given and not picked up, the partner sending them usually worries a lot. It is a "rejection" even if "coded" in a language that only the couple can understand. But there is no fooling the partner here. ***If you turn down your partner, always explain why.*** The "headache situation" is fine, as long as it is open and honest.

But think about this carefully; your partner will feel "rejected", even "embarrassed" and this can have huge consequences on his or her confidence. So, your "rejection" must be:

- *Calm*
- *Understanding and empathetic*
- *Specific in its reason*
- *Warm and not cold*

Something like, "Oh, sweetheart right now I have my mind on the electricity bill, I am sorry, I wish I could," then offer some ***intimate compensation,*** like a long hug, a cuddle etc....

The "Oh, no, I have just done my hair," followed by standing up to light a cigarette is actually painful (and unhealthy!) You see, at this stage, ***your main goal is not to hurt your partner's feelings.*** *Think about how you would feel about it!...*

Talking about which, what happens if it is your partner who turns you down? And how about if your partner does not behave as we just said? At worst, there's the "stop physical contact and move to something very cold and un-intimate" reaction. In this case, usually there is a serious problem within the couple, and it is time for a "relationship talk".

But in most cases the harm is done unconsciously. There are of course series of levels and reactions, from a simple "ignoring the sign but being sweet and intimate all the same" to "saying something that is too vague" etc.

Ok, here you need to approach your partner and have a chat about it. It is hard to say that you have been hurt. Especially on such intimate issues, there is a sense of humiliation and loss of face... But try to do it the very first time it happens, or as early as possible. ***Turning down offers of intimacy the wrong way cannot become a habit.*** That will start a really painful downward spiral that can ruin your relationship.

And, oddly enough, this is where you need to switch! Yes, you need to take on a *leading role* and start a conversation about what you expect of him or her in these situations. Now, note that you cannot say, "You cannot refuse my advances". That is not the point and make clear straight away that this is not where you are going. Doing this on its own will lower the barriers from your partner (s/he at this stage will be worrying about your "accepting the refusal" rather than the "how I did it was wrong").

Tell him that *the way s/he did it is hurtful*. Again, use the language of feelings we saw early on in this book: "When you stood up it hurt me, I expected a hug," or, "I felt bad because you didn't even tell me why you don't fancy it now..."

Don't be "nagging" but be firm on your right not to be hurt. It is not a confirmation but an "understanding each other moment". Basically, you need to teach him/her what you have just learned in this book. You too deserve a "rejection" which is calm, understanding, and empathetic, specific in the reason, warm, and followed by intimate compensation (a hug, a kiss, whatever...).

You will turn each other down over the years; this has to be done without hurting each other. So, both partners will benefit from learning this "switching out" skill.

Intimate, Personal and Social Roles... and More Switching!

While ideally most of us want egalitarian roles in social and personal situations, not everybody likes this in intimate roles. Pause, take a long breath and reflect. This is one of the weirdest balances to achieve in a relationship.

Do you know what I mean? Sheila and Frank are fully egalitarian. They have equal roles in the home, they share tasks with neighbors, they decide everything fully together, both work etc. But... When night comes and they cuddle on the sofa Sheila likes to feel protected and she cuddles within his arms...

So, at this stage, it is Frank who takes a leading role. This is a small and delicate example. But the fact is that ***within the intimate sphere any consensual role is fully acceptable.***

One thing we need to understand is that being egalitarian and equal in the relationship does not, for example, mean having to have "egalitarian roles in bed". That is a different sphere where one partner may just want the other to take a leading role...

All rules apart from one are suspended in that sphere: *what you do must be consensual.*

Of course, these roles can be pretty wild. There has been a massive increase in fetish and S&M sexual activity in recent years... Things that were once "mythologically perverted" are now very common indeed. It is part of the ***process of sexual liberation*** that we have seen in the past decades (after the 80s in particular).

It has been brought about by pop musicians (Madonna being by far the biggest driving force of this revolution) and then with the advent of the Internet... We all know that things you didn't even know existed all of a sudden pop up in little (and may I say, quite insisting) windows out of nowhere...

Now sexual practices that only few knew existed in the past are within reach of young people as well... And in fact, that world has totally changed...

There remains the only untouchable rule here; ***all sexual acts and practices must be fully consensual.***

But apart from that, ***the more experimental sexual roles are, the more they require switching skills.*** There can be embarrassment, uncertainty and even confusion if the switch does not work well.

Having said this, it is not at all uncommon that the partner who has a leading role in bed may then have a following role out of it. There is no rule and when cheeky (nosy) people look at couples and "guess" what their intimate roles are, well, be aware that the way they behave in front of you may be totally different from what they do behind closed doors. But the key point would be that what they do behind closed doors is no one else's business...

What does a successful switch in these situations look like?

It is actually a very crafty skill. To be honest in the old S&M community they had clear rules... It's amazing how the whole world was perfectly regulated, with rules you would never break and even a form of etiquette. But that was a small and closely knit community. Now these practices have become more common, those rules have been forgotten.

Instead, I would actually stick to them very closely. They are all centered around ***consent and safety*** and they are designed to ***make the transition from one role to the other smooth.***

- They are *very ritualized.* The ritual is usually always the same; there can be a dressing item, or words, or assuming certain positions etc. Usually more than one element together.
- *The leading partner starts this ritual.* The partner who takes the leading role in the sexual activity is also the one who "celebrates the ritual". Whether it is saying certain words etc., this is very important. It is the "easing in the following partner" that allows him/her to feel at ease and safe in this role.
- *There is always a way out for the following partner.*

Usually the partners establish "the word". It must be a word with no sexual reference, and if the following partner says it, the leading partner stops immediately, no questions asked. When you "lead" you may not be aware you are going too far. There is no option of disrespecting that word. In a way, it's the "thing" that keeps an element of equality even at this level. And when we say immediately we mean immediately. In fact, any act done after that is technically *non-consensual.*

- *The leading partner repeatedly checks for consent.* It is the good characteristic of a leading partner to make sure the following partner is actually happy. In "unequal sexual acts" the leading partner keeps asking the following partner if s/he like what they are doing. It's a responsibility, not just a "kinky game".
- *The switching out is slow, long and very warm and intimate.* There is a lot of cuddling, hugging, looking at each other straight in the eyes etc.... when moving out of the sexual roles and back into the personal roles. This too is very necessary to ease the transition into an egalitarian relationship. While the switching into can be quick, the switching out of can take half an hour to a whole day actually...

As you can see, there's a solution to everything. Relationships can be very complex, and we really need to be thankful to the people who developed a whole tried and tested, as well as safe process of switching in very intimate situations.

On a dry but necessary side note, this set of rules also safeguards both partners. Passing that line of consent means moving into "rape area". And in sex especially if one of the partners is "in control" we need to be doubly certain that that line is never crossed, not even by mistake.

When to Switch, How to Switch

Remember Lisa and Paul? I said we would come back to help them, and I always keep my word. Actually, you know I am lazy, and I am going to ask *you* to do it. But now we have to do two things...

- Remind ourselves of what Lisa and Paul's problem was.
- Look at this problem from a much deeper perspective we have now explored.

Let's start from the second (I like starting from the back) ... we have now seen that even very emotional switches, literally like that from S&M positions to equal partners (and even if you want to "boss and employee" – and have fun thinking that these are the exact opposite of what happens behind closed doors) ***are*** possible, and that *there is a tried and tested technique to do this switch.*

Now, from this perspective, Lisa and Paul's problem may look very small. Do you remember what it was? It was that Paul (for what we identified as cultural "legacy") would not do things like the washing up, and this, rightfully, gave Lisa the "feeling" that he did not see her as fully equal in the relationship.

Now we remember can I say one thing? By now I fully trust that you have lots of ideas on how to help her... So, can I absent myself for another cup of tea? Green tea now as coffee is bad for nerves...

...

Green tea is such a wonder of Nature... By the way did you know that it's excellent to lose weight? Turmeric tea in particular. It allows your body fat to turn from white fat to brown fat. White fat is the fat we store, brown fat is the fat we burn. Turmeric turns white fat into brown fat... On average, half a teaspoon of turmeric in a cup of water every day will make you lose 1.5 lb. a week. Not bad...

Enough with getting ready for summer though... What can we say about Lisa and Paul? For sure Paul needs to understand that "equality" has many practical implications. While this may look like a "little problem" compared with the "seismic switches" we have seen so far, it does not mean that the problem is less painful. What's more, Lisa may not want to address it because the "realization of the problem" is not huge, it may look "venial" and "petty" to "make a fuss" about such things.

Instead, what do you reckon? Should Lisa confront him about it? The answer is, I am sure you will agree, a resounding YES! And how should she do it? There are basically two options; one is like a diplomat trying to get a logical point across, the other is by tapping into Paul's emotional side and good will.

In practical terms... Most couples in this situation end up with one partner saying something along the lines of "It is my right that you...," or "You are not pulling your weight." The problem with this approach is not that it is factually wrong... It is that it puts the two partners into a conflictual situation... And whenever there is conflict there is risk of losing face, and when there is risk of losing face there is a defensive position... By now you know quite well that we are heading towards a confrontation at this stage...

Instead, can I suggest a different approach? It is different from what we normally would use (and fail), but familiar to us. Look at these sentences as examples:

"When I do the washing up and you don't help me, I feel as if you think it's a job I should do because I am a woman."

"When I do the washing, I would love to have a hand, you see, it is much harder than you think; you need to kneel down, pick up heavy clothes etc.... And they get heavier when you take them out to hang them."

That's a completely different approach from, "You don't help me with the washing because you think I am inferior," which may well be what one day Lisa will end up thinking and even shouting unless she sorts out this problem early on in her relationship.

Let's pause a second, though, because we have reached a very important point: ***try to solve each problem in isolation in your relationship as soon as it arises or as soon as possible.*** Trying to solve more problems in one go is usually disastrous. The discussion ends up jumping from one point to the other without solving a single one (it's called "kettle logic" by experts).

What is more, if the problem becomes ingrained, it is harder to eradicate and when you bring it up there is always the "Why didn't you bring this up before question?" Though it may be legitimate, this question shifts the focus from solving the problem to a series of memories from the past and accusations and it sets the discussion back...

But back to our main point; using the ***language of emotions,*** once more is the best chance you have to make a breach into your partner's heart and mind, and, at the same time, it is the best way to trigger a rational conversation aimed at a solution, and not at finding fault with each other.

Look at this like an hourglass: if you start accusing you will only get a defensive and irrational response. If instead you start by involving your partner and expressing your emotions, you will get the exact opposite: an open and solution oriented rational discussion.

Let's look back for a moment. We have made huge progress. Really... Look at how many problems and situations you can solve now. And because we are approaching the end of this book, we now want to turn to a very positive chapter... And I will leave you with an "exercise"... In your opinion, what makes a perfect relationship?

...

10

THE RECIPE FOR A GOOD RELATIONSHIP

And we finally reach a fully positive, sunlit, breezy chapter... We have gone through lots of important things in this book, from understanding the dynamics within relationships, to how to talk about sensitive topics to how to face critical moments... You have also met almost all my "imaginary friends" and you have seen that there are so many different situations in relationships that the world is your oyster if you take this positively.

Now we are coming to the end of this book, we can look at all the *ingredients you need to have a successful relationship.* But before I tell you my ideas, I would like you to brainstorm yours... As usual, take your time.

...

So, what do you think you need to have a good relationship? Most people come up with values, like "respect", and they are right actually. But there are also some practical ingredients, like communication skills, and we have seen how much they can make the difference between a successful relationship and an unsuccessful one.

So, without further ado, off we go!

Respect

Let's start with this. Respect is so fundamental in a relationship that we cannot ignore it, can we? One of the main anxieties in relationships is in fact losing respect, or "not being respected enough". Very often even betrayals are seen as "lack of respect".

But in many relationships, it also happens that *respect is taken for granted.* This can be fine, but I would suggest that ***you keep expressing your respect to your partner and encourage your partner to do the same with you.***

If you mean it, say it! *Focus on your partner's positive traits and don't take them for granted;* if s/he does something good, praise him/her. Make sure your partner knows that you think highly of him/her...

You know by now that you need to ***constantly feed your relationship***, and words and small gestures are "the food" of healthy relationships.

Honesty

Another quality that can make or break a relationship. "But surely no one wants to be dishonest in a relationship," you may ask? Well... Let's say that in most cases, *we start off with an idealized, fairy tale and idyllic image of what our relationship will be.* This is great, but in many cases this very "fairy tale idea of our relationship" is what ends up ruining it.

Example... George and Melissa started off a few months ago, and it was all perfect to start with. But after a while, things didn't look as perfect as they expected. Nothing major, really, a very small thing... Melissa likes playing chess and George went along with it. You know, when you are in the infatuation phase you like everything your partner likes. We literally have a "morphed" perception of reality. We actually really believe in ourselves that we like certain things...

But then the infatuation wears off and that more "realistic" perspective of reality comes back. But *we don't want to lose the "fairy tale idea of our relationship".* And it is because we want to preserve this ideal that we often start doing two little things:

- *Lying to ourselves*
- *Lying to our partner*

These little lies seem justified at first. We see them as white lies... But lies they are and in a relationship, they can have consequences. So, George rang me up the other day (they still have old fashioned telephones that "ring" in the world of imaginary friends) and he said that he can't face another long and boring game of chess, that he is a "physical person who likes being active, walking, doing sports, not sitting down for days on end in front of a chess board!"

I could smell a problem and so I asked a few probing questions... It turns out that George followed a very typical pattern...

- At first, he actually thought he would love playing chess.
- For a few months he was fine – he sort of enjoyed it.
- Then he started getting bored with it, but he *told himself that he would like it again very soon.*
- That "very soon" has never happened...
- He has not told Melissa about it and he is scared that if he does, their "perfect relationship won't be perfect anymore."

You see, the first lie to oneself actually makes it hard to then be honest with the partner. But as you can notice it all happens perfectly innocently... but then you end up with a "secret" from your partner... And that's a problem. George hasn't lied to Melissa, but he is holding a secret...

Guess what I told him?

...

You guessed; I told him to come clear as soon as possible. You cannot bottle something up or it will end up coming out at the worst possible time (years later during an animated argument – so, it comes as a "weapon" and not as a solution).

He can always play some chess with her, of course, but he needs to be honest, with himself and with Melissa. He needs her to understand that *he has not fooled her by pretending that he liked chess.* This is a problem he correctly has. He needs to be very clear and tell her that he actually did enjoy it at first but now he just does not...

Then there will be practical steps to take (e.g., she will need someone else to play chess with etc.), but the point is that ***you need to be vigilant about situations where you "hide a small thing" from your partner.*** This may lead to more and more hiding and a downward spiral.

So, keep an eye on the small things and you will keep your relationship clean shining with honesty.

Flexibility

We spent a lot of time talking about how relationships change. But I want to look at this from a new perspective. Now, there is something that people would define as "magic" when a new relationship starts. Those moonlit nights and strolls in a park full of scented flowers are inebriating...

And we hold onto those moments with great fondness, but also with the worry that if the relationship changes, those moments will never happen again. It is the "fairy tale" image we talked about in the previous section... That very ideal image can be an obstacle to flexibility.

When things are perfect, we don't want to change them. The problem is that even when they are no longer perfect, we don't want to change them and if we do, we want to "change them back", not adapt them to the new situation.

That is not flexibility; that is nostalgia.

You should fully enjoy that fizzy and aromatic feeling you have during the infatuation phase. But please consider this: ***there isn't just one fairy tale, there can be many, and many beautiful stories too.***

I'll explain, the fact that the first phase will come to an end is inevitable. But instead of seeing it as "the end of a fairy tale" look at it as *"the beginning of a new story".* Maybe you have matured, and it won't be a fairy tale, but there are wonderful novels for adults too, full of passion and happiness...

Shared Values

This is one of the foundations of good relationships. Most of us, at least adults, look for a partner with the same value system as we have. A left-wing person will look for a left-wing partner; a vegan will hardly get on well with a butcher. You know what I mean...

"But hold on, there are couples who even have different religious beliefs!" You are right! In some places they are even fairly common, especially big melting pots like Paris or London. But there is one key thing they share: they have a religious or spiritual belief... That alone is a strong bond.

These couples have to negotiate impressive cultural and moral variables to be honest. Different traditions, holidays, often even languages... But religions have much more in common than most people believe. The core value system of a Christian, Buddhist, Muslim, Jew, Sikh, Hindu, or even an Animist is very similar. But there are of course lots of "challenges".

Having said this, records show that multicultural and multi-faith couples do work very well. Maybe the fact itself of having to find an agreement on very important and intimate topics makes them very strong indeed (and flexible at the same time)!

Once you have managed such a huge step, you certainly are ready to face the world with lots of confidence.

It is actually more difficult to find an agreement between an atheist and a believer, of *any* religious or spiritual persuasion. Usually, atheists and agnostics stick together and so do believers. But again, this is not a strict rule.

But in any case, ***shared values and beliefs are a strong bonding element within couples.***

You don't need to share absolutely all values, but a large section of values is really fundamental for a couple. To start with, you will avoid never-ending arguments (trust me on this!) You will also have a shared mission in some cases. A couple who loves animals can work together for charitable work or on campaigns for animal rights, for example...

If you "activate" your shared values, these activities can too become "food for your relationship". What is more, they will do a lot to preserve or increase mutual respect and esteem.

Independence

Once upon a time, women would get married and lose any independence. That wedding day was the beginning of a life where the husband provided for food, shelter etc. and the wife took her "role" as dependent on him.

This still happens in some cultures, but it would be totally unacceptable to most modern women. The fact is that if you fully depend on one partner, you will lose a lot of freedom. Many women born decades ago never divorced not because they didn't want to, but because they could not afford it.

I mentioned divorce to show an extreme case, a lack of freedom so big that the whole relationship depends on it. But even on small things, lack of freedom can become tiring and wear the relationship.

But what happens if one of the partners does not work? Or do both need to have an income? I'll tell you a story, and this time it is not about imaginary friends... It's a couple I know well, born in 1942 (both of them). The husband worked most of his life (they are both retired now). But you know what? He never managed his salary. He gave it all to his wife. And then it was the wife who gave him pocket money...

I find this a very creative solution. You see, having to ask for money to the partner who holds the purse can be problematic. But if the person holding the purse is not the "breadwinner", the whole process is reversed.

I am giving this as a hint, something to consider and adapt. However, ***if one of the partners has no income, the other should make him/her independent and not dependent.*** The difference is huge... Giving the partner a reasonable sum on a regular basis as s/he wishes is a good solution, without then using it as a tool to make him/her feel "inferior".

Forcing one partner to ask for money every time and even worse explain why s/he needs it is humiliating to say the least.

Variety

Nothing is as tiring for a couple as "the same all over again every day, day in day out with no end in sight." Sometimes one of the partners leads the couple into a very routine life pattern. Sometimes both do it.

The fact is that routines are comfortable, and we feel safe with them. And indeed, you do need to have *some routines in your life and relationship*. The problem starts when routines are too many, and one of the partners starts feeling a bit bored.

Boredom within a relationship is frustrating, and one of the most common causes of this is actually the television... That very handy box of entertainment is not a good friend of happy relationships. I know, it is comfortable, it is cheap, and above all, it is *there.* Gong to the pictures requires the "going bit" ... It is also more expensive, it takes time, you need to get dressed... Especially if you are tired from work, the television is far too tempting.

But how many couples spend virtually every evening in front of the television? And how often do you think a couple should go out?

I usually find that when the "going out" starts becoming less than once a week, we may be entering "boredom territory". Not necessarily. I base this on the average urban couple. In the countryside dynamics may be different. You see, if you are indoors in an apartment in a city, you end up stuck in front of the television. If, however you live in the countryside, the glass of wine or cup of tea under a star-studded sky is often much more appealing than a reality show or even a sitcom... Certainly more than the news!

That can be romantic, and I would count it as "going out". But keep that general rule as guideline: ***at least once a week try to do something different, go out, have fun...***

And don't do the same thing every week. That restaurant you love so much because you went there on your first date can skip a week and you can try something different instead.

And how about when you have children? Big question. If you live near your parents or in-laws, or if you have friends that can help, do try to keep this "once a week we have fun" pattern.

If you don't? Well, babysitters are an option, if you can afford one. Maybe a friend who needs some extra cash, a student etc. Or... Why don't you do a thing like "car sharing?" Let me explain... Why don't you find friends with a child roughly as old as yours? Then you can do like this:

- On one day, you go out and they look after your child.
- On another day, they go out and you look after their child.
- On yet another day, you can meet at yours or theirs...

You get the extra bonus of a social evening, which in any case is a good break from routine evenings!

Communication

Ok, this has been the focus of most of this book. Still, it is so important that it is worth repeating... But there is a key thing you need to understand about communication:

- ***It is easy to have good communication in a couple if you start off open communication early on in your relationship.***

So, if you are at the first stages of your relationship, or if you are about to start one, do not waste those first few months. *Get into the habit of talking things through amicably and openly as early as possible.* Once you have developed this habit try to keep it. Actually, do everything in your power to keep this habit alive.

Be careful, because if *there is a communication breakdown, and the couple "go silent" it is much harder to reintroduce it.* By now you must have realized that in psychology and sociology we can never underestimate *"the power of habit".* It's like smoking and all bad habits. We pick them up, often without even being conscious of them. But once something has become a habit, it is hard to break.

If you are in one of those relationships that "have gone silent" work on reintroducing communication over a long time and in small steps. Here are some tips:

- *Start with easy to face topics.* Don't start with the most emotional and problematic issue you have if it is possible.
- Have *short, friendly,* but *frequent chats.* One big open-hearted chat followed by months of silence will not become a pattern, a habit, a "new modus vivendi"…
- *Allow your partner to get used to it.* Be understanding and patient, people take time to change traits of their behavior.
- *Consider that your partner may feel some level of embarrassment.* There can be some discomfort with new habits and talking about intimate things after a long time can be embarrassing.
- *Always end on a positive note!* Don't leave any bitter aftertaste to your partner or s/he will find it even harder to take on this new habit you want to introduce. Instead, close with something very positive. Your partner must be able to look back on the chat and feel *comfortable about it.*
- For this reason, *have lots of chats about positive things.* We tend to talk about things only when there is a problem. Especially in relationships. But hey, find an excuse and have an open-hearted chat about something positive. A long but heartfelt compliment is perfect. "I need to tell you how proud I am that you have taken up the art class and I love your style…" This sort of conversation is perfect to restart the communication after long breaks but also to keep it alive. So, even if you are so lucky that you don't have any problem at all for months or years, find a positive excuse to keep this habit alive. It may come in very handy later on…

So, frequency, positivity, good endings, short chats, and then a bit of bonding are excellent qualities of these chats. And your relationship may well depend on them!

A Common Mission

A common mission can be a panacea for relationships. Remember when we talked about the dynamics of relationships? Some are closed onto themselves... What happens then? All stress coming from within and outside the relationship is released inside, pushed in, like when you pump a bicycle tire. This may well cause the tire to burst... actually, it is easier to make a relationship burst with pressure from outside than even a weak tire.

While if you have a common mission, you will have a valve, an outlet, or even better a channel to turn pressure from outside into something positive and constructive.

Some couples are actually formed around a common mission, objective, passion, or goal. If you met your partner through an action group or charity, then of course you will already share a passion.

But what about if you didn't? The answer is simple, try to find one as early as possible in your relationship. It can be a small, local cause like, even feeding the cats of the neighborhood, it does not need to be anything particularly serious, demanding and complex. Actually, choose something achievable. Wanting to save the world is all good but it might be asking too much of your relationship...

And this leads us to our next point.

A Sense of Complicity

Doing things together, working on a common project can keep alive that sense of complicity that great relationships have. Don't underestimate this. When you are in the role of accomplices, you are "equals collaborating towards a common goal". That greatly improves mutual understanding and even communication.

It is also a way of getting to know each other while at the same time *learning to trust each other.* And of course, trust is next.

Trusting Each Other

We all say that trust is indispensable in a relationship. And in fact, it is. Lack of trust can lead to sad situations and, above all, *unnecessary jealousy.* Losing someone's trust is also very damaging, because most people never forgive those who break their trust and never give it back. It is often a permanent choice, and a couple cannot survive unless trust is kept or, if it is lost, it is then regained.

But how can you make sure that your relationship keeps being a trustful one? There are many ways, and, of course the main is ***never to do anything that can cost you your partner's trust.*** Before you do something, think about the consequences.

On the other hand, sometimes trust "fades a bit" instead of dissolving completely all of a sudden like a snowflake in the Sun… There is nothing big and traumatic, like an affair behind your back, but little by little things may become "less bright".

On the whole the older a relationship gets, the more trust there is within it. But this seems to become more prominent after a few years (usually 7 – that watershed of most relationships!) Before this mark, it may sometimes wane a bit.

This can also be due to lifestyle matters. If one of the partners is often absent for work, one of the partners has a wide (working) social network, if one of the partners travels a lot, while the other does not have these things, then it may happen that the second partner may become a bit jealous and lose a bit of trust.

What can you do about it then? Oddly enough it is again down to communication. Have very regular and very ***frequent open and honest conversations.*** The topic can be whatever you want, from world affairs to your friends or even yourselves. But have them, short, open, no secrets... That alone can greatly improve the level of trust in a relationship and reduce episodes of jealousy.

Playfulness

Oh, yes! Keep feeling young inside, actually keep that childish playfulness alive in your relationship. We make strong bonds with our playmates, don't we? Then absolutely keep playing games. Very playful couples even invent "in games" which is games they play alone, and know how to play.

These are sometimes played at parties, with friends, and even practical jokes can be fun. But do keep in mind that when others are involved, you should always mean no harm...

Then again there are many games you can play when you are alone, and even when it comes to intimacy, a bit of harmless playfulness can be wonderful. It will help you make those famous switches, but it can also help you experiment and try out new things.

What is more, it can teach you not to take yourselves too seriously...

Fun and Laughter

Please, please, please laugh as much as you can. And do it *with your partner (not at your partner,* of course). If you like telling jokes, go ahead. If you like in jokes, build as many as you wish. But even if you are not a comedian yourself, try to share funny moments with your partner.

Here the television (or a video platform, or the old-fashioned VCR... it does not matter) may come in handy. Watch sitcoms, funny movies and stand-up shows. Indeed, make sure that you have a "laughing evening" at least once a week, and every single week. And please, do treat yourself to that stand-up comedian you love so much when s/he has a show near where you live!...

It will be a great night out with your partner, so, something great to do, but it is also a "serotonin therapy" for your relationship. And I cannot even begin to list the positive effects of serotonin (a hormone released when we laugh) on your health, mental abilities, mood, emotional life, stress level, and even on your social and personal relationships. And in fact, I won't – start that is...

Friendship

Finally, do keep that friendship side of your relationship always kindled and alive. Going out with friends helps that, but also, as we said, playing together. The important thing is that you always treasure your partner also as a friend.

In fact, in super happy relationships the partners also see each other and treat each other also as best friends. And when they are out with others, they don't so much appear as a "romantic couple" but as a "pair of beat friends". That in turn helps the wider circle of friends stay young, compact, and united.

I know, at this stage I usually tease you about the next chapter. But not this time. In fact, there is no other chapter at all... What follows next is a goodbye from me, or maybe it is au revoir?

CONCLUSION

Wow, wow, wow have we not come a long way?! Remember when we first met? I do, I remember the first steps in this book... And look at what you know now! You are now basically an expert of relationships. And I don't mean a person who's had many... I mean that you have a good understanding of what relationships are like, how they work, what they need, and how you can face them with confidence, without anxiety, and without insecurities.

Actually – let me tell you – I think now you are confident and competent enough to give some good and sound tips to your friends. Do you want to have a go? Shall we try out a final exercise just for fun (and because I have become totally addicted to tea by now...)

Think about some friends of yours who are in a relationship. Have you got any tips on how to improve it (or to straighten up some "creases" in their relationship)?

And I know you have come up with an awful lot of ideas... But this is not just to look back and see the huge progress you have made...This is also a tip for you... Yes, thinking about your friends' relationships. You don't even need to then tell them what you have come up with. That is, unless you really think they would accept it and benefit from it... No, the reason is that ***it is safer to "brainstorm ideas" for other people's relationships.*** It is safer for your relationship. It's just a mental exercise, while if you did it about yourself and your partner it would be "something more" already.

So, ***use being an agony aunt even if only in your mind, about your friends' relationships as training, to develop your own skills, and only then apply your best ideas to your relationship!***

I bet you did not expect a final "trick of the trade" in the conclusion of this book... You would laugh to be inside a psychologist's mind on a train... They often make little "thought experiments" with the passengers. Like working out if there is an issue, what the issue may be like etc... It is just training with a skill, with a technique. And you can do the same now.

Let's try to remember a few of the many amazing things we have discovered about relationships in this book... For example, maybe you came thinking that a relationship is fixed, that it should never change? Well, now you know quite well that this very thought is what causes lots of anxiety, insecurities, and even major problems.

In fact, now you know that relationships change and go through many stages. But that there are also many different dynamic types in relationships… Some are closed and some are open, some are inclusive, others exclusive, some one directional, others not, some are egalitarian, others are not…

And you now know that the key to a happy relationship is not to be nostalgic of the first phase, the infatuation phase… that is a fairy tale idea…. But have you noticed that all fairy tales stop as soon as the relationship actually starts for real? Then they don't tell you the truth about Snow White… Dear Prince Charming turned out to be an utter bore and she went back to the Seven Dwarfs! Joking aside, that is to remind you that ***to be happy within a relationship both partners need to be comfortable with it at any stage***. And this often ***involves changing the relationship.*** Things change and you need to change with them. You can't have the same lifestyle before and after you have a baby. Ask any mum or dad… Actually, you don't even need to ask, look at their eye bags for the first year or so and you will already guess that many things have changed, even in the bed department…

But now you also know that ***communication is core to relationships and their success.*** We have spent quite a lot of time learning how we can communicate effectively. Remember that there is a ***specific way to express emotions, even when you are having an important talk…*** But you also know that communication needs to be kept alive. Many, frequent, positive and honest chats are what keep relationships alive and happy.

Those relationships where the partners keep things to themselves for weeks, months – even years – then all comes out in a massive row that lasts for a full day and that people in the near town confuse for fireworks... Those relationships have serious problems. But those where the partners talk frequently in most cases never even get to that stage where the massive argument starts.

But in case, you now know the way ***professionals avoid, defuse, and de-escalate arguments,*** and you can apply it to your relationship. Or even explain it to your friends if you have some who argue far too much. They will thank you for it.

But again, you now know that there are many types, or archetypes as we called them, of relationships and ***being confident with your relationship also means finding the right recipe, the right balance of traits from all these archetypes.***

And again, we have seen how ***important it is to be able to switch smoothly in a relationship.*** It is in fact a technique that has been developed oddly enough by a very unexpected community, remember? But psychology is not judgmental, and we take lessons wherever we can get one.

Many other things have made this journey what it has been. I hope you found it useful informative, colorful, and sometimes even fun, because laughing helps remembering things! And I hope you liked all my "imaginary friends". On this topic, just an ethical point: psychologists have to hide the identity of their patients when they talk about them, even in formal academic studies, the names are all fake, but the stories are real...

And I certainly have enjoyed it, and I hope you have too.

And if you need me again, you know where you can find me... No – not in the cupboard; that's where I drink my addictive teas... you can find me on a shelf!

RESOURCES

And if you want to know more, if you want to develop an area we have seen in this book a bit more in detail, here are some very useful books for you to choose from!

April, P. C. (2020). *The Anxiety Getaway: How to Outsmart Your Brain's False Fear Messages and Claim Your Calm Using CBT Techniques (Science-Based Approach to Anxiety Disorders).* Mango.

Bancroft, L. (2003). *Why Does He Do That?: Inside the Minds of Angry and Controlling Men* (Reprint ed.). Berkley Books.

Berne, E. (2016). *Games People Play: The Psychology of Human Relationships* (Penguin Life) (01 ed.). Penguin Life.

Butler, G. (2021). *Overcoming Social Anxiety and Shyness, 2nd Edition: A self-help guide using cognitive behavioural techniques* (Overcoming Books) (2nd ed.). Robinson.

Deguchi, H. (2021). *THE REAL RICH LIFE: Unlock the Secrets of Relationships*. Independently published.

Douglas, G. M. (2013). *Divorceless Relationships*. Access Consciousness Publishing Company.

Evans, P. (2010). *The Verbally Abusive Relationship, Expanded Third Edition: How to recognize it and how to respond* (Third ed.). Adams Media.

Hill, C., & Sharp, S. (2020). *How to Stop Overthinking: The 7-Step Plan to Control and Eliminate Negative Thoughts, Declutter Your Mind and Start Thinking Positively in 5 Minutes or Less*. Indy Pub.

Kingma, D. R. (1998b). *A Lifetime of Love: How to Bring More Depth, Meaning and Intimacy Into Your Relationship (Lasting Love, Deeper Intimacy, & Soul Connection)* (2nd ed.). Conari Press.

Life, T. S. O., & Botton, D. A. (2018). *Relationships (The School of Life Library)* (Illustrated ed.). The School of Life.

Ma, C. A. (2017). *The Anxiety Workbook: A 7-Week Plan to Overcome Anxiety, Stop Worrying, and End Panic* (Workbook ed.). Althea Press.

MacKenzie, J., & Thomas, S. (2019). *Whole Again: Healing Your Heart and Rediscovering Your True Self After Toxic Relationships and Emotional Abuse*. Tarcher Perigee.

Odessky, H., & Duffy, J. (2017). *Stop Anxiety from Stopping You: The Breakthrough Program For Conquering Panic and Social Anxiety*. Mango Media.

Welwood, J. (2007). *Perfect Love, Imperfect Relationships: Healing the Wound of the Heart* (42095th ed.). Trumpeter.

Winston, D. (2017). *The Smart Girl's Guide to Polyamory: Everything You Need to Know About Open Relationships, Non-Monogamy, and Alternative Love*. Skyhorse.

EFFECTIVE COMMUNICATION IN RELATIONSHIPS & COUPLE SKILLS (2 IN 1)

33+ SKILLS, ACTIVITIES & QUESTIONS TO HELP YOU BETTER COMMUNICATE, DEEPEN YOUR CONNECTION & ENHANCE INTIMACY & PASSION IN YOUR LIFE

INTRODUCTION

Many of us are in an intimate, romantic relationship of some kind. And a lot of those relationships aren't exactly perfect. While nothing truly is, a lot of these relationship can be improved.

Miscommunication or a lack of communication is often the cause of the problem in couples' relationships. It is both symptomatic and causal of a variety of other significant, even life-threatening conditions. Lack of clear communication destroys relationships, and of all sorts; romantic, familial, friendly, and professional.

The fact is that, in this information-packed world, being able to communicate clearly is vital, crucial not only to our success but also to your happiness, even our very survival.

Yet surprisingly, better communications skills are still out of reach for millions of people all over the world. There are lots of causes, including overthinking, suppressed emotions, inappropriate displays of anger, and aggression. This can also be due to a number of conditions and disorders and even complexes.

It's vital to know what you're dealing with, why it's happening, when, and where this miscommunication happens. It's crucial to know how to communicate better and more clearly, to your friends and family and coworkers, and especially your romantic partner.

This is just the book for you! No matter where you are in the romantic cycle; between partner and determined to do better, or in the crux of a crisis moment that you're afraid your relationship may not survive. And you could be right!

We'll move quickly and thoroughly through the causes and cures for this communication breakdown and tell you just how to fix it in each and every case. We'll work through different communications techniques, discuss what the real motivations might be, deep-rooted causes, ways to recognize and deal with crisis points and breaking points, and other relationship issues. We'll take a look at when and where these points may occur and how to handle them. The book makes complex theories easy to understand, with examples and exercises to get you on the road to a better romance immediately.

We'll also give you tons of practical suggestions on how, when, and where to go to improve your relationships, a virtual handbook of romantic travel and adventure which may take you to Paris ... or to your own backyard.

We'll use journalism's classic *5 W's & an H* rule (*who, what, where, when, why,* and *how*) to take you through every stage of a relationship and show you precisely how to understand and communicate your wants and desires. We'll go through the nuts and bolts of communication at the early, middle, and crucial late stages of your relationship. We'll coach you through communication breakdowns and crises. The information contained here will give you the necessary skills to navigate a breakup and to recover from it efficiently. We'll offer tips and tricks which just may lead you right back into your ex-partner's arms, if that's what you really want.

We'll take you through various schools of psychological thought, a virtual primer in modern psychology and communication theory that will help you not only with your inner life, your intimate partnerships, but with friendships and professional relationships too.

We are dedicated to bringing the latest information to our readers to make their lives easier and better. We know everybody's life could be improved in different ways and we are happy to do all we can to guide, instruct, and encourage anybody who is willing to help themselves. We make dizzying concepts easy to understand and to apply! My own journey through life (like most people's) has had its share of communication breakdowns, on almost every level. But it was with my partners that I often had the most trouble, because those relationships are the most delicate and in a lot of ways the most important. But I've learned from my mistakes, and now you can too!

This book has innumerable exercises and techniques to help any couple communicate better. The information here has been proven to rescue failing romances, and it can do the same for you. But this book can also help you communicate better with your family, your friends, and your coworkers. It will give you a better understanding of yourself and may set you on a course of self-improvement which makes every moment of your life better, happier, and more fulfilled. This book has insights and information that will make any person more effective, more productive, and more attractive.

And I'm not the only one. Our books have helped thousands of eager and hopeful readers, and these techniques are time-tested, research-based, and can certainly help you in any number of ways. But not just you. They've helped people I know, and they help people you know. There's so much information here, so many different aspects of communication are covered, that you're certain to know somebody who could benefit from the data you're about to obtain. You may not have a God complex, but chances are you know somebody who does have one. Have a friend who's a perfectionist? Do them a favor and get them a copy. Are you a manager with workers, they should all read this and then discuss it. The tool and techniques included here will make any office or workplace run more smoothly, efficiently, and effectively. Because this book is about more than just communication, it's about relationships. Help clear up relationship issues in the office and at home! There's a lot more here than just communicating with your partner, but so many of us do have flawed relationships that this book is of value to just about anyone.

If you incorporate just one technique from this book, you could save your relationship. Using more or all of them will revolutionize your life and the lives of those around you. Because even if they don't read it, you'll be able to guide them with what you've learned, improving their lives along with your own and without them even realizing it. They'd probably prefer it that way!

Not only is this book certain to improve your life and theirs, but it's vital that you start now! The maladies this book remedies can be insidious and even deadly. Lack of clear communication is a creeping disease which can have fatal consequences. It's like a cancer that takes hold before you realize and then spreads to every other facet of your life. And it can be just as deadly, leading to depression, abuse, the consequences of ill-health, even suicide.

Don't let things go too far, don't let that cancer spread. You hold in your hands the scalpel you need, the cure for what may be slowly killing your relationship and ruining your life. Don't wait another second! Your relationship can't afford it, you can't afford it. And your friends and family may be suffering too. The sooner you help yourself, the sooner you can help them!

Don't get caught in the trap of analysis paralysis, don't overthink, don't let negative self-talk or a fixed mindset prevent you from opening up new doors in your life and your love. This book will make it all clear and it will revolutionize the way you think, feel, and behave. You've already begun your journey, and you're more than capable of taking the next steps to save yourself and your loved ones from the common traps that ruin so many lives. The next step is the first section, the first chapter, the first day of the rest of your life.

Let's get to it!

I

THE HOW, WHAT, WHY, WHEN, AND WHERE OF COMMUNICATING IN A RELATIONSHIP:

HOW TO SAY IT, WHAT YOU'RE SAYING, WHAT IT TRULY MEANS, WHO YOU REALLY ARE WHEN YOU'RE COMMUNICATING, AND THE EFFECTS OF YOUR ENVIRONMENT

1

HOW: EFFECTIVELY COMMUNICATING WITH YOUR PARTNER

WHY BETTER COMMUNICATION ISN'T JUST IMPORTANT, IT'S CRUCIAL

Experts believe that communication skills really kick in at around age two, when words are formed and associated with basic concepts. But a two-year-old's ability to communicate is matched by the depths of their desire. They have basic thoughts, almost always self-directed (*"Gimme, it's mine."*) They even refer to the two towering influences in their lives, their parents, in terms of their own wants or needs.

And that's fine for a two-year old. But we learn over time (hopefully) that the more delicate and complex interactions of adults require a more finessed way of communicating. If, for example, you go into your adult romance saying, "Gimme, it's mine," you could lose that relationship and even personal freedom.

In fact, we learn in stages, our ability to communicate developing, evolving with our experiences. Keep in mind that there are two basic mindsets among the general population; a fixed and a growth mindset. The fixed is a closed-minded view of the world, convinced that things are the way they are, people are the way they are, and these things simply don't change. The growth mindset holds that people and their circumstances can be changed over time according to experience.

Why is this important? In truth, it's important to all things in our lives and on virtually every level. Whether you are of a fixed or a growth mindset will affect every aspect of your life; personal, professional, and social.

A romantic relationship is unique among these things for a variety of reasons, the first one being fairly obvious. The physical and spiritual intimacy anybody shares with a romantic partner, by the very nature of that type of relationship, makes each person in the relationship far more vulnerable, and they invest far more in those relationships than any others. Your boss never sees you naked (hopefully) nor they you (ditto). You're not expected to lay around snuggling and sharing your intimate secrets with your coworkers, no matter how close you are. And just as you may drift away from coworkers after transfers or job changes, you're not so apt to drift away from the romance, sometimes even years after it's over. We'll discuss this later in the book, but to further make the point about commitment; people are likely to switch jobs (roughly every four years) than spouses (probably twice in your life, perhaps three).

So how we handle ourselves in our romantic relationships is especially important. It goes to the very core of who we are. There's an old saying which goes something like, you can judge a man by the way he treats his wife. It doesn't sound very #metoo, but the point remains. The way a person treats the one with whom he or she is more intimate and loving than anyone else is a good reflection and indication of how that person will treat others. If a man would beat his wife, what would he do to a total stranger?

I don't mean to simplify the concept of physical or marital abuse, of course. There's a lot more to it than that. A man may abuse his wife only because she is the only one powerless to stop him, for a variety of psychological reasons.

But it is true that the way we communicate in our relationships reflects the way we communicate in other facets of our lives. A person with a fixed mindset on one level is virtually certain to have a fixed mindset on all levels. A person who is a good listener and a measured communicator in their romantic life is almost certain to behave that way with their friends and coworkers as well. It's all intertwined. So, learning how to communicate on this level is crucial to anyone's overall success and happiness.

How do we know this is true? Statistics bare it out! Studies show that married couples are almost 9% happier than divorced or separated people. Single people reported being only 0.2% happier than divorced people. Every study shows that those who have never married die earlier than those who have been married, and much earlier than those who remain married.

So, a happy, healthy romantic relationship is no doubt in our best interests. And healthy communication is absolutely vital to any healthy romantic relationships. Another look at various studies reveals that the inability to communicate is responsible for 65% of divorces. The inability to resolve conflict leads to 45% of divorces.

The men researched in a particular study cited complaining and nagging as their top communication problem. We call that blaming or shaming. Women seemed most irked by their partner's failure to value their feelings or opinions.

There can be little doubt. Clear, healthy communication is paramount to every facet of your life, and nowhere is it more important than in your romantic relationship.

WHAT YOU MAY BE DOING WRONG

But what is it about a romantic relationship which can make clear and healthy communication so difficult? Just as healthy communication is central to strong romance, we've already seen the stats of the negative effect on unhealthy communication. But the flip side is that, while communication in these relationships is central, it can also be the most challenging, and both are related to the particulars of an intimate relationship.

As we've seen, a person is most vulnerable in a romantic relationship, and they tend to invest more in those relationships. As in many transactional situations, there's a risk-to-benefit ratio. There's more risk in a personal relationship (the risk of rejection, the risk of betrayal, a costly or painful divorce and a child or children who must bear the brunt of that divorce). There's also more reward (better physical and psychological health over a longer life, a satisfying family life, children to carry on your genes and maybe take care of you when you're old).

But being so vulnerable in the face of some of these risks can affect a person's perspective, their mindset, their behavior. Fear is a powerful motivator, and anybody can become fearful over time. With that fear, anybody may want to protect their vulnerability. If a person is afraid of infidelity, they may withdraw themselves and become physically and romantically introverted. Envisioning a betrayal, they seal themselves off from the vulnerability, which is in this case the intimacy. This, of course, can become a self-fulfilling prophecy, wherein a person is fearful of being betrayed and shuts themselves off and thereby inspires their partner toward a betrayal.

More is the pity, because a simple clear line of communication would clear this up! If one is fearful of betrayal, they're making a big assumption. Assumptions, by the way, are almost always wrong; we all know what happens when you assume. Reassurance and clarification could reverse this assumption. Misread signs could be straightened out.

Romantic relationships have their own communications issues. Over time, a romantic couple may become so complacent that they simply don't bother communicating. Long out of the courtship phase, perhaps deep into a marriage, there may be little to talk about. But anybody with a growth mindset will know that a person is likely to grow over time, to evolve with the effect of experience. So, there should always be something new to talk about, really. It just takes a new perspective and an open mind.

There's also another old saying (we'll be using a few, because they work) which goes, *familiarity breeds contempt.* After so many years of intimacy, of complacency, people can often get sick of each other, it's as simple as that. And instead of dealing with this problem as it happens, one or both may allow those feelings to fester until they become unbearable and the relation comes to a crashing and often acrimonious end. This is also avoidable. True, not every relationship is going to work out. Not every two people are compatible with one another, people do grow apart. But bad blood would never fester if one or the two were open with their feelings and knew how to communicate them in a healthy manner. Because it's not just a matter of being open with your feelings, as that can have disastrous results.

And it just happens to be another big particular challenge of communicating in an intimate or romantic relationship. One or the other may become prone to over-expressing, over-dramatizing, over-acting and over-reacting. This communication becomes haranguing, sniping, complaining, insulting, verbal abuse, and it can even lead to physical abuse in an escalating spiral of anger and uncontrolled temperament. These abuses, all of them, can go both ways. So, if you're going to be free with your communication, you must be disciplined with it, restrained, considerate of the other person's position. Too often, after a certain length of time, we may begin to feel that we've given this person enough, and now it's our time; for release, for attention, for whatever. If you want to have a fight, you'll be well-situated. If you want to have a friend or a lover or a spouse, you're probably going ninety miles an hour down a dead-end street.

One thing to consider is to keep in mind the difference between resentment and anger. Anger is more of a passing emotion, whereas resentment tends to linger. Often, when anger is not expressed, it becomes resentment. Anger is much easier to deal with, before it has had a chance to grow and fester. So, if you can know the difference, you can recognize each and deal with them in different ways. Anger is less destructive and can be dealt with more quickly, resentment takes more time.

Those in a romantic relationships face other particular challenges to communication as well. Research indicates that the most common source of conflict among married couples is money. A lot of failed relationships are due to arguments about money, because money has its own particular challenges when it comes to communication, especially in intimate relationships.

In America, as in a lot of countries all over the world, we are defined by our success or our failure. How many conversations get rolling with, *"So, what do you do?"* In the 1980s and beyond, when greed was good, success became even more vital to a person's self-worth, especially for men. It was a measure of his potency, of his vigor, of his strength, a sign that he was an alpha male. This all fell into the biological mandate of procreation and what the human psyche has been both trained and created to seek, desire, and do. Remember that women have only been in the American workforce for a few generations. But men have a nearly 10-000-year-long tradition of proving their worth to breed, and doing this by dominating their environment; the prairie, the Pacific and other theaters of battle, even the boardroom or the suburban block. The pressure for men to succeed is immense.

For years, this had been an upward spiral. Every generation had done better than the generation before it. That did little to alleviate the pressure, of course. But when the current generation turned out to be the first not to do as well as the previous generation, things took a turn. Jobs were harder to find, and the so-called *great recession* of 2007-2009 hit, pressure to succeed became pressure to survive.

After a historic recovery, things have taken a downward economic turn again. People are having a lot more trouble now, only increasing the pressure of money troubles. This time, the economic battering was so bad it resulted in widespread depression, substance abuse, and even suicide.

And to get back to the stats, talking about money is hard for a lot of average people even under the best of circumstances. It speaks to the center of how we see ourselves. Many of us men by a simple historical fact, though increasingly few by a simple contemporary fact. We're all suffering, prone to feelings of failure and an inability to survive. It can trigger feelings of having failed one's parents, dropped the ball on the entire country.

Economic pressures are often unrelenting. No matter how understanding and sympathetic, supportive, and loving any two people are, that won't pay the rent. It won't put food on the table or pay the car insurance bill. Those things hover over the heads of countless couples, married or not, and it can be crippling.

The ways it shut down clear, healthy communication shouldn't be unfamiliar. Tempers flare and self-control erupts into irrevocable outbursts, or fear and shame create great lulls of communication breakdown until a clear line can no longer be re-established.

These money worries resonate in even deeper ways. Think of the fixed or the growth mindset. Almost nowhere does this resonate louder than in terms of our private economies, except perhaps our romantic lives overall. But since we're looking at an even more central aspect of our lives, let's parcel this out.

First, why is money more central than love? What kind of monster would write such a thing? Is this Gordon Gecko himself? Well, I don't mean to put it that way. But our success or failure is often seen as a reflection of something within ourselves. The rugged American individual so deeply engrained in our minds, from Davy Crockett to Ronald Reagan, that we see ourselves as the stewards of the American dream. It's something we do or fail to do on our own, according to many. It's a notion which lends itself to a fixed or a growth mindset.

A fixed mindset is likely to see things which happen in his or her life to be a reflection of themselves and to be a measure of their worth. A growth mindset is more apt to focus on the circumstance and their best efforts as they relate to the circumstance. A growth mindset is more apt to be self-forgiving, because the growth mindset doesn't let the circumstance, a success or failure, reflect on the value of the person.

But both mindsets may embrace the individualistic way of doing things. It's not to say that anybody with a growth mindset must necessarily be a team-player. Some people interact well with others and find inspiration there. Others thrive on privacy and fewer distractions. It has a lot to do with whether a person is a *manager,* whose job puts them naturally into interaction with others, or a *maker,* who's job requirements generally include long hours alone. A team-playing manager might be a growth-minded person, ready to focus on the result and not the individual commitment, but they may still be fixed in their methods, trained by experience to manage chaos with a stricter sense of control. You'd likely be hard-pressed to convince a person like this that their methods are wrong, because they might not be!

Either way, you could be growth-minded or fixed-minded and still be either a manager or a maker; you still may have money troubles you don't feel comfortable with. Because a growth-minded person can be optimistic about the future but still not know how to deal with the present. The fixed-minded man or woman is likely to believe that things will never really change. This person may be less likely to advance, but they also have more stable finances.

This brings us back to my Gordon Gecko impression. We see here how central the concept of success is to how we identify ourselves, regardless of our mindset or the state of the economy. We use the phrase self-made man for a reason, and it's the American ideal.

But any romance necessarily involves a second person. It's about the other person's points of view, opinions, tastes, foibles, follies, goals, and regrets. A relationship is not found at the core of either of the individuals, but in the center of the space between them. It's a different balance of gravity. Surely, the one affects the other, but they're not the same.

And since we've seen the crippling effects of money troubles on romance, that's something to be particular careful of. We'll talk more about this later in the book too, but for now just keep it in mind! (Really, we'll be coming back to all these ideas as we work our way through the book, so don't skip over anything, you may only have to go back.)

KEYS TO CLEARER COMMUNICATION

It all seems like a lot to digest. It seems that, in order to better communicate with others, we have to get into closer touch with ourselves. That's very true, actually. We've already touched on a fixed mindset or a growth mindset. Which are you? Take a moment to think about it? Do you have a defeatist point of view, ready to anticipate a pattern of events to repeat no matter what external forces occur? Do your failures inspire you to try again, to try even harder, even knowing failure may yet be the result? You may never have given that any thought at all, but maybe it's about time you did.

And even if you're a fixed-mindset person, you don't have to stay fixed about it. Face it; you can't control everything; you can't be responsible for everything. Every success is likely to be the result of at least a few people, even if they were only your personal heroes, teachers, or mentors. So, every failure is likewise not your fault. Failures lead to successes, they're part of the process. Realize that the process can yet change the final outcome, that nothing is set in stone. That's about all you have to do.

But if you're a fixed mindset person and you want to remain that way, that's okay too. There are other ways, but as a fixed-mindset person you can at least make sure you always put away money, the same amount every month if possible. Stick to the systems which serve you; pay your taxes on time, always tell the truth.

And this is your viewpoint, know it going into the realm of intimacy and communication. If you have your ways and they're set in stone, start off by finding somebody who understands and accepts, and even embraces it. Or you might find a partner with the same rules, also set in stone. Good. Two fixed mindsets probably make a good match.

If you're a growth-minded person, you may want to avoid a fixed-minded person, or you may not. Perhaps opposites attract. But knowing what kind of person they are, and what kind of person you are, will make all the difference in whether you can communicate successfully.

Knowledge is power, after all.

There are other aspects of the individual, which should be examined when looking at communication in romantic relationships. Because the nature of intimacy and a shared life is so widespread, it touches on every aspect of ourselves and each other. Are you extroverted, on the go, a manager type? If so and your partner is too, you might actually clash, each trying to outmanage the other. Two workers may become simply a pair of introverts and fail to make a connection at all.

The way we deal with different types is different, and it's nowhere as important as in a romantic relationship. We have a much greater effect on each other than we do on most others. If you're a manager type and your worker partner are symbiotic, that's great. But the two styles may clash. Too much management may further isolate the worker-minded partner. So, understand that you communicate in a certain way and your partner in a different way. Some people are more naturally high energy, others more reserved. This can inspire, or it can annoy. Be conscious of how this may affect them.

When communicating, always keep the other person in mind above yourself. Your reactions will be easier to manage than theirs.

This is the essence of diplomacy, with will serve you well in every facet of your life. It's always the first line in every military conflict, and the first rule of diplomacy is to resolve conflicts while avoiding war. It may sound simple, but it's commonly forgotten and over overlooked. Because while sometimes a disagreement many resolve problems and strengthen a friendship, the basic fact is that we're very often not looking for a friendship, we're just looking for a fight. We may be a bit drunk or a bit fed up, but we go into the conflict seeing it as a war waiting to happen, and it almost certainly will. Too rarely do people engage with an attitude that they are entering a mission of diplomacy, not a fight at all. If they did, at least some of those fights could likely be avoided.

And how do you incorporate diplomacy into your romantic communication? Let's take a closer look.

First of all, select a time and place with privacy. Nobody should be nearby to hear it, or what is said may embarrass one or both parties. That third person maybe drawn into a conflict where they have no part. And it's crazy rude to argue in front of another person. Ever see a bickering couple at a cocktail party, maybe two drunken lovers having a fight in the middle of the frat party. Yeah, so just don't do that.

Start with what's working. Don't just tear into your list of grievances. Things can only go downward from there. But remind your partner about what's working in your relationship, what you treasure about your partner, the fond memories you have and the things you look forward to. It'll soften what's coming next and take the edge off any potential combativeness.

Remind your partner that you love them and like them and that all you want is for you both to be as happy together as you can be. That *is* the way you feel, right? If not, rethink the whole conversation.

Ask questions. It's often said that the best conversationalist in the world only talks about one thing ... you. You don't want to go on and on about your angers, your needs, your judgements. That will only lead your partner to demand that it be time for their angers, needs, and judgements. That's where diplomacy often ends. And there are times when you have to represent yourself and should take the focus of the other, we'll get to them soon enough. But for now, if you're going to talk about the other person, do it in questions. Don't tell them their feelings are wrong, don't tell them how you think they should feel. But you could and should ask them about their feelings, express, and demonstrate a genuine interest in how they feel, why they feel the way they do, what they think they could change in order to stop feeling that way. But don't put all responsibility on them! Ask them what you might have done to make them feel the way they do, what you can do (if anything) to correct it. Engage, but do it in a rhetorical way. This way you're not making any declarative statements which might seem aggressive or insulting.

Listen actively, not passively. Don't just sit there and wait for your chance to insert your perspective or make your point. Really concentrate on what the other person is saying, to the feelings behind those words. Don't offer corrections or opinions, just listen. It's not as easy as it sounds, and it may take some experimentation. In our fast-paced world, we can hardly afford not to be proactive at all times. Meditation is an excellent exercise for becoming an active listener.

Without getting too deep into it, transcendental meditation includes sitting quietly and focusing on something other than the clamor of the world. It may be your breath, focusing on the in and out as you breathe. Some focus on a single focus point, other on a muttered mantra. The idea is to focus on only this thing. It trains you to focus and naturally makes you a better listener. Try it and see if you don't agree. It has lots of other benefits too.

Be empathetic. Briefly, sympathy is the capacity to feel badly for someone. Empathy is when you can imagine the very pain the other is feeling. Sympathy is a social norm, but empathy involves real emotional investment. So, since you're there with your intimate partner, perhaps your spouse, talking about the very things which may be plaguing that person's soul, invest some empathy. Imagine feeling what they're feeling, feel it deep down inside you. You may not be used to expressing empathy, but it is probably well within your reach. Try it by watching *Casablanca* or *Love Story* and see if you're not moved.

If you do have to speak and you have to say things about your partner which you might consider constructive (not likely to land that way), observe this rule; address behavior if you must, not the person's character. If sloppiness is a problem, keep it to that; no reason to diagnose that sloppiness as reflecting the person being lazy or stupid. Never go personal with it. Also, those things can be argued, but if the toilet seat is up, then the toilet seat is up; there's no argument to be had there.

If you must address your partner's behavior, follow it up quickly with a solution, which you should already have prepared in advance. Don't just go in with guns blazing and hope you're going to get what you want. Be prepared. Chinese warlord Sun Tzu said, roughly, that the general who prevails knows *that* he's going to prevail because he knows *how* he's going to prevail. He was a big believer in diplomacy too.

When you move from questions to declarations, keep them about yourself. Nobody has a right to tell somebody else how to think, how to feel, or how to express those feelings and thoughts, no matter how repulsive they may be. You can always walk away, and more often than not, that's what happens. But you always have the right to express how you feel. They can walk away, but you're not transgressing on anybody in telling them how you feel.

Keep in mind that you don't have the right to expect people to give you what you want if you're not ready to ask for it. You can't just expect them to read your minds. The old *you should have known* routine just doesn't fly anymore. So, buck up and prepare to stand your ground.

Be honest, no matter if you're speaking or listening. Avoid being frank or terse, certainly don't be rude. But nobody can blame you for being honest. Furthermore, it won't do either of you any good. If you're not being honest, you're not having a clear line of communication, period.

And when you make your declarations, there are certain strategies you can use. For example, you wouldn't say, "I feel that you're completely wrong!" That won't do the trick. Even, "I feel that I am completely right, and ... seem to feel otherwise." You can't cheat this, and getting it right really isn't as easy as it sounds.

Try something like, "I feel that I'm not being heard," or "I feel tense, more and more," or even, "I feel that something is wrong between us." Hey, you feel how you feel. All the other person can do is say how they feel. It's a great way to de-escalate things if you can, even to prevent them from going haywire. Take responsibility for your actions, your place in the scheme of things between you, for your own feelings and emotions.

But watch out, as there's a hitch; some people hear the word feelings and they become insensate! You've suddenly become a so-called *snowflake,* as if you have no intellect at all and are acting only from emotion. But I find that most people who instantly aggress on the word feelings isn't an intellectual but a bully who is a slave to their own feelings, which they can almost never understand. Mentioning your feelings is a trigger for this kind of bullying attitude. It doesn't mean you shouldn't do it, but be prepared.

If somebody does get triggered in this way, the best thing to do is walk away. If this is your romantic partner, you might not be a good match. If you want to try to make it work, know what kind of communication just won't get through to that person and be prepared to accept it. Of course, this is symptomatic of a fixed mindset, and a fixed mindset can be changed, as we've seen. But that change almost always has to happen from within. A person with any mindset is likely to hold onto it only until they decide to change it. They'll cling to it all the more in the face of intervention from somebody else. Really, you can't change a person.

This person may also be an abuser. There are various types of abuse; physical, sexual, psychological. If you're that frustrated in a relationship, this person may be emotionally abusive. If they are withholding affection, show no remorse, are unusually controlling or blameful or disrespectful of your feelings, you're probably in an emotionally abusive relationship. I think you'd be hard-pressed to find anyone willing to suggest you try to change this person or the relationship. This person could have any number of psychological disorders, problems you can't solve, if they can be solved at all. Almost all abusive relationships must be escaped, not saved.

But if you're both sound of mind and truly interested, there are lots of ways to keep it going smoothly. Reflect on what your partner has said, rephrase it as you delve deeper. "I know you feel this way, that your voice isn't heard ..." or whatever it is they said. It shows that you listened, understood, and that you've taken it in as a part of your personal responsibility.

Respond, don't react. Keep it reasonable, avoid emotion. When a person comes from an emotional place, they cannot be reasoned with. Likewise, emotion cannot really sway reason. It's about the brain and how it functions.

Our brains' prefrontal cortex controls logic and decision-making while the limbic system is where our emotions are found. When the prefrontal cortex inhibits the limbic system's emotional reactivity, we're all quite reasonable. But when emotions run eye, the prefrontal cortex loses control. But they operate on different levels, and once the imbalance is struck, it takes a while for the brain to recalibrate. But just know that, for practical purposes, an emotionally revved-up person just won't listen to reason. So, when things are too emotional, think about walking away. You won't get anything accomplished from that point forward, and you're likely to go on to do further or even irrevocable damage.

If that happens, don't ever be afraid to walk away from a conversation and don't let anyone pull you back in. Nobody has the right to demand that you do that. They can speak, but you don't have to listen.

When you *are* speaking, however, use collaborative language like *we, our, us.* It's a bonding technique, demonstrating that you are not only in it for yourself, that you have a shared goal. If you don't have the shared goal of keeping the relationship happy ... and alive ... then you've got other problems.

If you're still on an even keel but diplomacy doesn't seem to be working, there are other considerations. You've asked about your partner, you've expressed yourself, now what? Take a look at your environment. The environment has a huge effect on the psyche. Be constructive about what you each can do to improve the situation. Don't be judgmental, but there could be physical things which will affect your behavior and your feelings. Is it time for a good Spring cleaning? Maybe that activity will give you a chance to work together and get closer. It'll give you time to look over those old souvenirs you've got laying around, and that could lead to rekindling old feelings, reminding each of their love when it was at its fullest. Does one of you feel cramped or smothered? Perhaps an area set aside for private activities, like reading or journaling, can be set aside. Maybe a vacation together will reinvigorate a waning sex life or maybe a separate vacation would be good to correct too much familiarity.

Be creative, but be reasonable. If a vacation won't really help, it could actually hurt. The question is really about identifying the problem, which we'll look at soon. If your problem is a cluttered homelife, a weekend in Las Vegas won't help that. You'll still be coming home to the same problem. If you're wrestling with a gambling or drinking problem, Vegas *definitely* won't help that. And if money is your trouble, well, there's always a good ol'-fashioned Spring cleaning.

Think before you speak. This is something we should all do more often, but it's crucial when things get heated between you and your partner. And it's altogether too easy to speak too quickly, to say too much. And some things just can't be unsaid.

Some other great communication tips include keeping your voice down; voices escalate, one with the other, so keep it down and you'll keep it cool. Don't interrupt; listen quietly and respectfully and really listen, it may be your last chance. Be sober; don't have any big talks about anything important when either of you is under the influence. Be kind; no personal comments about the others' body, face, hair, mother, friends, pet, anything. Be brief and don't repeat yourself; if you didn't make your point after one or two tries, maybe the other person just isn't listening. Be aware of your body language; don't point, snarl, lean forward, thrust your chin, bite your lower lip, grit your teeth or clench your fists. These things will have an affect on your voice, which will feed an escalating spiral of uncontrollable rage. Be happy; come at the communication with a hope to make things better, not the certainty that they're about to become worse. Look at it as a mission of diplomacy.

Along these lines, make yourself comfortable. Don't stand face to face in the center of the room, that's the posture of combat. That's how boxers and swordsmen and barroom brawlers stand. But you're there as a diplomat, to prevent the fight. So, sit down, and in a comfortable way. Avoid power postures, like sitting somebody down in a chair and then sitting on the corner of the desk, looming above them. Don't sit them down while you stand. Don't sit them across a table from you, that's a confrontive position. Sit down side by side if you can, on a couch with nothing between you.

Make eye contact. This works in all kinds of communication, from legal and judicial interrogations to the psychological area. It's quite common in the corporate world, a direct power move. It shows that you're focused on the other person, that you're listening. Looking away makes you seem distracted, disinterested, or worse confused or dishonest.

But be careful with the eye contact, as it's a serious technique. Some may find it disquieting. If they fidget under your gaze, look away. And if you're angry, this is a particularly jarring technique and can even seem threatening.

Think good thoughts about your partner during these conversations and in general. I'm not saying anybody's a mind-reader, but these kinds of things manage to get through on a subconscious level.

Lastly, don't be afraid to apologize. It's really quite a simple thing, but some people just can't or won't do it. Research indicates that people who refuse to apologize include those who fear being seen as weak or fear retaliation or rejection that they won't be forgiven upon their admission. Some are perfectionists who feel this small failing will define them. If you're one of these people who feels this way, you might want to reconsider. It takes a real mature adult to apologize, especially when they are wrong. And we're all wrong a lot more than we realize.

It doesn't make you or anyone a victim to be on either side of an apology. We've seen that a person has to ask for what they want, they can't resent another person for not reading their mind. It doesn't make anyone a victim for asking for an apology either. It's a personal declaration and a pretty modest one at that. Chances are, if somebody believes they are owed an apology, they probably do deserve one. If you were perceived as being rude, let's say, and offended somebody inadvertently, then you should apologize for misspeaking or for being inadvertently offensive. If you meant to be rude, you definitely owe an apology, or if you've come to see that you transgressed, just apologize. It's a sign of strength to apologize.

Though if you're in a situation where you're constantly having to apologize, there could be a real imbalance there.

So be careful when communicating with your romantic partner, be mindful of the hidden traps, and use those helpful tricks.

2

WHAT: NEEDS AND DESIRES

This takes us on a trajectory going deeper, from ways of communicating, or the *how*, downward to the next level, the *what*. Because it's important to understand what you're expressing before you can express it clearly.

Basically, human motivation can be categorized as either a group of needs and a group of desires. Are you expressing a need or a desire? Let's take a closer look at both.

NEEDS

Needs are the things you must have to survive.

Abraham Maslow (1908-1970) created his hierarchy of needs as a five-tiered pyramid of the things the human psyche requires for a fulfilling life. It begins with the bottom level, the broadest and most basic but also the most requisite. These are the physiological needs of food, water, warmth, rest. Without these things, none of the others are necessary or even possible, because life cannot progress without those basic physiological needs.

Note here that Maslow himself admits that there's some overlap here. The safety needs may occur at the same time as the physiological, the physiological with the belonging and love needs, so they may not progress in a strictly orderly fashion and can't necessarily be dealt with in that fashion.

But in the basic model, only when the first level of needs is satisfied can one move up to the next tier, safety needs such as security, safety. This includes shelter. It's not strictly necessary, but it's the next step upward after the basic necessities. In less strenuous times, shelter would have been considered requisite, and it still is for a fulfilled psychology.

The third level up includes the belongingness and love needs, which include intimate relationships and friendships. Once these are in place, one may progress to the second level from the top, esteem needs. These include prestige and feeling of accomplishment.

Once one has worked through all four levels, in order, they may arrive at the top tier, self-actualization, which brings a person to achieving their full potential, with a balance of professional and personal successes.

And the entire hierarchy, all five tiers, can be divided into three categories. The first two, physiological and safety, are considered *basic needs*. The next two up, belongingness and love needs and esteem needs, are considered *psychological* needs. The upper tier, self-actualization, is a *self-fulfillment* need.

So, if what you're expressing is a need, which one is it? It's likely to be one of the psychological needs, but what if it's really a self-fulfillment need? Your partner can't be responsible for your self-fulfillment, but they do take some part in your belongingness and love needs, so it's fair to approach them on those grounds. Though they're both considered psychological needs, do you have esteem needs or the more basic belongingness and love needs? When you're in a relationship, it's important to know the difference. Also, keep in mind that in intimate relationships, a belongingness and love need, is as important to you as to anyone. It comes before esteem and well before self-actualization. So, know the value of what you're trying to preserve.

But there's even more to this fascinating psychological model. Because the five tiers can also be subdivided into either *deficiency needs* or *growth needs*. The first four, the basic and the psychological needs (physiological, safety, belonging and love, esteem) are considered deficiency needs. The top tier, self-realization, is a growth need (sometimes called a *being need*). And this only makes sense. If you lack the first four, you're deficient in them. Until you have all four, you're just catching up, not getting ahead. The fifth, top tier is where real growth happens, where advancement is achieved.

Now that the hierarchy of needs is clear, the waters muddy up again. Because the model has been modified for the modern era to include three more layers! A new fifth layer above the fourth, *cognitive needs,* includes understanding and knowledge, exploration and curiosity, a need for meaning and predictability. Think of the existential questions of identity and purpose. These things are generally resolved before the higher, self-fulfillment growth need of self-actualization.

A new sixth layer is just above cognitive, aesthetic needs. These include an appreciation of nature, the search for balance and form and beauty. Then comes self-actualization needs at number seven, with a new top layer, an eighth layer, above that; *transcendence needs.* These include values which go beyond the self, beyond the existential questions of personal place and identity to more transcendent notions of eternity, God, religious and spiritual matters. Experts would say that a truly fulfilled psyche would first need some self-actualization before being equipped to have any transcendental understanding, so that one goes at the top.

Of the new, eight-tier pyramid, the first four (physiological, safety, belonging and love, esteem) are considered deficiency needs and the upper four (cognitive, aesthetic, self-actualization, transcendent) are considered growth needs. The new hierarchy breaks down into the familiar three categories in more or less the same way: The first two, physiological and safety, are still considered *basic needs.* The next two up, belongingness and love needs and esteem needs, are still considered *psychological* needs. The upper four tiers, cognitive, aesthetic, self-actualization, transcendent, are all considered *self-fulfillment* needs.

So, what happens when a person reaches those growth needs and become self-actualized? Self-actualized men of history include Abraham Lincoln and Albert Einstein. But while anybody can theoretically become self-actualized, few people manage it. Maslow himself suggested that only two percent of people become self-actualized. So, let's take a look at what happens at the top of Maslow's hierarchy. This will help you gage where you and other people are in the hierarchy and that will help you identify needs and then be able to satisfy them.

This is especially crucial when dealing with intimate partners.

Are you self-actualized? If you've bought this book, you probably have an intimate relationship, that puts you at least at the third layer. If you're also imbued with sufficient self-esteem, then you're ready to progress upward and become self-actualized, if you don't consider yourself that already. Let's take a closer look at what a self-actualized person looks like.

According to Maslow's research, self-actualizers can tolerate uncertainty and have a clear and efficient perception of reality. They accept themselves for what they are. This means perfectionists and overthinkers, those with various complexes, are unlikely to achieve self-actualization because their perceptions of themselves and of reality is so skewed.

Self-actualized people tend to be spontaneous, they live in the moment and are not caught up in either the past or the future. They don't over-consider every option until no option at all is selected (sometimes called *analysis paralysis*).

Self-actualized people center on problems, not people. With a growth mindset, they know that failure does not define the person, and that their own efforts are not as important and the end result. In the case of failure, they learn from their mistakes and work onward toward the next challenge.

Maslow found that self-actualized people have a sometimes-peculiar sense of humor. They delight in what they think is funny, not in what they think others will find funny. They're not as concerned about what impressions others may have. They also tend to retain their individuality, they're not prone to cultural trends; though they're also not deliberately outrageous or rebellious.

Those who are self-actualized tend to look at life objectively rather than subjectively. They have a clearer perception than those who see the world only through their own experiences and perspectives. In this way, the self-actualized person is apt to be both sympathetic and empathetic. In a like vein, they tend to be concerned for others' welfare and for the future of humanity. They have transcendent concerns, but they also have deep appreciation of the basic life experiences. They may have their head in the stars, but their feet are firmly on the ground.

Self-actualized people tend also to be highly creative. They establish fewer relationships in life, but those relationships are more meaningful and tend to last longer. They tend to have had peak experiences, memorable heights to look back on. Yet they generally have a need for privacy and little need for holding the spotlight.

They also tend to have democratic social and political views and high ethical and moral standards. How many did you check off your list? Which ones are you lacking? You can remedy almost any shortcoming on the list. Don't consider yourself highly creative? Maybe you just haven't found your medium. Being creative doesn't strictly mean being artistic. You could be a creative problem-solver, for instance. Are you more politically conservative than liberal? That doesn't mean you can't be self-actualized. Don't let the list limit you, let it open doors you didn't know were there.

Let's make it easier. Instead of looking at the behaviors of self-actualized people, let's examine behaviors leading to a place of self-actualization. If you want to become more self-actualized, try doing what they do.

Try to experience life like a child, absorb everything and have curiosity and an open mind. Try new things and embrace new experiences. Listen to your own feelings, evaluate things and experiences based on your own perspective, not the common perception or that of some authority. Think for yourself.

Be honest and avoid fakery or game playing. Stand by your views even if you risk being unpopular. This is called integrity, the measure of effect a thing undergoes given the same external pressures. It's an aeronautic term, referring to how much a wing will bend given the same height, altitude, temperature, wind, and other external forces. If the wing reacts the same way given the same circumstances, its integrity is intact. Self-actualized people are reliable.

In the same way, self-actualized people take responsibility for what they do and say, and they work hard to do and say the right things, things they're prepared to stand behind or beside. But being self-actualized is not to be perfect (in fact it is to abandon perfectionism), simply to know that one can be better.

A self-actualized person also has the clarity to see their own shortcomings and work to resolve them. They have the growth mindset which allows them to change and grow even after having achieved self-actualization. But remember that self-actualization is a growth need.

It all comes together so neatly, doesn't it?

That brings us from needs to desires. Here's where things get fun!

DESIRE

Derived from *desiderare,* Latin for *to wish or long for,* desire is our constant companion in ways great and small. It's a part of our life in every way, and it can be both inspirational or destructive.

Sigmund Freud (1856-1939) divided desires into roughly two categories of urges, libidinal (sexual) and aggressive (death). When each is suppressed, sexual urges often create productive or creative results while death urges often inspire depression or other destructive behaviors. He also noted that there could be some overlap, with sexual urges often becoming aggressive and death urges often having sexual undertones. Years later, the spectrum of strange and violent video images available on the internet bears this out.

Before we go any further, let's say simply what desires are not; needs. We've already looked at those, which are necessary for a fulfilled life. Desires are things beyond those needs which we crave, things we want.

When we lack desire, our lives are consumed only by necessity, and that is not a well-balanced life. Desire motivates us, and without it we can become bored or aimless and endlessly dissatisfied. This can lead to depression, poor health and sleeping habits, related physical and psychological complications leading to early death or even suicide.

One problem is that, for the first few formative years of our lives, our needs and desires are basically the same, the basic physiological and safety needs. A child both needs and desires food and drink and can't differentiate one inspiration from another. Then, when we mature, we often can't let go of that childhood parallel of need and desire. To the untrained, undisciplined mind, need and desire are still one. And so, one may feel they need a new car, or can't live without that pair of shoes. They've neglected the difference.

This is particularly striking in intimate relationships. You may come to need each other financially but not desire each other. You may feel you need an extra-monogamous partner, when this may simply be a desire. Do you need an apology, or do you simply desire one? It's a critical criteria for choosing what to ask for and how to ask for it.

You can always use an if/then construct to figure it out:

> *What if I don't get this, then what will happen?*
> *What if I do have this affair, then how will I feel?*
> *What if this doesn't happen, then what will I do?*

It helps you visualize the future and gives you clarity to make a better choice.

THE PROBLEMS OF DESIRE

Now that we're clear on our needs and, in this case, our desires, let's take a closer look at this complex and often contradictory impulse.

It's not surprising, perhaps, that the life force desire is known roughly as *destroyer of self-realization and knowledge* and *the great symbol of sin* in the Hindu tradition. Buddhism's Four Noble Truths proclaims lust, itself one of the purest forms of desire, is the cause of all suffering. The Old Testament's Adam and Eve had desire for knowledge, and we all remember how *that* worked out.

Still, let's take a more contemporary view.

We are taught early on that we must control our impulses. Sigmund Freud introduced the psychological model of the id, the ego, and the superego. In this model, the id is the part of the brain which is ruled by desire. This the impulsive, childhood part of the psyche which seeks immediate fulfilment without thought of others or of the future. The ego is the practical part of the psyche, the part which deals with the outside world and knows what is required, what is needed. The ego must govern the selfish, impulsive id. This is the central struggle of the psyche, the need of practicality wrestling with the wants of selfishness.

Only when the ego has gained control of the id, when the practical psyche has firm control over irrational desire, can the superego be achieved. The superego looks beyond the self of the id, beyond the social practicality of the self, and looks outward and up, toward the moral and spiritual good. Freud would argue that a psyche which fails to govern its own impulses and desires can never attain a clear moral perspective.

It's important to keep in mind that all three elements are necessary, they work together. The ego does not crush the id, as the id serves great purpose to the psyche. The id brings spontaneity and whimsy, creativity, a lot of the traits of the self-actualized person. But the id must be governed by the ego, which also has a vital purpose. All three work together.

So, we're not here to demonize desire, only to better understand it so that we can better control it. This will help you better understand your partner's desires and deal with them more effectively as well.

THE CYCLES OF DESIRE

Though it can be said, and often is, that suffering can be framed in terms of desire. There's a cycle to this, and if you recognize the cycle in yourself or others, you'll be better equipped to interrupt it. It starts with desire, which is unmet. Unmet desire is painful, pain causes fear and anxiety of more pain. Fear and anxiety may disrupt desire or radically misplace it, causing more desires to go unmet, which causes more pain and that triggers more anxiety and fear, creating misplaced desires which cannot be met, and so forth.

Here's an example: You desire the company of an attractive individual, but this person is married so your desires must go unmet. It's a reasonable position, but pain is an emotion and not a reason, so you feel the pain of the unmet desire. Now you may fear that no partner will accept you, you may have anxiety about what you might have done differently or what you still might do to change the outcome. This may give you the desire to interfere with the marriage, derail it in order to irradicate the problem. But that's not going to work, your desires will only go unmet. You're likely to have anxiety about what you've done, and fear of retribution. Looking for a clear conscience, you decide to move to another town. But your conscience will never be truly clean, so that desire goes unmet. It's an even worse pain to know what kind of decisions you've made, you're fearful that your life is ruined and anxious about what to do next. You desire a drink with the desire of somehow eliminating the pain. The next morning, that desire goes unmet, and so on.

It may sound extreme, but these things do happen. You might know somebody with a similar story. But that really doesn't matter to us. What about you? What are your desires? Might they lead you down this path? Try a few if/then exercises to know you're not heading down a dangerous and destructive path.

There's another destructive cycle of desire to be cautious of, one which is just as insidious. Desire can be a motivator; for success, for achievement of all sorts. We desire a big home, a nice car, a good job, an attractive partner.

But once these things are attained, all too often they become obsolete, insufficient. The same drive may push an individual to desire a bigger house, a nicer car, a better job, a more attractive partner.

The problem here is that one may fail to recall that desire is a motivator, it is not the goal. Desire feeding itself will never be satisfied. Once the objects of desire have been achieved, the energy of desire should be redirected; a desire to be charitable, a desire to help others, a desire to find greater forms of expression.

Because too often the things we desire are material things. This desire can blind us to what really motivated us in the first place, the things that truly matter. A person may desire the trappings of success, but to what end? Self-actualization, growth. But desire upon desire is not grown, it's just expansion. That's sideways growth, and it's really the same thing as going nowhere at all.

This kind of desire quickly becomes greed, and despite what Gordon Gecko and I said before, greed is *not* good.

THE WORLD AS WILL

Arthur Schopenhauer's *The World as Will* draws human society into two layered worlds; above is the world of appearances and, beneath that, lay the world of will. The world of appearances is the conscious world, the ego-driven world. The world of will is a blind process in the search for survival and reproduction. Schopenhauer tells us that the will is the formative world, the world of appearances merely a cluster of manifestations of that will.

Even the human body is designed to manifest the world of will. The mouth and stomach are hunger made manifest, genitals are the fundamental form of lust and desire to procreate. Nothing in the natural world can be separated by the will which inspires it.

This world of appearances is meant to appeal to our intellectual sides, we too are merely manifestations of our own will.

What does this mean to you? If world as will theory holds, everything in your world of appearances is really just a manifestation of your will. We've already discussed how the environment reflects and influences our mental state (see how it all comes together?) and now we see that concept taken to the limit. The environment isn't merely a reflection of the psyche, it is created by the will, subject entirely to its power. In this construct, it's a one-way exertion of influence.

Does your world reflect your will? What is that will? Put that will through the 5 Whys technique or a few if/then exercises to get to know that will better. But you may not have to do more than take a simple look around your immediate environment. Isn't your computer a manifestation of your will to succeed? What about those video files you downloaded? What part of your will do they manifest?

So, according to the World as Will concept, we don't shape our desires, our desires shape us. We can't choose them; we can only come to understand them and thereby control them. And as lofty as this theory is, it does make a lot of sense. Think about it; tastes and desires are formed when we're children and they rarely change; they're imprinted in our formative years. You like what you like, you want what you want, what turns you on simply is what turns you on. You can't really change it and you shouldn't deny it either, just understand it.

It's not always easy to understand our desires, as they are very often only in our subconscious minds. And we often are conflicted and even troubled when those desires become conscious. Conflicted sexuality or gender identification is a good example of this.

TYPES OF DESIRE

Desires rarely occur on their own. In fact, there are two types of desire and they usually work together. There are *terminal desires* and *instrumental desires*. Instrumental desires act in support of terminal desire. For instance, if I want to go get something to eat (a terminal desire) I desire to get dressed and find my car keys (instrumental desires).

Terminal desires are generated by feelings, in this case hunger. That makes them powerful desires. Instrumental desires are more reason-oriented and less impacting on our psyches. They're also more fleeting by nature, as it may take a dozen instrumental desires to get to one terminal desire. Instrumental desires are not intended for our pleasure, but the terminal desire is. Some desires are both instrumental and terminal, such as your career (if you enjoy it) or your home.

Both terminal and instrumental desires are considered healthy, positive desires.

Most terminal desires are also known as *hedonic* desires, which leads to pleasure in avoidance of pain. The craving for a cocktail is a hedonic desire, for example. Not all terminal pleasures are hedonic, however; there's the desire to be charitable, for example. Some may argue that any thing enjoyed is hedonic because you derive some pleasure from it, but I'm skeptical of such a jaded perspective.

Desires can also be divided into two other categories; *natural* and *unnatural*. The physiological desires are natural desires and are limited by their nature. Hunger is a desire sated by feeding, thirst by drinking. Unnatural desires, for power or fame or wealth, are unlimited. The desire for these things will never be sated. To paraphrase Epicurus, natural desires easy and pleasurable to be satisfied, so they should be satisfied. Unnatural desires are neither easy nor pleasurable to satisfy, so they shouldn't be.

A Fifteenth century Indian poet and philosopher Kabir described desire as constituting humanity's true wealth. Kabir believed that the person with the most desires were the poorest and seldom succeeded. Kabir considered them the saddest and most superficial of people, overwhelmed with too many desires which are of too little value.

Others are born with the same desires, but focus on only a few and manage to achieve at least some of them. These people are happier and considered successful.

A third group are born with fewer desires, and naturally focus on excelling at them and accomplish their goals to achieve their desires. These become great world leaders, scientists, and artists.

The rarest individual has only one desire, for transcendence. We've already seen how lofty a goal that is. And Kabir tells us that as emotional development grows, the number of desires decreases. Meditation (which we already touched on briefly) is a good way to reduce ten thoughts to five, five to two, two to one. This is one way meditation helps achieve transcendence. And anybody can meditate if they have just a few minutes, even one minute of focusing on your natural breath can be beneficial. You may not transcend, but it's a good start.

There's a direct correspondence between emotional development and desire quantity. Those with many desires are emotionally volatile. They're not committed to much, including their own emotions, so they don't last. However, just as feelings of anger pass quickly, so do feelings of joy or satisfaction.

People with fewer desires tend to have more passion. They have more energy to spread out over fewer pursuits and are more likely to succeed and achieve.

When all goals and desires meld, Kabir calls it *singular passion devotion*. This is the true goal of self-actualization, when all needs and desires are satisfied by the same pleasurable satisfaction.

Which type of person are you? If you feel you're overwhelmed by too many desires, make a few lists ranking them in importance, on a scale from one to ten. Leave yourself only the three which you are most likely to accomplish. They don't have to be the three most vital or most challenging. Achieve those desires and move on to another three. You may also consider cutting a few, either those that are too grand or too petty.

What stage of desire do you find yourself in? Are your emotions volatile? That could be a sign that your desires are too many and you have to pair them down. Get out your pen and start making some lists!

Though meditation is a good way to do that, suffering is another. Those who suffer more desire less and focus on what's truly important in life, forgoing unnatural desires. First-responders, combat veterans and other POWs are good and honorable examples.

3

WHY: DEALING WITH ROOT CAUSES

While it's vital to know how to conduct yourself when communicating in your intimate relationships (and any relationships really), it's time to go deeper. We must look past *how* we are communicating and even past *what* we are saying, and go all the way to the root causes, the *why* of what we're saying, feeling, and doing.

Any personal transformation starts with the center of the body and soul. The existential questions of a person's self-dentification, of their place in society, are central to who they are and what they think on virtually every level. (We'll get back to existentialism later in this chapter.) A person with a fixed mindset who self-identifies as a loser, they will only embark on a downward spiral into self-fulfilling prophecy, missing out on opportunities, overthinking things and demanding perfection which is unattainable. A person with a growth mindset who sees themselves as resilient will likely be resilient, and they'll overcome failure to achieve great success.

So, this is one of our core concepts, the things from which other attitudes and behavior springs.

But it's not the only one.

SIGNS AND ROOT CAUSES OF NEUROTIC BEHAVIOR

The term *neurotic behavior* is as broad as it is misunderstood. It may sound like a cheap insult, a catch-all diagnosis for someone's behavior you may not like, or for a person you may not like. But it includes a number of very serious conditions. So, if we're going to get to the root of miscommunication and the other things which destroy relationships and even entire lives, a little time must be spent on neurotic behavior.

You might be inclined to skip this section, but I strongly recommend you don't. A lot of people exhibit neurotic behavior, and in ways they may not even understand. And even if you don't consider yourself neurotic, your partner may exhibit these behaviors, and the whole purpose of this book is to arm you with the tools you'll need to deal with a variety of challenges, neuroses included.

Neuroses are not psychoses. To be admittedly quite general about it, a psychotic loses the ability to distinguish fantasy from reality. The neurotic is actually hypersensitive to reality. A true psychotic may believe they are being followed or conspired against, though there is no conspiracy. A neurotic is more concerned with germs; and while there are germs, their danger is imagined.

The tricky part is that there is a lot of crossover. Disorders like borderline personality and bipolar may seem more like neuroses, but they go much deeper. Some believe borderline personality disorder can't be treated at all.

But there are some common signs to keep an eye on if you're looking out for neurotic behavior.

One common neurotic behavior is unstable emotions. Neurotics can fly into a rage (also common to bipolar disorder.) Another common neurotic behavior is a so-called addictive personality. The research is all over the map as to the roots of an addictive personality, and it could have as much to do with parental imprinting as it does with a chemical imbalance in the brain. Both could be true. But surely, addictions are a neurotic behavior. The neurotic is hyper sensitive to the pressure of life; overwork, boredom, negative self-talk or a negative self-image, a sense of futility which comes with a closed mindset. But it's a big red flag for neurotic behavior either way.

Perfectionism is a classic neurosis. Hyper-sensitive to reality, a perfection for a sese of control, to define his- or herself in the best possible terms. Anything short of that may nag at them, rob them of the joy of their efforts and prevent new efforts. Perfectionists, like others on this list, tend to go toward negative self-talk and overthinking, the replaying of previous events or the imagining of upcoming or possible events. This plagues perfectionists, fixed-minded folks of all sorts, and it's a very common neurotic behavior. If you overthink things, you can easily deal with this by accepting your imperfection and the chaotic nature of the world, let go of the past and the future and live only in the present. Meditate. But beware of this deadly duo of perfectionism and overthinking.

Chronic stress is also a common neurotic behavior. We all get stressed out now and then, but if a person is constantly stressed then they probably lack the coping skills, and they should read this book. Chronic stress is a common result of overthinking. And like a lot of these neurotic behaviors, stress can have terrible effects on the body. Internal inflammation, a common result of stress, can cause heart attacks and strokes. Behaviors associated with common stress are also common to the others; food and substance abuse and the health risks that go along with it, including premature death. Stress and other of these neuroses have psychological effects too, including depression, sleep disruption, and suicide.

Envy is a neurotic behavior. It creates obsessions of inferiority and jealousy and pent-up resentment and may inspire kleptomania and other anti-social behavior. Those who exhibit envy are often fixed-minded people, more concerned with how they appear to others, successful or not, more than how they see the world.

Being over-dramatic, which we've already touched on, is a classic neurotic behavior. It happens as a result of excessive sadness or anger, often rooted in some small problem. But it results in a fit of rage, a temper tantrum which the person often can't control. At least they never learned to; they could if they tried. But this kind of overacting is a leading cause of breakups, and it's also a very common neurotic behavior. It's also wildly anti-social. Forget losing your love relationship, if you're a temperamental person to outbursts of rage, it won't be long until you're entirely alone.

Hopelessness is a common neurotic behavior too, in a lot of ways it's the flipside of being over dramatic. It leads to depression, substance abuse, and suicide. But starts off simply enough, just an extended melancholy born of a fixed mindset which is certain that nothing will ever work out. Well, if you were dead sure nothing would ever work out, you'd probably be feeling hopeless too. But hopelessness can be related to stress, to a passing crisis like an illness or the death of a friend or loved one. I can be born of disappointment, the loss of a job or a romance. But it can also self-sabotage a career or a relationship. Nobody wants to be around a sad sack Debbie Downer, right?

NEUROTIC BEHAVIOR'S OWN ROOTS

But neurotic behavior is more than just deep-rooted and liable to cause all manner of other problems, it can also be traced back to other behaviors and conditions. Some people believed, and many still do, that neuroses are genetic, handed down from one generation to the next, symptomatic of disorders like schizophrenia. Many more modern researchers believe they're acquired behaviors. Traumas are often cited as the root of various neuroses, and others are the result of parental imprinting.

Child abuse is a common cause of many neuroses, including perfectionism and chronic stress. A lot of adults live striving to correct whatever mistakes they made in the past to inspire the abuses of their childhood.

Because neurotic behavior is so widespread and varied and often hard to identify, it's a much more widespread problem than it need be. And with our recently turbulent world, there's even more anxiety and the neurotic behaviors which are likely to result.

As long as we're looking at the part neuroses play in our lives and in how and what we communicate, especially to our romantic partners, we should go one step further. Because once you've looked at some of the neurotic behaviors, let's take a look at some of the even more deeply rooted complexes which are often associated. Not by coincidence, these are also among the most commonly reported complexes blamed for failed relationships in various studies.

The Oedipus/Electra Complex is when a person has an almost sexual attraction to the parent of the opposite gender.

A deep affection for the parent of the opposite sex. Oedipus, of Ancient Greek myth, fell in love with his mother and killed his father. Electra, on the other hand, was attracted to her father and blamed her mother. These days, the complexes are a lot more conservative in nature. But there are many cases where an unnaturally strong bond between mother and son (for example) can result in an emotionally stunted adult child unable to truly step into an adult role. It's also a common killer of romantic relationships. No woman wants to deal with that, and why would she? This complex leads to perfectionism and overthinking as the child fixates on the parent with eternal efforts to impress and win their love and approval. It can lead to a lot of negative self-talk and overthinking as the frustrated child constantly scolds his- or herself over failures to do better, to truly win that parent's love.

It's a shame, because a more growth-oriented mindset would help the adult child abandon the fixed mindset they may have acquired during childhood; that the child is and should always be the central figure in the parent's life. As a result, these adult children tend to treat their adult partners poorly; neither can live up to their unreasonable childhood expectations, which themselves are doomed for disappointment. Men may abuse their partners; women may retire from social interaction entirely.

The Madonna/whore complex is a way to describe the perspective of men who see women as being one of two archetypes; a virginal young mother (the Madonna) and a ravenous, sexual beast (the whore). The complex has been played out in countless works of fiction and comedy; it's driven into our collective conscience. You need go no further than Ginger and Mary Ann of the 1960s sitcom *Gilligan's Island*. They were the Madonna/whore complex come to life, and it was and remains powerful iconography.

Another, more modern take on the complex states that men with this complex truly desire both archetypes in one person, a schoolteacher by day and a stripper by night. They're meant to be all things and also in turn.

Men who suffer from this complex are often unable to maintain a relationship because few women are either one of the extreme types, and fewer more are actually a combination of both, which is what a lot of men truly want. This unrealistic expectation is, as most, almost always doomed to end in disappointment.

Men also seem to have a hard time differentiating one aspect from the other, and the whore persona may contaminate the schoolteacher/homemaker side of her dual persona. Or he may want only the whore but discover she is much more that that. He may feel cheated, but of course he was only let down by his unrealistic expectation.

Men with this complex are often alone and lonely, imbued with desire and vision but with no reasonable way to find satisfaction. This man is often of a fixed mindset, seeing women as one type or the other, his own situation eternally stifled. Perfectionism is also a red flag for this common complex.

The God complex can be particularly irksome for lovers. One of the two may consider themselves answerable to nobody. It's their way or the highway. Not only are these people commonly arrogant to the point of being insufferable, they're prone to perfectionism, other complexes like the aforementioned Madonna/whore complex, believing they deserve it all, and all of it perfect. But this person may also be prone to infidelity. So, if your partner leans toward a God complex, be on your guard. Really, any of these common complexes should probably put you on your guard.

Someone with a persecution complex has an irrational fear of hated, mistreated, persecuted. This complex, related to paranoia, is common among overthinkers and those with negative self-images. It leads to chronic stress, self-medication, an exaggerated panic reflex, and sleep deprivation. And in relationships, a person with this condition will be suspicious of the other, they'll project their insecurities onto the behavior of the other. Very often, this person will suspect the other of something themselves have done or might do; the liar imagines everyone else lying, the thief will suspect you of stealing, the cheater will assume you're doing the same thing. It's almost always unreasonable and irrational and can kill a relationship as fast and as certain as anything else.

Those with a martyr complex rely on suffering for sympathy and attention. The martyr appears selfless, but the longsuffering soon become the longwinded. Those who go on about their sacrifices are really just languishing in self-pity. Often, they're making excuses or blaming others for a lack of their own achievements. The martyr will never take responsibility for themselves. The sufferer of this complex is often of a fixed mindset, believing they must always play that role, that it is the only way they can get ahead. But they're often afraid of trying, afraid of failure, and wracked with a lack of self-confidence and little confidence in the notions of change or progress.

This person can be insufferable to an intimate partner, robbing their relationship of its joy to replace it with the guilt and drama that they martyr complex requires.

The inferiority complex leaves a person feeling unable to succeed or even survive. They feel they just don't have it in them and they never will, that they're destined for failure. And the law of the self-fulfilling prophecy suggests that, sadly, they're right. This is a kind of perfectionism turned on its ear, call it *imperfectionism* if you will. The sufferer is so vastly convinced of failure, perfectionism is so far from them, they can only see their own imperfections, the imperfections in their lives and their futures.

People who suffer this complex often suffer depression, lifestyle issues, physical and psychological issues stretching across the spectrum.

The flipside to the inferiority complex is the superiority complex. This person believes they're naturally superior, not inferior. Also, a perfectionist, this person may see everything they do as perfect. Similar to the God complex.

Those with a guilt complex blame themselves for everything and anything which may go wrong. Just as the inferiority and superiority complexes are closely associated, and the superiority complex is a close cousin to the God complex, the guilt complex can be hard to differentiate from the inferiority complex.

The man with the Don Juan complex sees women strictly as a source of pleasure. This is a womanizer with no interest in long-term relationships. I'm sure there are instances of this with women who suffer the same complex with men. The condition is actually called hypersexual disorder, sometimes called sex addiction. These people are often emotionally distant, overthinkers, and they're just not good candidates for a monogamous relationship.

Lastly, there is the hero complex, wherein the person, man or woman, positions themselves at the center of attention by virtue of their accomplishments. Often indulging in false humility, the person with the hero complex brags about his or her accomplishments (this is what the term *humblebrag* means). This person is often fixed-minded, as they put the focus on the individual's qualities instead of the final result and the common good. The hero complex is not apt to be generous with sharing credit, and can seem selfish and self-promoting, because they are. The person with a hero complex is not likely to be a good listener, or to be empathetic, since so much of their attention is on themselves. The hero complex is similar to the superiority and the God complexes, and in a way to the martyr complex, which also seeks to draw the full attention of the others. In fact, a closer look reveals that all of these complexes put the person at the center of the action, from various angles and in both various and consistent ways.

Whatever the complex or cause, there is a handy, almost-universally known way to get to the bottom of it, and that's something you should know before we move even further into the root causes of ineffective communication in relationships.

THE 5 WHYS

Back in the 1930s so-called *father of the Japanese industrial revolution*, and Toyota Industries, needed a way to make work at his factories more efficient. He developed the now-famous *5 Whys* system. If any worker were to come across a challenge, they only needed to ask why to five consecutive answers. His theory is that one is never more than five steps from finding the root cause to any problem. It was then a matter of resolving the fifth answer.

Here's an example to make things a little easier:

A worker has arrived late to work. The first question is, "Why?" That's *why* number one.

A (1): "I couldn't get onto the factory grounds."

Q (2): "Why?"
A (2): "The man wouldn't open the gate."

Q (3): "Why?"
A (3): "It was malfunctioning."

Q (4): "Why?"
A (4): "It wasn't serviced properly or promptly."

Q (5): "Why?"
A (5): "Because the country has not set aside a budget for maintenance."

The root of the problem, setting aside budget money for maintenance of the gates, can now be solved.

Let's try it when it comes to something more contemporary and perhaps more relevant to you. One person may ask another, "You're upset, honey? Why?"

A (1): "I'm depressed."

Q (2): "Why?"
A (2): "I lost my job."

Q (3): "Why?"
A (3): "My poor performance."

Q (4): "Why?"

A (4): "I've been partying a lot lately."

Q (5): "Why?"

A (5): "I just can't stop drinking."

It's an amazingly effective technique, one you can use at any time, on the spot and one with which you can find the resolution to virtually any puzzle or quandary. It should help you in helping your friends or partners in crisis as well.

EXISTENTIAL ANSWERS?

Remember when I said we'd come back to existentialism? Well, here we are. Any philosophy poses a question: What is the nature of the heavens? What is the nature of mankind? When these questions are answered, they cease to become philosophies and become sciences (in this case astronomy and biology).

But the prominent philosophy of the Twentieth century, existentialism, will never become science because its questions are so particular to the individual: Who am I? What is my purpose in life? When those questions are answered, lives may be secured, but not sciences. The reason is obvious; unlike the mechanics of the Universe or of the human body, the answers to the existential questions are different for every person who asks.

Existentialism was born in the Age of Enlightenment at the end of the Nineteenth century (romantic-era writer Mary Shelley's *Franken-*

stein is an early existentialist tome). But existentialism came of age in the mid-Twentieth century as a result of the horror of World War II. The cruelties of the German concentration camps led many to believe that there could be no God if such horrors could go on.

Later existentialist philosophers like Kierkegaard, Nietzsche, and Sartre, believed that life had no purpose, and so nobody had any real purpose either. We're born, we live, we have suffering and pleasure, perhaps we marry and procreate, and we die. No heaven, no purpose, just mold clinging to a rock floating around in the cold vacuum of space.

Fun crowd.

But few of us can afford to be so detached. We have to live our busy lives and find some reason to keep on keepin' on. To think we're working so hard for pretty much nothing is more than a lot of people can stand. Anxiety is a common symptom, as is depression, negative self-talk, overthinking, and a lot of other negative behaviors.

Existential psychology examines these connections between mental health and existential crisis. Research into patients with a range of issues and personality disorders as well as terminal illnesses such as cancer revealed a strange common denominator. They longed to maintain meaningful and truly nurturing relationships with others. Instead, they tended to use their relationships to cope with existential anxieties.

Existential anxieties tend to take root during youth and may last a lifetime. Isolation constantly recalls the suffer that they were born and will die alone. A fixed mindset and negative self-talk assures the sufferer that living alone is natural and inevitable. Freedom reminds us that we are unrooted, disconnected. Feelings of meaninglessness are only strengthened by years of searching for a purpose which we may never find simply by virtue of our certainty that meaning and purpose are illusory.

Luckily, we have a handy remedy! Use the 5 Whys technique to move away from the puzzle of the crisis and get to the root of it. Take more than the five if you need to, but if you keep asking why, which is a fundamental question in existentialism, the simple answer will slowly come to you.

The patient can't sleep and has constant anxiety, and the doctor asks the first *why:*

A (1): "I'm afraid I'm going to die alone."

Q (2): "Why?"
A (2): "Because I can't find a spouse."

Q (3): "Why?"
A (3): "Because I'm unlovable."

Q (4): "Why?"
A (4): "Because I'm so messed up."

Q (5): "Why?"
A (5): "Because life has no meaning."

And there's the solution! If your life has no meaning, find some meaning for it. Volunteer a food bank and you'll realize that to help others is one of the things that gives life meaning. It's hard work and that'll help you sleep, which will make you more pleasant and alert. And that will come in happy when you meet a likeminded single at the food bank, who perhaps was also just looking for a little meaning in their lives.

I mentioned *Frankenstein* earlier, and it raises an interesting point. The creature asks the existential question of his own identity, but he allows society to define him as a monster and so he becomes a monster. He does not answer the existential questions for himself. But existentialism fairly well demands the seeker find a solution before society does, or the self-actualized mind can never be achieved.

And this brings us to our next chapter, WHO. You may think you know the answers to that, and what you've learned in this book so far may have enlightened you even further and sent you on a voyage of self-discovery that will change your life. Bravo or brava, my friend! But knowing about narrative therapy will make your journey a lot easier and less perilous. It's a significant advance for almost anyone in mental or emotional crisis, but it's ideally suited for applications in the area of relationships.

4

WHO: NARRATIVE THERAPY IN COUPLES' COMMUNICATION

You may never have heard of narrative (or cognitive) therapy, as it is a modern school of mental health treatment. I use *narrative* because the focus is on the narrative of the person's life. A person's expressions of the stories of their life experiences shape their view of themselves in the context of those experiences, of that story, of that narrative.

The key to narrative therapy is that people tend to tell themselves this story of their lives time and time again, reaffirming that narrative and their place within it. It's a fixed mindset which is secure that no change is possible.

They may see themselves as a loser, for example, after years of losing significant things in their lives; parents, lovers, jobs, opportunities. In answering the existential question of identity and purpose, this person has answered the question and resolved themselves to the answer. In their version of *Frankenstein*, they are the creature, the wretch.

Others may see themselves as the doctor, young Victor. Victor's best intentions create a set of circumstances he cannot control. How many of us have that feeling of helplessness, hopelessness, that we'll fail no matter what we do? It's reminiscent of the martyr complex and both the inferiority and the superiority complexes and, in its own way, the God complex too.

Some may see themselves as the Victor's betrothed, Elizabeth, a victim of male abuse which has made her ugly, wretched, worthy of death.

Not that everybody sees themselves through the prism of this particular story. Everybody has their own story of which they are the central character. Charles Dickens' great *David Copperfield* begins: *Whether I shall turn out to be the hero of my own life, or whether that station will be held by anybody else, these pages must show.* Sometimes we are the villains of our lives, sometimes the fool.

But this role is not prescribed, even by the pattern of one's experiences. A fixed-minded person would tend to see the pattern as determinative of the future, a fatalistic view which abandons responsibility. A growth-minded person sees the narrative as fluid, the role subject to interpretation, that failure can lead to success.

In a nutshell, not only can a person change their role in the middle of their life's story, from fool to hero, but they can rewrite the entire narrative to change the character from the very start. Changing the narrative changes the role and that changes the perspective and that changes the life.

Developed by Michael White and David Epston in the 1980s, narrative therapy separates a person from their behavior. This way a person who committed a crime can identify themselves as a person who made a mistake, not a criminal and therefore, unworthy of a normal and happy life.

This therapeutic model features three main conceptual protocols. It is respectful, treating clients as individuals and not the sum of their mistakes. The approach is likewise non-blaming, focusing on outside factors and the influence of circumstance and deflecting any sense of blame or shame against the client. Lastly, narrative therapy views the client as the expert. In narrative therapy, the subject comes to the conclusions through a series of answers. The client is never instructed or dissected; they are guided to discover these things for themselves.

Now wouldn't your next emotional or intimate conflict benefit from just that paragraph alone? Worth the price of admission right there. But there's more!

Narrative therapy distinguishes between an individual who has problems with an individual who is problematic. It's an important difference, because an individual with problems can correct those problems, they can be changed. The problematic individual cannot be changed.

Here's how narrative therapy keeps the focus on the difference between the problem and the person.

Our interactions with others impact the way we experience reality. That reality is communicated through and influenced by language. Different languages can actually influence different interpretations of the same events or experiences. Stories and narrative help us understand reality and our place in it, answering the basic existential questions.

Narrative therapy focuses on subjective realities. Instead of an objective reality or truth, the truth is interpretive. And it is accepted that one person may interpret an event one way and someone else another.

It's akin to postmodernism, a school of thought which holds that there's no objective truth, that reality is changing, shifting, a personal concept instead of a shared set of facts. Norms and facts have their place, but they're more influential than causal.

So narrative therapy sees individuals in a postmodern context. There is no universal reality, the truth belongs to the individual, who creates his own reality. And, lest anyone suffer the sad fate of Frankenstein's creature, he or she must construct that reality, or allow the pains of letting somebody else construct it instead, to suffer the consequences.

Narrative therapy provides these very same story-retelling skills.

COMMON NARRATIVE THERAPY TECHNIQUES

The first step is telling the story by putting together a narrative. The therapy seeks to help the client find their voice to tell their own story (or this might be you). Storytelling is the way a person may find meaning and purpose from our own personal experiences.

The story may need guidance through questions to discover for themselves the meaning and the healing and to recreate a new identity, and reshape the narrative. A narrative can be altered, flipped on its head, or rewritten altogether. Interpretation can create countless narratives from a single narrative, as we saw with *Frankenstein*.

The second step is the *externalization technique*, which separates the questionable problems or even behaviors around the client from the client. The problem is not the person. And it's easier to change what you do than who you are. So, separate the two and fix the easiest one first. It's easier to change your behavior than your feelings, we've already seen that; same thing here only more so.

If you're quick to anger, for example, that's behavior. If you see yourself as an angry person, that's something else again. Learn not to be so temperamental, change your behavior, and you'll change your identity as a temperamental person. Change the behavior, change your persona.

It all sounds very theoretical, but it really works. Let's look at a few other techniques of applying narrative therapy, and then we'll get down to the emotional communication aspect of it all.

The third technique is the *deconstruction technique*, which deconstructs a problem to reduce it to insignificant parts. It's another way to break down a big task into smaller tasks, classic technique for a variety of applications. It also gives almost anyone the chance to see the bigger picture, the forest for the trees.

Deconstructing can reduce overgeneralizing and make an issue more-specific and easy to handle while clarifying core issues. It can really bring you to the core of almost any issues, and it works well integrated with the *5 Whys* technique, which can be helpful here, as it is on so many occasions.

The *unique outcomes technique* is the way one changes their own storyline. It's a way to reframe their experiences, which you cannot change, into a different interpretation, which you can change. You can turn a living nightmare into a life-affirming story of survival, a victim into a hero, just by adjusting the perspective even slightly. And it's more than just positive thinking, it's changing the entire worldview. It's not avoiding the problem, its reimagining it.

And this technique can include multiple storylines as well, for us and for others involved in our stories. Remember, there is no objective truth in this school of thought, and that leaves a lot of room for subjective truth. And a disaster in one narrative may seem insignificant in another narrative, so the possibilities of this approach are expansive, if not endless.

I'll bet you figured that existentialism would be the last big technique of narrative therapy. It re-asks the questions of identity and purpose, allowing the client (or your friend or yourself) to change their minds about who they are and answer it in a different way, a way which will shape their lives in a positive and not a negative way.

Here's a great narrative therapy exercise you or anyone else can do. It may be extremely helpful, and it just might be a little bit fun.

Imagine you're writing your life's story. This will help you separate yourself from the events of your past and giving you a wider perspective of those experiences and your life as a whole. Now do the table of contents; seven chapters which encapsulate major eras in your life. Then come up with at least one subhead, or a line which describes what the chapter is about. You can use this book as an example!

But you might write something like:

I GUESS I DESERVED IT I GOT A TERRIBLE DISEASE AND DIED ALONE

Expressive Arts are the third principal technique of narrative therapy. We all have different ways of expressing ourselves. Some are visual, some audio-oriented. Painting and sculpture work just the same way, or even interpretive dance. This technique works great with kids, but it could work great with intimate companions as well, as it provides fun and interactive practices. Art is well-known to have positive energy and various therapeutic powers.

Yoga and meditation are great shared and private activities which can help anyone redefine themselves and change their narrative.

Visualization is a powerful technique. Imagine the new narrative, the new character, the new future. Write it in your mind or on a vision board. That's another fun shared activity to draw or keep a couple together. Make sure to include your partner on your vision board!

So, how do you put narrative therapy to use? Try encouraging answers with some questions like these: "It sounds like this problem might be a part of your life. How long have you noticed this? What effect does it have on you and your life? Does this affect your energy or distract you from your daily duties? Does this impact your daily life? Does it affect your child's life, or your partner's?"

Remember to differentiate the problem from the person with questions like, "Do you accept the effect of this problem? If you do, why? If not, why not? Why do you take that position?"

Remember to keep things moving forward, toward a new narrative and a new future with questions like, "What would you prefer? How would you rearrange things if you could? What do you think you might do to rearrange these things so that they'd be as you prefer?"

So, when you're speaking to your intimate partner, your romantic intended, or just about anybody, you can always start such a conversation in this way (or something like it):

"Do you remember the last time this wasn't a problem? What did that feel like? What happened at that time, in those first few minutes, and what happened after that?"

Then move on from the past to the future, make it constructive. *"Do you want more moments like that? What can we do in order to recreate those things now? How would you feel if we did those things?"*

It comes to another type of visualization of the future, a technique we've already seen to be powerful and motivational.

But how can you use all this in your own intimate relationships? It's really simpler than it seems. Is your partner serially unfaithful? Instead of being accusatory or confrontive, you adopt the narrative therapy techniques of being non-blameful and separating the person from the deed. This is not a serial cheater, but a person who makes the same bad choice over and over again. What are the reasons for this behavior? Perhaps there are triggers which can be avoided by a slight alteration of behavior. What feelings do these behaviors inspire in your partner? Can they envision a different set of circumstances which might create a different inspiration and so, change their own behavior? Can you imagine something else which might give you the same feeling? How do you or your partner see yourselves in that circumstance, when they're being unfaithful? How do they see themselves? Is that how they want to feel? Do they want to change the circumstance so that they can feel differently?

The client is expert and with the right guidance they can find the answers.

But it's as important to ask yourself these questions as it is to ask anyone else. You may be trapped in a narrative that constrains you. Remember that narrative therapy is not about blame, but about accepting reasonable responsibility and being willing to act on it and pro-actively make the necessary changes.

NARRATIVE THERAPY AND COUPLES

We've already seen how narrative therapy allows us to reconsider our life stories and our places with that context. It allows us to externalize the person from the problem, and that helps clear up a lot of issues for individuals and couples alike.

Couples tend to see their problems as being part of their identities as a couple. The problems become internalized into their *couple-hood*, if you will. A person may believe that the problems in their lives come from within and are endemic *("I'm a criminal")* instead of external *("I'm a person who has made mistakes")*, a couple may come to feel the same about their pairing *("We're just a bad couple" instead of "we're good people with some relationship issues")*.

In a couple's situation, many of the same techniques apply. The problems should be externalized, made separate from the identity of the clients. Even behaviors should be externalized, because behaviors can be changed.

Some behaviors do come up as a result of clashes of personalities. They both may be manager types and are overmanaging each other. One may have a complex which clashes with the other. In any case, those clashes can be externalized.

One trick anybody can use is to identify these problems and then call them by a name. It can be anything from The Beast to Prince Albert, it really doesn't matter. The point is that it makes the problem separate from the clients.

Questions are vital for a couple. Once separate from the problems, they must stick together as a couple to solve those problems. They may ask, "How can we change our behavior to resolve this issue? What kind of need or desire are we looking at?"

Blame, criticism, defensiveness, and closedmindedness are often problems between couples, but externalizing and questioning can help. You might try something like, "Is your anxiety rooted in trust issues about us? How does the criticism damage our relationship? Is blame threatening our shared dreams? Should we listen more to one another?"

Now that we've gone deep into the *What* of couples' communication, it's time to move on to the Where and the When, both of which are crucial to consider in greater depth.

5

WHEN: RECOGNIZING THE CRISIS POINT AND THE BREAKING POINT

Every relationship has little bumps along the way, every *life* does. So, putting two people together to share a life is, in reality, a matter of putting twice as many bumps on a single, shared road.

And in each case, the person or a couple may simply brush these things off. They may say, "Sure, I drink a little," or "We bump heads sometimes." And those things are acceptable in moderation. But when do these behaviors become a problem which has to be dealt with?

Of course, the best thing is to start off with an open line of communication from the very start. It's best not to let silent resentments build up, not ever to use blameful language or to be overtly confrontive. And we all go into our relationships believing this will be the case.

But if it were, you wouldn't be reading this right now.

It's possible that you're about to start off a new romance and you want to get off on a good foot. Excellent! Everything in this book will help you out. Maybe you're between relationships and you're determined not to fall into the same cycles the next time. Also, excellent! Be growth-minded and use this information to move onward toward your future successes.

It's also fairly likely that you are in a relationship right now and that you're urgently hoping to rescue it. Excellent. This book may help you do just that.

But how do you know if you're at that crisis point? Nobody wants to be the overthinking worrier so afraid of having a bad relationship that they enact a self-fulfilling prophecy and wind up creating a bad relationship from a good one. On the other hand, if you stand by and watch your relationship go sour, it's as much your fault as your partners because you failed to act when you could.

And just when *is* that?

THE CRISIS POINT

A breach of trust is not something you can ignore. It can be major, like cheating, or something like divulging a secret or humiliating your partner in public. It could be a money matter. One partner entrusts another with the safekeeping of these things, and violating that trust has to be dealt with.

On the one hand, it's very egregious behavior and it will not only continue but it will get worse if allowed to go unchecked. More money will disappear, more public humiliations will alienate partners and also friends.

On another hand, such things cause deep-rooted resentment which is sure to be corrosive to the relationship. That's not a bump in the road, it's a sinkhole.

Frequent arguing is a bad sign. Of course, couples disagree about things, and may even flare up from time to time. But if it's become a regular thing, it has to be dealt with. If you follow the guidance in this book, of course, you'll never have to have another argument again. But constant clashing has to be addressed. It's not healthy and it's not clear communication.

In fact, not having clear communication itself is a bad sign. Overt conflict isn't always the problem. Sometimes people just sort of shut down, then close up. When asked, everything's fine. But it's not, and it's only going to get worse. Complicating this is that some people close off, consciously or unconsciously, because they are self-sabotaging and creating a self-fulfilling prophecy. They won't communicate, and then they complain that there's no communication.

You might be doing that yourself, or your partner may be. Consider what one of you might be doing to encourage the other down this destructive path and how you can change your behavior in order to change course.

It might be a matter of something being wrong, but you just can't put your finger on what it is. That happens a lot. People are complicated and often emotional to the exclusion of being rational. They're generally resistant to change or compromise, they harbor all manner of complexes and exhibit a spectrum of negative behaviors.

Along the lines of a lack of communication, there may be something you want your partner to know, but you just can't bring yourself to say it. Maybe you're worried about their reaction, maybe you're not sure if you're right to bring it up.

Hey, it happens.

Have you figured out if it's a need or desire? What kind of need, what type of desire? Is it a natural desire or an unnatural desire? Those and other analytical techniques in this book should help you figure it out. But if you're wrestling with it, then there is definitely a communication problem somewhere along the line. Finding out where that blockage is will be your true challenge.

If either or even both of you become dysfunctional when you have a conflict, it's a big problem. Conflicts do arise, of course. But if one or the other or both start shouting, drinking, throwing things, slamming doors, and closing themselves off, that dysfunction needs to be addressed. It's probably a deeper-rooted issue than whatever the current argument is about.

Life-changing crises may create a breach between partners which needs to be addressed. The deaths of family members, loss of job or career, disease, these can throw a person into a different mindset. A formerly growth-minded person may become fixed minded in the face of grief for a devastating loss. They can readopt a growth mindset or retain the fixed mindset, that will be up to them. But great loss can create stunning changes in perspective and behavior.

Have you or your partner suffered a devasting loss? Keep that in mind when evaluating their behavior or your own. Make allowances, but don't let those changes become permanent. People often fall into these patterns if not corrected, while others fear rebuke if they are indelicate during moments of great loss. It's a high wire to walk, but it's also a long fall off of either side.

If you feel like you're stuck in patterns of harmful or negative behavior, it may be time to talk things out. Locked in a party cycle that's wearing you out? Do you find yourself engaging in negative self-talk more than you used to? These patterns have all kinds of ramifications and consequences and can send you both down a bad spiral, as individuals and as a couple. That's something you should talk out.

If there's a severe dip in your emotional intimacy, that's a problem that has to be addressed. Sure, no couple stays in the honeymoon period forever, that's fair enough. But there can also be a sudden chasm which may open up between two people well into their relationship. It could be because of something physical, like weight gain. But it may not be that one couple is repulsed by the other's weight gain, but that the person gaining weight is suddenly self-conscious and apprehensive. Or it could be due to an attraction to a third person, or any number of things. But emotional intimacy is crucial to a healthy romantic relationship, and one is not likely to survive without it. Don't let that go too far without addressing it.

Along the same lines (and probably in direct connection) is a dip in physical intimacy. These things work together, and the loss of one is almost certain to lead to a loss of the other, and if you lose both your relationship is in mortal danger. Physical intimacy, as we have seen, is what makes an intimate relationship so special. That's the thing you reserve only for your partner. You may share your charm or your experience or your grace, but not your physical intimacy. It has special value. That's why infidelity is so painful, because it destroys that thing about the other which is most rare and exclusive. The amount of trust, the importance of which we've already discussed, is greater when the risk is greater, and physical intimacy involves one of the greatest risks an individual can take in society.

When physical intimacy wanes, it creates insecurities, feelings of rejection which make them protective of their vulnerability to shut down further, close themselves off even more. That downward spiral is the death knoll of any intimate relationship.

RECOGNIZING THE BREAKING POINTS

We're here to help you either rescue, manage, or create an intimate relationship. And we're going to keep trying. The second section of this book is jam-packed with exercises, lists of things to do in order to bond or re-bond with your partner or future partners. You might have fun doing them alone!

Those are ways to identify and deal with the crisis points.

But for a moment, we have to take a look at what happens when a relationship just won't work out. Just as you have to know when to take a stand, when it's important to put effort into saving a relationship, you should also know when to walk away and invest your energies and passions elsewhere.

So, let's move from the crisis points to the breaking points.

THE BREAKING POINT

First of all, if you've been trying and trying, using all the techniques in this book, perhaps even gone to therapy, and there's no real progress, perhaps it's time to move on. You can't fit a square peg into a round hole no matter how hard you try.

We talked about abusive partners, who create abusive relationships. There are various types of abuse, including physical, sexual, psychological, and verbal. The basic cycle of abuse includes friendliness, anger, abuse, contrition. Things start off well enough (friendly), then somebody gets resentful and perhaps drunk (angry) then they let loose (abuse) and later they beg forgiveness (contrite). Once forgiven, they're friendly for a while, later angry, then abusive, and of course being contrite gives them license to repeat the cycle.

If you're the perpetrator of this cycle, you are an abuser. Your partner cannot help you, and the best I can do is to make you aware of what you're doing. Get serious help from a therapist. If you're the victim of this cycle, just get out. True, this abuser you're with may ultimately find good care and become a better person, but it's more than likely that they won't. And you should neither spend your life suffering under the abuse nor should you legitimize the abuse by playing the role of victim. Also, your leaving may be the only thing which jars the abuser enough to convince him or her to get the help they need. For your sake and your partner's, get out of an abusive relationship as soon and as quickly as you can.

If you know in your heart that there's just no future in the relationship, then what are you fighting for? If you know you don't want to marry the person, won't ever have children with them, if you know they love you and you're simply ambivalent, then you're not doing either one of you any favors. You're only making each other miserable and restricting yourself from finding better relationships with more fitting partners. Also, the longer you stay with somebody you know you'll be leaving, the more you're actually taking advantage of them, exploiting them for whatever they have to offer while you're waiting for the right next person to come along. Looking back, your partner is bound to feel lied to and abused. As they say, *when you know, you got to go.*

Different values and beliefs may also be insurmountable. You might have thought those religious differences wouldn't be a problem, but they may be coming up again and again. Some personalities simply clash. A tree-hugging hippie and a corporate shark may simply be a miss-match.

If one person seems to be making no effort, or barely any, that may be a problem which can't be solved. You have to want a relationship, value it, both parties do. If one party doesn't, they may never. It could be that they can't help it. Some people just can't access that part of themselves. Others are so hurt or simply disinterested. It hardly matters. It could be that they're narcissists and are truly only interested in themselves. You won't be able to change those things, not even with the techniques in this book. It could also be, frankly, that he or she just isn't that into you.

If your partner has an addiction, it may be time to give up and get out. Addictions are red flags of other serious complexes and personality disorders. They create unstable and violent behavior. Addictions can also be addictive, and if you've got addictive inclinations yourself you may be triggered into bad behaviors you've worked hard to avoid. And as with a few other things we've discussed in this chapter, your leaving may be the impetus for your partner to get the professional help he or she may desperately need.

Your partner may fall short of being a narcissist, but he or she may also prioritize themselves above you. Is your time together filled with his or her friends or favorite activities? Are your interests given the short-shrift? You might be able to work this out through clear communication, but it could also be that this partner is subconsciously trying to drive you away and end the relationship in an indirect, passive/aggressive manner. Isn't it better to take a stand and just leave instead of being subverted?

We've talked about how important physical intimacy is to an intimate relationship. And this can evolve, have ebbs and flows. But there some things which just can't be overcome. Some people just aren't attracted to their partners. They try to be, they may convince themselves that they are, but there's a certain chemical attraction between lovers which can't be replaced and cannot be manufactured. One may think they'll get used to the other, but they won't. It's a big part of a downward death spiral of almost any relationship.

There is also the question of sexual taste. Among lovers of any gender or identification, sexuality is a complex part of our lives, both inner and outer. And the spectrum of sexual fetishes is vast and wide and seeming to become more so every day. So, it's really possible that two doms have found each other, that one has a fetish or fantasy that the other simply cannot or will not satisfy. It's possible that one has desires which he or she cannot accept or express. We can't help what we want, as we've seen, only what we do. So, if the other person just can't give us what we want, or we can't give our partners what they want, at least we can all control what we do, and just leave.

Trust issues may just be your undoing. We looked at trust as a red flag for approaching one another with an eye toward clear communication. But even after that, the behavior may continue. If a person is a serial cheater or thief, then they have deep-rooted issues you can't reach and shouldn't be expected to try. Let them deal with it themselves and start practicing some serious self-care.

If your mutual families don't get along, that could also be a serious problem. Forget the grumpy, judgmental mother-in-law of yesterday's sitcoms, it could be a matter of a child who rejects a partner. Or it could be radical cultural differences which make family interaction simply impossible.

It could also be that your partner is a *splitter*, a term for a partner who seeks to separate an individual from their other family and friends. This often happens with people of some money or resource, wherein the partner wants control of those resources. One by one, family members are dopped by the wayside. Their more aggressive attempts are more aggressively rebuked. Lawsuits are filed, power of attorney documents are signed. It happens in a lot of families, and there's really no way to stop it. You can demand that your mother and siblings be allowed back into the house, but splitters are smart and will try to convince you that they're bad for you, that only your partner is truly on your side. Of course, your partner is on one side only; their own. Learn to recognize this situation early on and if you can't stop the pattern from recurring, take what you still have and go … or kick your partner to the curb and give them what they deserve; nothing.

Some of the other behaviors we've mentioned can be more than crisis points but also breaking points; breaches of trust, lack of physical or emotional intimacy, lack of communication.

6

WHERE: RECONSIDERING YOUR ENVIRONMENT

We've already taken a look at how impacting an environment can be on an individual. The environment both reflects and influences the state of mind. It's even more particular with couples, because it's two individuals who would have been used to their own environments. Just as a union is like putting more bumps on the same road, it's like parking two cars in a one-car garage.

We've talked about solutions of being crowded or fighting the feelings of being "suffocated". Private areas, nights out with friends, even separate vacations can be a great way to change the environment in order to affect feelings and behavior. Absence makes the heart grow fonder.

But there's a lot more to it than that.

You may think about a bigger apartment, for instance, if that's how you live. It could be that the environment you share can't be reshaped to make more room. It's a big move, but it could be a good one.

A move together, however, may trigger certain feelings. It's a major turning point, and it may instigate questions and insecurities about the future. One big decision may lead the mind of either partner to consider other options, not ones which will keep the relationship alive. If one partner owns the property and the other, a cohabitant, wants to sell and buy something else, legal complications may enter into it. It may also call into question potentially threatening perspectives of their achievement. It may seem legally invasive too, as if one person is selling out the others small house or condo, let's say, to spend that money in a way that suits themselves. And if you're married householders and genuinely want to stay together but move up to bigger property, you simply may not be able to do so, depending on the economy, the housing market, and interest rates.

Money, am I right?

So, your environment may not be so easy to change as you may wish. Still, it may have a powerful effect on your relationship. If you live in a stressful city, that stress is bound to infect your personal interactions. If your jobs require you to be in the city and you can't just or don't want to head for the suburbs or do a year in Ecuador on the cheap, your options are limited.

Or are they?

One significant question of *where* when it comes to romances is the office or workplace.

Most people under normal circumstances spend a third of their day at work with other people. It's easy to form friendships and even romantic relationships under those circumstances. Human Relations offices in various companies are designed to cope with that common fact.

How can this environment affect your relationship? If your relationship was created at the workplace, it could have all manner of complications. If the relationship goes bad, the crucible of the office will keep proximity tight and tensions high. That disruption could result in job loss, career failure, a downward spiral which could handily result in depression, abuse, ill-health, suicide and death. There could also be legal ramifications, harassment suits and even worse.

There's also the complication if you're otherwise committed, married or in a monogamous relationship, and you begin a third-party flirtation with somebody at the workplace. Even if you don't, jealousies can arise from presuppositions.

Workmates may also take offence to a workplace romance. Promotions may be doubted, other resentments can fester.

Still, these romances do happen and they're not always destructive. But they have to be entered into with caution and reason amidst the heady passion. Here more than anywhere, you have to be aware of the *where*.

But we don't live in the workplace.

What other environments may create romance, either wanted or unwanted?

Family visits are a change of environment which can have a sharp influence on a couple. Going to the house of one relative or another can raise issues of insecurity and defensiveness. Families don't always share the affection that partners do, and things like the Oedipus/Electra complex can be brought right to the surface. Arguments break out under those pressures, and so too do behavior like shutting down.

So, be careful when you're in those environments. Reassure each other that you're there for each other, not for them. Remind the other and yourself that you love each other more than you love the others ... if you do, that is. If you don't, that's a different issue. After all, boyfriends and girlfriends may come and go, but siblings are for a lifetime, that's true. But you don't live with your siblings in your adult years (hopefully) and you may very well live with your romantic partner or spouse (hopefully). Keep that in mind and don't let a three-day change of environment damage a three-year relationship.

Vacations are a big trigger for sexual activity. And that only makes sense, as everything about the marketing of the tourism and hospitality trade is geared toward a romantic ideal. The commercials for cruise ships, resorts, and casinos promise romantic perfection. We're trained to think of big vacations as life-changing indulgences in debauchery (Spring break, anyone?)

People go on romantic vacations sometimes to re-ignite a waning romance, or to find a new romance quickly. But both are illusory, really.

A lot of people hope a romance will save their relationship, but it's rare enough that any deep-rooted issues are going to be resolved on such a trip. They're only being put aside temporarily, and ultimately there's no solution. It's a fool's errand.

And meeting somebody while on vacation can be just as treacherous. You're meeting this person in a world other than their own. As we know, environment influences our behavior. Therefore, if you meet somebody in an alien environment, their behavior will not be the same as it would be in their normal environment, which is likely to be quite different. If a person's behavior is changed in proportion to the difference in their environment, then their normal behavior may be radically different than their behavior in their vacation environment.

As they say, what happens in Vegas … stays in Vegas.

However, there are splendid honeymoons and lovely trips for couples all over the world, and that's great. Travel is an important part of any life, but of a pair of lives in conjunction even more so.

People fall into ruts, it's just a fact. They become bored. And variety is the spice of life. Trips together provide that variety, of place and experience. It can refresh a couple's interest in their world and in each other. Changing the environment may change behavior, it almost certainly will. And these travels may bring out fascinating aspects of one or the other which had gone undiscovered or forgotten.

Date nights are a good way to change the environment to refresh or revitalize a relationship. They lack the escapism of a vacation (which a lot of people just can't afford anyway) but still give two people the chance to interconnect on a personal level. It's a small trip out of the house, a change of scene, a chance to put aside the scramble of the day and be pampered and served just a bit. Recent events have made this an even rarer treat than before, but even under normal circumstances, a nice dinner out and maybe some dancing is a luxury most people overlook to their detriment.

Date nights also have the added benefit of reminding both partners of earlier days, when love was fresh and exciting. One may come to see the other in that old, forgotten light.

Don't forget to dance! Dancing is an erotic exercise. It is liberating, the exercise of a growth mindset which is unconcerned with the judgment of others, Dancing excites both parties, letting go of their inhibitions and letting their instinctive, primal selves take over. It's easier to cast aside the overthinking and negative self-talk when the music drowns it out. In those flashing lights with all those swaying hips and chests on the dancefloor, it's a good way to reconnect on a basic level. And of course, the environment is crucial to the effect.

The same would be true, by the way, in a fancy ballroom, a tango studio, or dancing in a sunny field of daisies. All would be great, actually.

Religion offers couples (and individuals and families too) a new environment which can have tremendous impact on interrelations. Without favoring any particular religion, as there is no need to; the communal and spiritual pursuits of any religious institution can have far-reaching benefits.

We've already mentioned volunteering at a food bank as a good way to increase your self-esteem and to find satisfaction beyond feeding your own desires. Desire to help someone else, right? Well, that brings us to your local church or other institution. This is a way to change your environment in order to change your thoughts and behavior. If you introduce some spirituality into your couple-hood, it could take your focus off your own grievances. There's nothing like hearing about the suffering of others (Jesus, Elijah, Mohammad, the Buddha, Gandhi) to put our own suffering into perspective.

And, as meditation gives us something else to focus on, so too does religion; at least an hour or so per week when you're not thinking about the pressures of the workplace or of the home.

Religions of all sorts also tend to promote the tenants of couple-hood; loyalty and honesty and pure passion, the hallmarks of the ancient family structure of any ancient religion.

First, a word about environment, the *where*. Places of worship, whatever their orientation, are different environments than either our homes or our workplaces or even our recreational centers. They are palatial and ornate, bedecked with stained glass or mosaics. They have a power, a sense of serenity, an empowering and an intimidating presence. And they are designed that way, they always have been. From the Islamic shrine The Dome of the Rock to the Wailing Wall to the Church of Nativity in Bethlehem; from your neighborhood church or synagogue to your local mosque or Buddhist temple, these places are designed to inspire calm and open one's mind and heart to the messages of true transcendence.

Religious institutions also offer support with new friends who are like-minded and who have endured similar challenges. There could be great advantage to enjoying the mentorship of others whose guidance could make all the difference. They're also filled with children and their excitement and youthful glee, always a positive influence on a young couple, married or not.

There are lots of different religious organizations, one to fit every world view. If you're interested in biblical history but too secular-minded to embrace the mystical aspects of biblical lore, that's okay. The wisdom to be found in the two Testaments is well worth knowing, whatever your feelings. If you believe in the Word but have lost faith in the Church and the fallible men and women who run the churches which function in His name, then follow your own path. There is no prescribed path which you must follow. Religion is there for you until you decide that you are there for it.

Whatever your religious perspective, you just may find what you're looking for in simple attendance. At least it will get you to stop thinking about how angry you are at each other, and maybe the reasons why. It's a new and fun activity, if nothing else.

And if you feel uncomfortable with that, which may happen, consider our other previously discussed idea of volunteering. That may put you into other and more temporary interactions with various institutions. Who knows? It may widen your social circle, which may either introduce new and invigorating inspirations that will keep both partners happy, or enlighten each as to the pressures the other is facing. Plus, you'll both have the benefit of having helped others, which is an inspiration which burn internally and which you can take you wherever you go.

And as long as we're talking about *where*, let's take a closer look at places to go, things to do, ways to bring your romance back to life and keep it strong or ways to get that new romance started off right. We've done our homework. Now in the book's second section, let's go out and play!

II

THE HOW, WHAT, AND WHERE OF MAINTANING A STRONG RELATIONSHIP:

HOW TO DO IT, WHAT YOU'RE DOING, AND WHERE IT'LL WORK BEST

7

CLASSES BRING COUPLES CLOSER TOGETHER

You spend a lot of time with your partner. And though you were drawn together by a series of fun mini-adventures known as dates, you've probably settled into a bit of a rut. It's easy enough to let happen, and there are a lot of good reasons for it. Our busy lives are demanding, often requiring two jobs or long gig-economy hours at home. Money's tight, and dating isn't cheap. It's also easy to reason that the courtship phase of the relationship is over, and all that energy naturally goes elsewhere.

But it's crucial to keep your lives amusing. Working too hard and too long has proven effects on physical and mental health. It leads to feeling of burnout, isolation, depression, overthinking, perfectionism, poor diet and sleeping habits, even premature death.

And it's important to amuse yourselves together, embark on activities which will draw and keep you together. So, while separate vacations have their place, it's not in this chapter.

Vacations together can be great too, a classic way to bond and create memories you can treasure. But vacations can also fail you in this effort, so let's take a quick look at that.

You should definitely take vacations together, don't get me wrong. But you can't take a vacation every week, and we're looking for things you can do on a more regular basis. You're lucky to get two weeks a year for a vacation. Also, as we've seen, people aren't quite the same when they're on vacation, and that can be a good thing. It may not be. Vacations can be stressful on a relationship if things go poorly or quarters become too tight. If you're having trouble with your relationship, it's a long shot bet that a vacation will correct those things, unless you're at a couples retreat of some sort.

Let's agree that vacations have their place, but not really in this section. Let's take a look at some things you can do in your day-to-day life, things that will bring you together.

Taking a class together is a great way to spend fun time together and get closer. There are any number of classes available at your local junior college or community center. You may have met your partner in a class of some kind, and that could instigate fond memories. It could remind you of shared interests or inform you of shared interests which you didn't know you shared. You may discover talents you didn't know you had.

Yoga is a great way to spend time together and it has great health benefits. Any exercise class would have the same benefits. There's also the physical charge you'll walk away with, all that testosterone and endorphins which will need release (and at the same time, too).

Meditating together will have a lot of mental and physical benefits, though meditating is a more individual endeavor. Unless you're concentrating solely on each other, meditation may not be perfect choice for a joint activity. It has great benefits though, and doing it together certainly couldn't hurt. It's just not that interactive.

You might think about a martial arts class. That's interactive and steeped in calming philosophies that are bound to inform your personal relationship. You'll each have a practice partner, a support source, and it will give you the same physical rush as a vigorous workout. You'll also get the benefits of all that wisdom and the ability to defend yourself or your partner should it ever be necessary.

Massage classes are an amazing way to spend time together in this manner. It's a joint activity which creates a mutual focus and is physically invigorating. And massage has a benefit few of these other classes, and that's the necessary intimacy involved. You're touching parts of the other's body which most don't ever touch (and may likely never even see). You're touching deep, creating sensations which go straight through the body and into the mind. You are bringing calm and healing. It's practically a type of foreplay (and very often winds up being just that). You'll also learn a lot about the human body, which is a fascinating subject. So, your brain will be excited even as you are a force for relaxation and calm. You'll be able to use your new skills on your family and friends, and you'll be the most popular person in the room. If your boss has a kink in his or her neck, it may even help your career. It's a great thing to practice at home, and think how good it will feel to have all those massages.

You might consider a language class. You'll each have a ready practice partner, and you'll get all the benefits of learning a new language. That excites the brain, sharpens your thought processes, and stimulates the synapses. Learning a second language can be a real career boon too. Being bilingual makes you much more valuable in any number of industries. It could be just what you need for that promotion you've been hoping and working for.

Dance classes are very popular among couples, and for good reason. They include a vigorous workout, they encourage teamwork, they put the dancers' focus on each other. Dance classes can be a lot of fun, and you don't have to be great at it. But you may discover a talent you didn't know you had. Being a good dancer does instill confidence and a certain personal style. Men and women who can dance carry themselves differently.

There are classes for all styles too; tango, flamenco, ballroom, swing, line dancing, modern, tap. Dancing has very sexual overtones too, as hips sway and shoulders roll. It could be just what you need to keep things intimate and frequent.

Some couples enjoy fencing as a hobby. It's physically vigorous, requires hand-eye co-ordination, it pulls the focus of one onto the other. It has the competitive edge of sport the way the others don't, and it's a neat thing to talk about at parties. Tennis, racquetball, even ping pong would have the same positive effects. Tennis may be a bit hard on the joints, but ping pong's pretty harmless. I don't know that you can take ping pong classes the way you can take tennis lessons, but you can still just buy a ping pong table and start playing. It's fun and funny and will give time focused positively on each other.

Art classes are always fun. Painting or drawing are calming activities which, like meditation, draws focus away from the clamor of life. Creative minds are more active. Creativity is one of the signs of a self-actualized person and a growth mindset, which is a key facet of a successful person.

But it's also an activity that you can physically share. Set up your easels next to each other, support each other's work, learn from one another. You're working toward the same goal; you're spending time without fighting or complaining. You may discover a hidden talent or sharpen old skills. If you're handy with a brush or pen, you can show off for your partner, impress them again, the way you did when you met. That alone may be helpful.

Also, painting is a great exercise in goal-setting to achieve an ultimate goal. And you'll have the satisfaction not only of having achieved a goal (painting a painting) but you'll have the satisfaction of having created a piece of artwork. Art has a tremendous positive energy, and so does creating it. Sharing that positive energy can only be good for any relationship.

As long as we're talking about art classes, pottery or sculpture can be a great pastime. The clay is slick and yielding and tactile. You remember the movie *Ghost,* right? If not, go to YouTube and search *ghost pottery* scene and you'll get the picture.

Cooking classes are a fantastic way to spend time together. It requires teamwork, preparation, and creativity. Cooking appeals to all the senses; touching the food, tasting, smelling, hearing the sizzle and crackle, savoring the colors and presentation. It's a great exercise in breaking one big task down into little tasks, each milestone featuring its own small reward on your way to the satisfaction of the final meal.

You also get to eat the meal, which is its own satisfaction. You can happily practice at home, and all that proximity, combined with the sensual delights of the culinary arts, is famously romantic. Countless movies have used a cooking scene to get the characters into bed ... or onto the dining room table.

Cooking lessons have other benefits too. Prepared food is cleaner and healthier. You'll lose weight and look better, and that will have physical and mental health benefits. You'll be more confident; people will react more positively to you. You'll be able to control exactly what goes into your food, make sure it's made just the way you like it. Cooking is an important but sadly neglected skill in our fast-food, pre-prepared world.

You can also clean up together afterward, more time to spend together on a common goal.

Acting classes can be a fun way to be together in a positive environment. Acting is a team effort but also a personal accomplishment, and it can be quite exciting. You and your partner can assume different identities, utilizing externalization and other techniques from narrative therapy. It's a good way to abandon your inhibitions. It's a great way to express yourself without feeling vulnerable (once you get over your initial nervousness). And since you're not yourself and they're not precisely your words, you may be able to express the real truths of your life in this way. That's what good fiction is all about.

Improv classes have much the same positive effects and for the same reason. Improv also keeps you thinking on your feet, and that excites the brain and keeps it sharp. It's okay if you're not that great, and you're not alone on the stage so you'll always have support (that's one of the tenants of improv). And improv classes are all over the place, so they won't be hard to find. They won't be expensive either.

Stand-up comedy classes are common too. Unless you're doing a doubles act, you'll be working alone. But if you both do it, you'll be there to support the other, you'll be able to guide each other, work on material together (which you can't do with improv).

You might try a writing class. Writing is also a fairly isolated activity, but it's frequently done by two people. I've collaborated several times with great results. And the practice often strengthened my relationship with my collaborators. Writing is challenging, requires breaking one big task down into smaller milestones, it's a team effort. It's something you can set a timeline for, an activity which can take as long or as short as you can reasonably manage. You can write fiction or nonfiction in any one of countless subgenres. Whatever you enjoy, you can write.

Or you can take the same class but write different projects, each reading the other's for guidance and support. That can sometimes be tricky, giving notes to a writer. But it's a great way to apply some of the communication exercises and techniques you've learned from this book.

Poetry classes are also a superb way to spend time together. Poetry is famously romantic, and for good reason. It can be a fascinating subject; it's filled with history and colorful figures. It's reflective and meditative, and it may allow you to express things in ways you couldn't do before.

Mixology classes are always fun for couples. You'll learn to make all the most popular drinks, which will make you great fun at parties (but watch out you don't get stuck behind the bar). It's a fun thing to practice together, even if you don't drink! They're easy to find and fairly inexpensive, and you don't need a lot of art or sports equipment. But please ... mix responsibly.

You might be interested in a home improvement course. Even if you're not a DIY-type in general, it does reconnect a couple with their home, so important for a stable psyche and a happy life. You could pick up skills that save you a lot of money down the line. And you may come out of it with a nice table or spice rack.

Maybe a Kama Sutra class is what you need. The ancient Indian text is a masterpiece on eroticism, sexuality, and emotional fulfillment. The book is famous for its many sexual positions, and that alone could put the kick back in your relationship. Even if you're all good as a couple, things could get even better!

Along these lines, classes on tantric sex are custom-made for lovers. You'll have a (hopefully) ready practice partner, you'll learn amazing things you never thought possible, and you may just wind up a sexual superstar. There are numerous techniques, tricks, and aspects to this ancient school of sexual thought which has only recently become known to the common folks.

Classes are great and have a lot of benefits. But there are other ways too! Let's take a closer look at some other fun activities for couples.

8

PERFECT VACATIONS FOR COUPLES

We went over why vacations weren't the best way to clear up communications in your relationship. But vacations do have their place, as we've seen. And some vacations actually can bring you and your partner closer together instead of simply forestalling your lingering problems. Let's have a look.

First let's visit some of the most romantic cities in the United States, where a lot of us call home. In fact, let's look at the places you actually did call home!

You might consider going to one another's hometown. Meet their old friends, see their old haunts. Share your own! It's bound to give you both insights into the other's past, it may explain a lot about why the problems which have come up are still coming up. And nostalgia is a potent force for positive feelings. Any time you're together and the feeling is positive, it's a good time. Besides, perhaps it's been a while since you've been back, seen the old gang, shown off your awesome partner. What could be better than that?

Maybe Las Vegas, Nevada, which remains one of the world's most glamourous cities. It's packed with fun things to do, places to eat, hotels to visit. It's a place made for couples. The lights and sounds are designed to bedazzle, and the place exudes sexuality at every turn. The showgirls, the pop stars, the place is bound to be a boon to your libido. But don't keep looking too long! Vegas may provide temptations you don't want to have excited. Know your boundaries and your triggers. If gambling is a problem between you, maybe not. Otherwise, you can fly in from anywhere in the country and stay at some of the most luxurious and renowned resorts in the world. It's really quite affordable if you don't gamble, and even more affordable if you gamble really well!

New York City, New York, is also spectacular for lovers. It is steeped in legend and lore, a place where dreams are said to come true. It is the living, breathing personification of the American dream, and it's empowering just to be there.

Sure, the big apple can be intimidating, but it is swarming with great hotels and some of the world's best restaurants. And Manhattan has delights all year around; Spring in Central Park, Christmas on Fifth Avenue, Autumn uptown, summers off the Hudson River. There's really no other American city like it, and it may inspire you to new depths of mutual understanding.

Broadway shows and museums are great ways to spend time together while broadening your horizons. Museums are a great way to spend time together back home too, and though you may not have as many Broadway shows, you've probably got some community theater.

Yosemite National Park in California is gorgeous and secluded, charming and relaxed. If you're a rock climber, another pursuit a lot of couples share, this is the place for you. But for others, there's the amazing wildlife, lush forestry, and of course the big rock face, *El Capitan*. Hiking, skiing, biking, there are all manner of fun couples' activities. It's a photographer's dream, and that's another great way to get closer to one another. Photography is creative and still physical. It's a personal experience but can be easily shared. Each supports the other, the brain and body are activated. The focus is not necessarily on one another, but it's a meditative practice which provides great personal satisfaction. And with digital photography, it's much more affordable than ever before, and you'd be surprised at the results you may come up with.

Wyoming's Yellowstone National Park features over 2 million acres of gorgeous wildlife and the famous geysers Steamboat and Old Faithful. The Lake Yellowstone Hotel & Cabins is the the oldest hotel in any national park and features a stunning view of the lake.

Where else can you take a safari searching for large herds of bison and possible sightings of elk, gray wolves, and pronghorns. Cody, a frontier town, brings you back to a different time, when the town was founded by Buffalo Bill Cody.

Santa Fe, New Mexico may not be on your list of great places, but it's truly great for partners. Not only are the skies and desert landscapes breathtaking, but the town is also an artist's enclave. It is packed with galleries featuring stunning paintings, pottery, sculpture. There are lots of top-notch restaurants and a healthy community theater scene too.

The mysterious spiral staircase of the Chapel Loretto and the Georgia O'Keeffe Museum are not to be missed!

Savannah, Georgia is charming, Spanish moss hanging from the old oak trees, historic town squares and stately mansions. The weather is warm year around, and the restaurants and nightclubs are among the country's best. Forsyth Park, River Street and a walking ghost tour make Savannah a fun and romantic excursion to the American South.

Unlike the more popular islands and cities of Hawaii, Molokai enjoys a slow pace and less touristy feel. Called the friendly isle, Molokai gives any couple time to reconnect in the splendor of the tropics without being crowded with tourists and mega-resorts. Hiking through Halawa Valley, staying at the Hotel Molokai, canoeing, picking flowers for a handmade lei; this is about as romantic as it gets.

With its soaring cliffs, craggy caves, waterfalls, and lush forests, Ohio's Hocking Hills remains among one of the American Midwest's premiere destinations. Old Man's Falls and Ash Cave are highlights of Hocking Hills State Park and are great fun for couples. You can zipline through Hocking Hills tree canopy above Hocking River, repel down cliffs, enjoy the cozy luxury of the Inn & Spa at Cedar Falls.

Snowmass, Colorado is a lovely alternative to the more crowded and touristy Aspen. It's a quaint, small resort town, uncrowded and cozy. With 300 hundred days of sunshine and the balloon festival in the summer is a colorful and fun way to enjoy each other's company.

California's Big Surf has some of the most gorgeous coastal views in the world, with lots of quaint little towns that are perfect for lovers. Julia Pfeiffer Burns State Park features the post photographed waterfall in the *golden state. Treebones Resort* is rustic and gorgeous, and the *Eselan Institute* provides workshops for couples!

San Francisco, California is one of the great romantic cities, with the gorgeous bay, the streetcars, and the famous pier. The delicious crab and incredible hills and the foggy mornings are worth seeing. Key West, Florida, is hot and tropical, with all kinds of boating and fishing and some of the best biking in the whole state. It's steeped in history and lore, famous for legendary figures from Jean Lefitte to Ernest Hemingway.

Historic downtown Charleston in South Carolina offers historic mansions, cobblestone streets, the sweet smell of magnolia in the air. It offers goat yoga classes (yeah, you read that right), the colorful houses of Rainbow Row, and the 500-year-old Angel Oak Tree. Don't forget Shell Island for a fun time searching for sea shells together. They're wonderous and pretty and great souvenirs, and the search is a great way to spend time together.

A trip to Lancaster, Pennsylvania is like stepping back in time and gives any couple a chance to do some shopping for unique furniture, rugs, and famous quilts of the Amish. Their food is rich and hearty, and there are lots of fun activities to forge memories while learning more about one another. You might try apple picking in Maine too, or in any number of states, you'll learn how pies and sauces are made. It's bucolic and seasonal, surrounded by the colors and smells of the changing seasons.

A trip to a vineyard is a great way for a couple to get away from it all. There's lots of wine tasting, fine foods, a lovely environment, and homey surroundings. They're very popular locations for weddings too!

This brings us to the relatively new concept of agro-tourism. This is the notion of vacationing on something like a working farm, for instance. You take part in various things around the place, learning the skills and traditions; be they table-making or tobacco processing. Agro-tourism goes on all over the world, and it may bring you to Israel, Ecuador, Costa Rica, Europe, Africa, all over the world.

And speaking of going all over the world, if you've got a little more money (maybe more than just a little) or if you're cagey about getting good travel bargains, there really are amazingly romantic places to go.

Paris, France is among the most romantic cities in the world. The famous *city of lights* offers one amazing experience after the next. The greatest art museum in the world (The Louvre), incredible sights like Notre Dame, the Arc de Triumph, the Eiffel Tower. The world-class shopping at the Champs-Élysées, the incredible restaurants, the winding cobblestone streets all make Paris a must-see for lovers.

Venice, Italy features the canals and gondola rides which epitomize the romantic pinnacle of Bella Italia. The ancient buildings and incredible food make a trip to Venice an amazing experience which truly cannot be replicated anywhere in the world. Gothic landmarks, St. Mark's Square, and Murano, the glass-blowing region of Venice, guarantee a memorable stay.

Santorini is considered the jewel of the Greek Isles, with white buildings and jagged cliffs and azure waters of the Aegean Sea.

Thailand's Krabi offers incredible blue water, delicious and affordable flood, Thailand has become the playground of the rich and fabulous, with Krabi considered the most romantic of its many beach communities. Krabi is popular among twenty-somethings, which might be perfect for you, or perhaps not so much. But the limestone formations, mangroves, boulders, and a variety of natural wonders will be attractive to anyone. Boating, snorkeling, and five-star resorts make this one of the most romantic destinations around.

South Africa's Sabi Sands Game Reserve gives couples a chance to see a world they could likely only imagine. Find a leopard in a tree or a diamond in the rough, or just rediscover each other, a genuine African safari is a bucket-list item for a lot of people, and seeing all that majestic wildlife in its natural habitat can be a life-changing experience. Surely there is little that gives us a feeling of being intrepid and adventurous. No guns though, please. Take a picture, leave a life.

The Berkshires' Laurel Lake in New England is gorgeous and tranquil, mist clinging to the water. Early winter or even autumn are the best times of the year to be there, when the leaves are bursting with yellow, red, and purple hues. No place in the world is quite like it. Cozy B&B's, big, homey breakfasts with homemade waffles and syrup make this place a snuggler's dream.

In the Indian Ocean, the Maldives is comprised of 26 micro islands clustered together. Swimming, snorkeling, boating, surfing, amazing views and spectacular beaches, it's one of the most beautiful and desired honeymoon spots in the world. When you go, make sure to spend the day in Male, the capital, to walk the main street, Majeedhee Magu.

Maui, Hawaii, is much better-known than the Maldives, and a bit more crowded. But it features amazing sites and lots of things for couples to enjoy, including Kaanapali Beach, the Hana Highway, and Haleakala National Park, The Pools at 'Ohe'o (aka the Seven Sacred Pools).

Italy's Amalfi Coast overlooks the Tyrrhenian Sea, sharp cliffs and mountainside villas make this such a breathtaking region. Moderate climate makes it a great destination year-around, and the fishing villages and beaches are almost as welcoming and nourishing as the Italian people themselves.

Back in the United States, Aspen, Colorado has long been the winter jewel of the jet set, the ski town extraordinaire. Those gorgeous mountains and resorts have earned every bit of its reputation. The quaint downtown area features unique restaurants, boutiques, and even an opera house from 1889. And nothing beats on outdoor hot tub with your partner, especially in the snowy winter!

Santiago, Chile, might not have jumped to your mind when thinking about romantic getaways, but that's part of what makes it so special. Though it's not nearly the only thing. The

Neptune Fountain at Cerro Santa Lucía, the view of the Andes Mountain range, a big city, the Chilean coast. The incredible Plaza de Armas to the Metropolitan Cathedral is a one-of-kind experience. You can hike in the summer and ski in the winter.

While we're in South America, Quito in Ecuador is the gateway to the Amazon Rainforest, a must-see for anyone. Lush jungles, rivers teaming with piranha and snakes and caimen, exotic birds and monkeys in the trees. The indigenous people are welcoming and share the knowledge and wisdom of their traditions. Bathe under a waterfall, enjoy amazing local fruits and meats. It's one vacation which is certain to last in the hearts and minds of any couple. And it's so gorgeous and memorable, it really has to be shared.

This brings us to actual couples' retreats, combinations of vacations and therapy. Here are few of the better ones.

The Northampton Center for Couples Therapy (NCCT) boasts a fully licensed, on-site team which is dedicated to couples counseling. It's the only one in the US which does. It's known for a variety of restoration methods, including Brent Atkinson's PEX-T model Gottman Method to Emotionally Focused Therapy.

It's not cheap, but it's important to keep in mind that none of these places are. But if it's the right move for you, it may be worth the investment. All of these retreats run a few thousand dollars a day or more, and that may or may not include travel. It's part counseling and part romantic vacation.

Sedona Soul Adventures in Sedona, Arizona is as much about counseling as it is about renewal and revival in a spiritual and customizable experience.

Mexico, Texas, Utah, and California offer Life Marriage Retreats. The principles of perspective, commitment, forgiveness, accountability, and trust. They're designed for marriages in crisis and offer a hands-on approach over a four-day retreat.

Sonoma, California offers the Healing Couples Retreats for a blend of hands-on coaching and research-based interventions. They offer a shared group retreat and one-on-one private counseling.

Beautiful North Carolina offer the Marriage Rescue in Huntersville, a Christian-centered counseling retreat. It offers 3- or 4-day retreats and six months of telephone support to follow up. Their programs are completely private, which is what many couples prefer.

Kokomo, Indiana's Relationship Rescue Academy works couples through an incredible six-month course in an even-more amazing three days and all sessions are completely private.

The famous Marriage Boot Camp is as much for unmarried couples as married couples, perfect for preparing and educating the partners for marriage. It also services married couples in crisis.

Make sure to avoid retreats which embrace a neutral stance. You're not going there for a neutral stance. You need help and you're paying for it. Find a practice which will avoid hot-button issues. It's not about fighting, it's about *not* fighting, right?

Your marriage retreat of choice should respect your personal boundaries. Select a retreat that honors your personal goals for your relationship. You don't want to get caught up in a cookie-cutter approach, and that can be common among retreats which don't have private sessions and even some that do. You are individuals and as a couple you are unique, and you should make sure whatever retreat you select understands that.

Make sure the approaches are tested by research. There are a lot of fly-by-night retreats that will take your money and give you nothing but a lot of hot air. You'll want a place with a hands-on approach.

Try to choose a place that will offer practical follow-up care. You may have great success at your retreat, but the weeks and months that follow will be crucial. Without follow-up you may backslide into your old habits and lose all the ground you've gained together.

Now that we've looked over vacations and retreats, let's take that closer look at things you can do around your neighborhood. They're not as committal as a class and not as intense as a vacation or a retreat. They include all kinds of fun things which are perfect for couples, in crisis or not.

9

FUN ACTIVITIES TO KEEP THE RELATIONSHIP FRESH

The important thing is to keep your communications open and your relationship alive. Prevention is worth a pound of cure, they say. So, it's vital to keep life enjoyable on a continuous basis. It's important because it's all too easy to allow the negative things to build up; the time pressures, the self-doubt, the lingering resentments. And with our busy schedules, recreational things like things we're going to look at are often the first things to go by the wayside. A lot of us have so many responsibilities to others that we neglect the responsibilities we have to ourselves. But we have to be conscious and conscientious about how we spend our hours, our days, our weeks.

And if you've found yourself with some problems which have been gathering, these are good ways to get closer and clear up those communication breakdowns. They're basically all very affordable, creative, and are proven to work. They can be done repeatedly, in combination, and you definitely shouldn't stop at just one. Check 'em out!

You might think about having a no-tech day. You'd be surprised how much tech dominates your life. Between your smartphone, your computer, the television, screens are everywhere. And with the internet, there are endless distractions to come between you and your partner. Also, all that unnatural light is bad for your eyes, sitting at a computer for too long can give you a blood clot, and watching too much television can cause depression, lethargy, weight-gain, poor sleeping habits. So, shut it down for a day. And it's not like you have to go to an amusement park as an alternative. Have a house-cleaning day, another great thing to do as a couple as we've seen. Enjoy the quiet of the house. Have some small talk. Take walk outside, do some gardening. Read a book to one another, that will give your partner a chance to hear your voice in a positive context, wrapped around exciting words of romance or adventure. It enjoins you both on a fictive adventure without ever leaving the house. Or just take a nap; anything other than high tech. You'll feel refreshed, trust me, plus your house will be clean.

Making plans for your future is a nice way to get closer, because the whole nature of it is based on the idea that you're both still committed. It's also a great way to engage the Pomodoro method of breaking up a big goal into smaller, attainable steps. Those little victories will boost your confidence as a couple, just as they would in an individual pursuit or as when a team is involved. You might be saving for your wedding, for example, which means making a time table and a schedule, making deposits into the savings account together, researching locations. It's fun and constructive and keeps the two walking down the same path in the same direction.

A couple's massage is a great idea, like a mini-mini-vacation. You'll lay together and be pampered, savor the sensuality of a deep-tissue backrub, luxuriate in a mud bath side by side. It's relaxing and rejuvenating and refreshing. It's more than a date, and what more is that it's time you're spending together which is guaranteed to be positive time and leave you both feeling great. That's what you need to achieve and maintain clear communication and keep that hidden negativity away.

Going on a double date is always fun, and something we may find ourselves doing less and less. It's nice to see friends again, and to watch our partners connecting with others. Bonding with others helps a couple bond with one another. Other people may bring out things in your partner you've forgotten about; a little laugh, the turn of a shoulder, a surprisingly quick wit. Their flawed romance, seen objectively, may just look more fondly on their own relationship, which they see subjectively.

Stargazing may sound like an old-fashioned way to spend an evening, and it is. Perhaps this is so because our cities and towns are increasingly big and brightly lit, which blanches out the starlight from below. But there's always the rooftop, or a quiet hillside spot somewhere outside of town. Check the internet for a good spot. But it's really relaxing and romantic. Since mankind first looked up, he was gazing into the stars. It's the birthplace of all philosophy, and astronomy is the father of all sciences. Nothing can make a person quite so reflective as looking up at the stars. And when there's a meteor shower or something like a blood moon, it's a truly spectacular sight.

Along these lines, watching the sunset together is also a calming and bonding experience, and one you get to do every day if you like! There's oftentimes nothing more breathtaking than a beautiful sunset, all those colors streaked across the sky, changing right before your very eyes. It's almost meditative, and it's an experience you share with your partner.

Some couples write live letters to each other. It may sound corny, but it's potently romantic. And let's face it, there are some things that are just harder to say. Writing them down still gets them out, and it gives them additional power. Those words can be read and re-read, sinking in deeper each time. They're lovely keepsakes too, and could be powerful reminders of your love in times of conflict or crisis.

Or you could play naked Twister. I know, it also sounds corny, but like couples' game night it's good, clean fun. Well, maybe not so clean, but you may not realize that when the game originally came out it was lambasted by some conservative groups as being overtly sexual.

Unless you really swing, you might want to leave Twister on the shelf for couples' game night. But this is a great way to bond with friends and with one another. You get all the benefits of a double date while getting the stimulation of a couples' activity. Charades or other participation games of the sort (like Pictionary) are always great, and a quick search on the internet will handily deliver plenty of these to get you through the evening. Trivia-based games are perfect for couples' game night, as are murder mystery role play games.

Binge-watching a new series or having a movie marathon is always fun. That's a day lying around in bed or on the couch, comfort foods and cocktails, all the comforts of home. There is tons of content out there. But choose that content wisely. Classics and romances and sultry thrillers may all be good choices, but avoid argument dramas like *Who's Afraid of Virginia Woolf?*

Some couples like to make a scrapbook, which is a fun and endearing way to spend time together. It's creative, keeps the focus on one another, and helps you visualize your relationship, which gives it its own special power. This scrapbook, like your love letters, may come in handy later when doubts and suspicions come creeping up. A few nostalgic moments with the scrapbook could be just what you or your partner needs to be reminded of what's so right about the relationship.

Then have sex in every room of your house. Not all in the same day, necessarily (but it's something to think about). But you might make it a personal challenge to do the entire house over the course of a given month (February, perhaps). Don't tell your partner either, just let it happen. After one particularly romantic meal in the dining room, throw the dishes off the table and have at it. One night after doing the dishes, do it up against the fridge. The living room's easy to wrangle, and the shower is right there in the bathroom. Just do it. The spontaneity is bound to thrill, the change of environment has a big impact on the act (as we've seen) and you'll be certain to obliterate any sexual rut you may have fallen into.

Singing a karaoke duet is great fun, something couples do all the time. You can go up there and clumsily shamble *Summer Nights* or *Islands in the Stream* or *Up Where We Belong,* or you can really practice it at home and blow your friends and coworkers out of the water. It's a fun practice activity, because you can do it around the house, as you cook or clean. Just download a karaoke track from the internet, pop it into your smartphone, and play it anywhere. You may be a better singer than you think. Karaoke is a good couple's activity anyway. One person is there to support the other, it's expressive and there's no pressure. There's liquor too, if that's your thing, and often these bars serve food. It's like a date and game night and a musical performance all in one.

A lot of couples sext each other. This, of course, is dirty talk over a text line. Imagine sitting in a boardroom meeting or a lecture class to be interrupted with a naughty suggestion from your partner, and you return it right there and then. There's a certain voyeuristic appeal to it, it's a dirty little secret. How much fun is that? Some people send naked pictures, often very close up, of particular parts of the body, but we can't recommend that. The pics may come back to haunt you or your partner. Doesn't mean it isn't hot as hell, it is; we just can't recommend it.

Make a logo which represents your couple-hood and leave it on little notes or when you sign your love letters. It might be a combination of your first initials. My brother Eric and his wife Christine have one, a lowercase *c* which curls into a lowercase *e*. They wear theirs as a small tattoo which each of them has. I recommend Post-It notes for now, but hey, you do you.

Creating a new tradition is good, because it's predicated on the idea that you're both in it for the long haul, that you're building a future together. You might take any of these fun activities and do them on a regular basis and boom, it's a tradition. Sunday singalongs? Tradition. Game night first Saturday of the month? Tradition. It gives you something to look forward to, a goal to achieve together.

Silly though it may seem, playing a round of mini-golf is a fantastic way to reconnect and stay reconnected. There's no pressure, like karaoke, the worse you are at it, the more fun you can have. It's colorful and amusing and cheap, and it can really bring you back to earlier days, frivolous and childish, beyond the pressures and stresses of the world.

Some bars will have trivia night instead of karaoke, and that's great too. Everybody plays with every question, it has teamwork and pits your wits against the others, bringing you together. You'll learn a lot and you may even know more than you realize. If you've got a head full of facts, this is a great way to remind your partner how smart you are!

We mentioned amusement parks, and those are perfect for reconnecting. Chances are, you went to at least one amusement park when you were dating, and going again will bring back a taste of that honeymoon period. The rides are exhilarating, the whole experience is engaging in every way. Your brains are excited by the colors and figures and shapes surround you. All is cheerful, you're surrounded by smiling children and proud parents, which can only help you visualize your own future. If there's a Ferris Wheel, take it and then kiss at the top. It's a moment for a picture postcard. If you're lucky enough to have fireworks going off in the background, you're in heaven.

Bowling is a great recreation for couples. It's a physical activity, mutually supportive but individual at the same time. It's slightly competitive. It allows time to sit and chat and eat and drink. And there are usually pool tables nearby, another fun couples' activity.

Bingo is fantastic for couples. You play as a team against the others, so it's a bonding experience. It's mentally engaging without being too challenging. There's a competitive aspect, the thrill and rush of gambling and sometimes even winning! You may find it at your local bowling alley, actually, with automated systems on big television screens.

Riding a horse on the beach is great if you've got a beach nearby. That's something straight out of a romance novel, and it's like a tropical getaway that's really no farther than your nearest beach. If you haven't got one, a ride through the desert is just as spectacular in its own way.

Taking a spontaneous road trip is a great little getaway. I know we've already mentioned vacations, but these are more like weekend getaways. The key is to do them in the spur of the moment. Or you may do a little planning first and then just come up with it on the spur of the moment (as far as your partner knows). Either way, think about getting in the car and heading off. A road trip is fun and adventurous, and there are lots of B&Bs and places to stay, just for a change of environment and a change of pace. It's the spontaneity which give it its punch.

Go to a rock concert or big show. Make it a glamorous night, with a nice dinner and fine dress. Have a night at the theater, a play or a symphony, or the opera. Or rock it out with Paul McCartney next time he comes to town. A big show is a special thing, that makes it a special night, and that makes each member of the couple feel special, it makes the *couple* special.

Have sex in some exotic place. We're not suggesting you break any laws, of course. But an erotic night in someplace like Las Vegas has its own allure. One aspect of this is the famous Mile High Club. To join this exclusive number, you have to have sex in a plane (and that's all you have to do). Generally, a couple will each go into a certain lavatory separately, have sex, then step out one at a time. I suppose others may charter a plane just to fly around while they have sex in the main cabin. Either way, this isn't the most economical excursion, but it could be well worth it. And really, a flight from Burbank in Los Angeles to Las Vegas is only a hundred bucks round-trip, so that's two sessions for two hundred bucks, not much more than a hotel room. And you can have a meal in Vegas before flying back, refreshing yourself and replacing your electrolytes.

You might try making love while you bungee jump, but I'm not sure I can recommend that. However, the big B is popular among couples. It's something you do together, it's invigorating, and the rush it creates is bound to be powerfully impactful on both partners.

Handsome cabs are a charming way to reconnect and stay close. A horse pulls you through Central Park or some comparable place, the conversation flows as the sites drift past. It's like stepping into a different era, one of charm and romance.

Camping is always a fun time, and there are campgrounds near almost every big city or suburb. Getting back to nature is refreshing, a drastic change of environment. The quiet of the woods or the desert or the sea, the crackle of a fire, the way the food tastes. If you're near to a hot spring, that's its own big boon. It will leave you empowered in ways you've never imagined, that I can tell you.

Speaking of that, while you're at home, spend some time cuddling up by the fireplace. Fire is mesmerizing, it's warm and colorful and comforting. What's more romantic than cocoa by the fire, or a nice snifter of warm brandy, or a hot buttered rum, curled up and snuggling. It invokes a sense of heart and hearth; home, family, love.

Have you ever thought about recreating your first date? You can work it out ahead of time and surprise your partner with it. Take him or her to the same place, eat the same things, go to the same movie theater or come home to watch the same movie you saw together that first time. The power of the nostalgia will be amazing, but it will also show how much you remember that first night, how much you think about your partner and your relationship, how valuable it all is for you. That will make it, and you, more important to your partner.

Doing a jigsaw puzzle can be fun. It's an open-ended pursuit, you can't really time-log it. But you can spend a lot of time together working toward a shared goal. And you'll have the satisfaction of having finished it and having done so together. And you'll have a cool picture worthy of framing. It will serve as a reminder of what you can do when you work side-by-side, creating a thing of beauty despite the many little challenges.

And of course, there's the classic breakfast in bed. Surprise your partner by getting up early, present all the colors and shapes and smells of a hot breakfast lovingly prepared and presented. And make enough for yourself so you can climb in and enjoy it too. All of these activities are for both to share, after all. And speaking of activities which are for both to share, let's get into the next chapter. Do you really need me to say it?

10

SEX AND COMMUNICATION AND HOW TO BRING IT ALL TOGETHER

We've already established how important sex is to an intimate relationship. It is the most intimate expression of our thoughts and desires, it reflects everything that we are and very often everything that we hide. It's often memorable, though not always for the right reasons. It's the manifestation of our drive to reproduce. It's at the very core of our beings in our fears and desires. It reverberates through our organs and blood and genitals. It's on our very surface, in our skin and hair and clothes, faces and fashions. It's in everything we see and everything we're sold. It's the measure of our success and failure, beyond the mere money and power. We're obsessed with it because we're trained to be.

People between 18 and 29 years old have the most sex according to recent studies, having sex roughly 112 times per year, or roughly two times a week. After 30, the number seems to drop to around 86 times per year. After 40, it's just under 70 times. But that doesn't mean you don't want to have it, whatever age you are. Because let's face it, when it's great, it's *great.*

And no book about relationships would be complete without a look at sex. But there have been volumes written on the subject. There are volumes on the psychology of sex, the underpinnings of certain fetishes, ways to introduce those things into your lives. So, there's no real reason to discuss the psychological subtext of bondage or role play fetishes or any of them. That's a different book for a different time.

But there are some things which are independent of whatever you or your couple may or may not be doing. They're not about getting to the bottom of why you like what you like. As we've seen, you can't really control what you like, only what you do. So, if you enjoy wearing a red clown nose, have at it.

What we're talking about here is a way to approach sex which centers on communication between couples. After all, clown nose or nurse's uniform or what have you, sex can often become a very isolated and isolating experience. Despite being as physically close as two people can be, despite being closer emotionally than with essentially any other, we're often little more than two people slapping against each other in the dark. Even in that most intimate moment, we're often alone in our own thoughts, our own world. We close our eyes, we retract, interacting only physically.

So, let's take a look at some of the practices we can take into the bedroom which rely on and accentuate clear communication. You may also be about to learn the most potent sexual techniques you will ever know.

DIRTY TALK

Probably the clearest and most basic form of sexual communication is dirty talk. It can take the form of sexting, as we've seen, or phone sex, which was quite popular only a few years ago and there's no reason it shouldn't be even more popular now with the ubiquitous nature of smartphones in our lives. Facetiming is probably the future of that practice, but hey, whatever brings and keeps people together is a good thing.

But we're looking at dirty talk in person. It entails hearing the voice, your partner's and your own. It's about giving power to your feelings by speaking them. It's about the strength that wells up with language you wouldn't use otherwise. Because the first thing you should know is that dirty talk is *dirty*. It's not loud, it's not mean, but it's not polite either. But in dirty talk, you're abandoning civility, you're throwing your inhibitions away. You're communicating your deepest desires, your truest self; you're declaring, in your way you're demanding.

And because that language is so anti-social, it carries with it the thrill of rebellion, of wildness. When you speak that way, you're not speaking as you're civilized self, and you're not speaking to your partner's civilized self. You're speaking to each other the way only you two could. If a waiter or coworker threw some dirty talk at your wife, you'd be furious and (hopefully) so would she. But this is a private thing, like sex itself, something you reserve just for the other.

It also has a tendency to bring out the most primal aspects of our nature, that part which rejects the norms of society and be willing to do anything, anywhere.

I know what I said.

Next, dirty talk doesn't have to be restricted to the bedroom. Next time you're at your couples' game night or even at your partner's parents' house, try siding up to him or her, leaning in and whispering something like, "I want to ___ you so hard right now, take you in the bathroom right here and now." Then just walk away. Because you're not demanding that you do it, just putting the thought in their imagination. Then your partner will be thinking about it too; they won't be able to think of anything else! They may just pull you aside and make that happen, though you'll probably be as quiet as you can in that instance. Still, that repression of sound, that lack of communication, is a powerful thrill all its own.

But let's go inside the bedroom. Nothing is as powerful as dirty talk in the bedroom. This is true because we so often retract into our own worlds. Men may be doing math or employing other techniques to maintain their stamina, a woman may be trying to well up an orgasm practically on her own.

Let's also take a minute to discuss what dirty talk is not. It's perfectly healthy to tell your partner what you want, and what you want may be dirty, but that's not dirty talk. It's okay to guide a lover to where and when and how hard, and that's closer. But it's still to civil, too practical. Dirty talk is animalistic, primal.

Say how beautiful your partner is while you're engaged, in any stage of your lovemaking. Tell them what parts you like best, say those words with extra zeal and relish. Remember, these are not things you say to everybody all the time, and words have meaning. Search for and find all the meaning you can just in the way you enunciate the word. It also matters where you say it, close to the ear. It's intimate in every sense, that means being close. Part of dirty talk is how your voice resonates in your partner's body, that's what makes it such a potent form of communication.

And remember that they're beautiful in the dirtiest sense. Use the dichotomy of words like *beauty* and *gorgeous* with the sharp frankness of the expletives you'll use. The contrast will be mind-spinning, I assure you.

Let that primal beast in you rise to the surface. You're climbing to the pinnacle of ecstasy, not ordering a steak dinner.

You can actually control your own and your partner's performance by using dirty talk. Escalate your voice as the passion escalates. Increase the tenor of your demands. Insist upon interaction, don't let dirty talk go one way. Ask a rhetorical question, one about your mutual satisfaction, and demand an answer. Then demand it louder. Just the act of speaking, of hearing one's own voice, is empowering and creates a connection between the two of you during what might be an isolating exercise. Instead, it only brings you closer together.

VERBAL FANTASIES

Before we get to the more complex communication-based techniques (just be patient) it's time to talk about the communication-based fantasies. How do they differ from non-communication-based fantasies? Beyond simply dirty talk, these fantasies require communication in order to take their proper effect. For example, a threesome is a popular fantasy for a lot of couples and individuals alike, but it doesn't require any real communication, just three willing people. Likewise, a bondage fantasy may require no communication at all (just consent).

The soul mate fantasy, on the other hand, hinges on communicating, on speaking. Here, the dirty talk isn't used merely to excite and flatter, but you're taking a subtle kind of control over your lover's mind. And that's powerful communication.

The soul mate fantasy is simple. You're already using your dirty talking skills to drive them into a physical and mental state of ecstasy. But then you turn your dirty talk away from the superficial and toward the soulful. You're not going backward into the romantic, that's not what I mean. You've already flattered and engaged them. Now is the time to tell them that you're meant to be together, that you fell in love with him or her the moment you saw them (or whenever that was, there's no need to lie). Say that you're soulmates, that you'll always be soulmates. Make sure you get an answer and one in the affirmative. It will only really work when they respond in the affirmative. Just as you have to say it in order for the other to believe it, your partner must say it in order for him or her to believe it.

Same thing for the pregnancy fantasy. In this fantasy, you're building toward creating a pregnancy. As you make love, you cajole your love to admit that they desire to have a child with you (you can do this even if you're the female partner). You work them up, tell them how much they need it, demand they answer you. If they deny it, challenge them, assert your growing personal power.

Tell them that you can feel that it's going to happen, you can feel all that energy building up in both of you, new life ready to explode. Tell your partner how great the child will be, how perfect a childhood, that this young life will go on to save the whole world! Tell your partner that they're the only person who could make it happen, that your pairing is the only magical one which can create this life.

Give it power by giving it words, by giving voice to it. That will be infectious and it will carry from one to the other and then back again. Your partner may even take over the experience, but once you've taken control you should hold onto it. It doesn't matter where you are physically, above or below, in front or behind. The center of the power is squarely between the two lovers.

But be careful with both of these techniques. When you can control what a person is saying, you can control what a person is thinking. And these two fantasies in particular reach down to the center of a person's psyche, two of a person's most primal desires; to be loved and to procreate. So do not engage in these fantasizes lightly. You'll get a terrific result to be sure, but you could also be making subconscious promises which you'll be consciously held to keeping. Anyway, it's manipulative if you don't mean it. Clear communication is open, honest communication. Lying is the exact opposite.

A variant on these fantasies is the virgin fantasy, wherein one pretends to be a virgin and the other extols the virtues of initiating their partner's journey into sexuality. From here we slip into slutty schoolgirl fantasies, weird incest-things, and other matters I'd just as soon leave to some other writer of some other book. Either way, there's little denying the powerful influence of verbal communication in sexual intercourse. And we're only really just getting to the good stuff.

VERBAL EXERCISES

Unlike verbal fantasies, verbal exercises are more intense, deeper, resonating far beyond any fantasy, as potent as they are. But these verbal exercises can be truly life-changing. This is as close as we come to the tantric models of sexual self-control, and this is only a brief visit to a subject you may want to deal with in greater detail. But in terms of sex and communication, you're about to set into the final frontier.

The first verbal fantasy is known as the *orgasm on demand.* It's a bombshell for women who've never had an orgasm, and this may just be the key. Because when you can control their language you can control their behavior, you can control their bodies, and then do what they cannot do for themselves or what others cannot do for them. And when you can do that, you've used communication to secure your relationship, instead of to destroy it.

Observe:

You're making love, slowly ramping up the energy and the passion. You're using dirty talk in order to excite your partner's primal, anti-social instincts. Your partner is answering in the affirmative, and the energy is increasing.

Now, instead of turning your attention to a fantasy, turn your attentions toward that orgasm. Tell your partner that you know they're thinking about it, that they want it. Promise them that they'll have it if they trust you. Demand their trust and promise an orgasm. Demand that they acquiesce. Now draw their attention to different parts of their body, tell them to feel their legs, their arms, always accentuating those parts of the body in your dirty talk ("Feel those long, pretty legs, feel that heart pounding in your chest ..."). Draw them from every part of their body until you've focused their attention on their genitals, the orgasm which will be lurking beneath it.

Tell them it's there, but they just have to find it. Demand that they do. If they can't demand they try harder. It doesn't matter, as you'll encourage them to feel it growing, feel it rising up and soon enough they *will* find that. Tell them they can feel it growing inside them, that you call feel it getting bigger, even if they can't feel it yet, you know it's there.

Keep the physicality of your intercourse strong, getting steadily stronger if possible. Tell them that you can feel it coming on strong, encourage as much as you can. Keep your partner encouraged to drive that orgasm higher, higher, telling them it's getting bigger and bigger. It will.

Then refuse them. Change course. Keep up the physicality, but tell her (or him) that you won't let them have that orgasm. Absolutely forbid it with every bit as much command as you used before.

Command that they refuse themselves, deny themselves even as your body works harder to make it impossible to refuse.

Note how crucial the act of communication is here, and how particular it is to intimate couples.

The contradiction between the physical inspiration and the verbal refusal will have your partner's head spinning around. Do not let them have that orgasm, whatever you do. Tell them to wait, to forestall it as long as they can even while you do everything you can to bring that orgasm to life.

Then make them beg for it. Make them beg for you to allow them this simple, natural expression. Because you've taken control of their body, their mind, their will. Demand that they beg and they will. Now, instead of being unable to have an orgasm, they're almost unable *not* to have one.

Almost.

Because you deny them. You refuse them until they beg louder and you go on driving your partner's body over the point of no return. They'll beg until they're screaming for release.

That's the time you grant it. In fact, you demand that they have an orgasm. It's happening anyway, so you retain control and make yourself the cause. Demand that they absolutely explode! Use all your dirty talk, the dirtier the better. This is a moment of blinding lack of reason, of pure primal instinct. It's the least social moment of your week, so make it that times a thousand.

You'll produce that orgasm, and if you don't keep going until you do. It will come in the denial phase. If it takes one or two tries, so much the better. Practice makes perfect!

A variation of this exercise is known as the *countdown to ecstasy* or sometimes *the 10 count to orgasm.*

Take yourself back to your dirty talk. Once you're both excited and you direct your attention toward that orgasm, you build up just a little bit, but don't go off the rails, because what's going to happen is carefully calculated.

Begin a nice, slow pace and let your whispered but commanding voice begin to explain that you're going to count down from 10, and when you get to one, your partner will have an orgasm. Remember you've got ten counts to go, so start off nice and slow and give yourself room to build.

Pause on each number, don't rush from one to another, but pick up the pace just a little bit with each descending number. And linger on every number, stay on nine for a good long while before counting down to eight and cranking things up just a little more.

Sprinkle in lots of dirty talk between counts, flattery and aggressive lust. You're in control. Don't be afraid to get creative: *"Seven now, angel, sexy seven ..."*

Keep increasing the base at a very incremental rate. Your partner will be likely to be focusing inward at this time, measuring their bodies and waiting for that one. Don't let them. Demand that they open their eyes and look right at you. It's an amazing power move, and it will keep your partner directly engaged and focused as much on you as on themselves.

Count down slow even as you ramp up the pace. It's the contrast of the frenzied action and the elongated suspense which will excite the psyche. You'll be getting closer to the final count, but you'll be getting to them more slowly, stretching out the time even as you deliver a frenzied pace.

They'll start to beg as you withhold the four, the three, the two …

Then taunt your partner, as for them to beg for it, demand that they do. They will, they'll shout out the number for themselves.

Deny them.

Go back to ten and start again. It's important because, like the orgasm on command, you assume control of your partner's orgasm. In this way, you become the only person who can control their orgasm, or give them one at all. They'll associate you as being the gatekeeper of their own bodies, their souls, their lives.

And why? Effective communication in an intimate relationship, just what this book is all about … life, too.

But sometimes your best efforts aren't good enough. Something more is wrong, nothing is working. Why, and what do you do next? The next section of the book will answer those questions and more. But it's a lot less fun than reading about visiting Ecuador.

III

THE HOW, WHAT, WHY, WHEN, AND WHERE OF COMMUNICATING IN A BREAKUP

11

THE ELEPHANTS IN THE ROOM

There are some things which can challenge a relationship and can be dealt with in a number of ways. It only seems right that we take a look at them here. They go a bit deeper into darker territory, things which may well spell the end of your relationship.

ERECTILE DYSFUNCTION

The old phrase refers to the subject everyone is aware of but which nobody wants to talk about. But if things just aren't going right, if all the tricks and techniques are still coming up with one of two predictable outcomes, it's time to just take a frank look at them both with frankness and honesty.

A lot of men suffer from erectile disfunction, or *impotence*. Some ED is common from time to time, especially in times of distress.

Occasional ED isn't uncommon. Many men experience it during times of stress. If it happens chronically, though, it could be a sign of significant health problems which have predictable remedies. It could also be rooted in psychological or emotional problems. Let's take a look at the easiest ones first.

An erection is what happens when blood flows into your penis. When it doesn't, you haven't got an erection, you've got a problem.

The most common physical causes include diabetes, high blood pressure, cardiovascular disease, high cholesterol, kidney disease, obesity, stress, age, low testosterone or imbalances of the hormones, anxiety, relationship problems, and depression.

Other known culprits include medications for depression or high blood pressure, sleep disorders, substance abuse, certain diseases such as Parkinson's or multiple sclerosis (MS). Pevronie's disease (scar tissue in the penis) or pelvic damage may have the same ill-effects. So will certain prescription medications, such as those used to treat high blood pressure or depression.

ED can be caused by only one of these factors or by several of them. That's why it's important to work with your doctor so that they can rule out or treat any underlying medical conditions. Learn more about the causes of ED.

Treatment will depend on the cause; it may require medication, change of diet, or therapy.

Some common pharmaceutical treatments for ED include sildenafil (Viagra), vardenafil (Levitra, Staxyn), and avanafil (Stendra), and alprostadil (Caverject, Edex, MUSE). Low levels of testosterone may require testosterone therapy (TRT).

If you're interested in the so-called *talking cure*, or *talking therapy*, you might look into a number of programs designed for this very problem. You'll be looking into anxiety, stress, post-traumatic stress disorder (PTSD), and depression. Expect to talk about feelings about your sexual well-being and be ready to visualize what it is you really want.

Symptoms of erectile disfunction include trouble getting or maintaining an erection, reduced interest in sex, premature or delayed ejaculation, inability to achieve orgasm (anorgasmia).

Of course, the causes may be psychological rather than physiological. A person facing the psychological aspects of ED may be prepared to answer questions such as the following. Ask yourself:

How often, per month, do you have sex and has this changed recently? How firm are your erections, and why? What contributing factors are there? Do you have erections in the middle of the night or in the morning?

What is the state of your relationship? Happy and sexually active? Are there any changes in that recently? Are you currently under a lot of stress?

Are you currently taking medications or using tobacco, alcohol, or illicit drugs? Are there any underlying conditions, such as a heart condition or diabetes or pelvic injuries?

Other diagnostic tests may include ultrasound to test blood flow, a nocturnal penile tumescence (NPT) test, injection tests, urine and blood tests.

Kegel exercises may be helpful and not nearly as invasive. Just identify your pelvic floor muscles. Do this by stop peeing while in midstream. You'll feel those muscles at work that's your pelvic floor. Now contract them for three seconds at a time. Do that 20 times in a cluster, three times a day. Kegels may be easier to do lying down at first, then try it sitting or standing up. It could be as simple as that. Guaranteed it will strengthen your muscular core in any case.

Around three hours of weekly exercise for roughly six months could also lead to a decrease in erectile problems! Boom, price of admission yet again!

Diet can reduce inflammation and constriction of blood flow, to allow more blood circulation to the penis. Fruits, vegetables, whole grains are all good. Red meats, processed sugars and full-fat dairy are to be avoided. Alcohol should only be used in moderation.

Herbs and supplements for ED include asparagus racemosus, dehydroepiandrosterone (DHEA), ginseng, L-arginine & L-carnitine, and yohimbe. Zinc and horny goat weed may also help. Talk to your doctor before taking any supplements or drastically changing your diet or exercise regimen. Some of these supplements, like yohimbe, may have dangerous side effects.

Some people use acupuncture to cure ED, but *I* wouldn't want to try it!

Much more attractive seems prostatic massage, which is a form of massage therapy. It couldn't be much worse, right?

Studies indicate that about 30 million American men have erectile disfunction, and it only increases with age. With each decade, the average of ED sufferers increases by 10%. But it happens among a lot of younger men too, largely for different reasons.

True, ED does tend to increase as a man gets older, but there are ways of dealing with that, such as a more nutritional diet and more exercise. Testosterone is the natural inspiration for an erection, and the body creates it simply by requiring it. It's needed to propel the body through physical activity. So, get some exercise and your body will create the fuel it needs for that exercise and for other exercises as well.

There are lots of medications and treatments available, but you might be well-advised to avoid them. Pills can have all kinds of side effects and some devices (pumps and implants) can have terrible results which cannot be remedied.

ED can be traced back to several common conditions, and controlling it could be a lot easier than you think. Here are the best tips and tricks to prevent or reverse erectile disfunction.

First of all, try to keep any medical conditions like diabetes and heart disease under control. Get regular exercise and maintain a healthy weight. In your weight regulation, focus on a healthy diet and not on binge fasting. Manage or reduce stress in your life and keep a close eye on feelings of depression or anxiety.

If you smoke cigarettes, stop doing that. It's bad for every aspect of your body and mind and is especially detrimental to proper erectile function. Excessive use of alcohol can have the same reaction. And keep in mind that different body chemistries react differently to different alcoholic influences. Same for drugs which aren't prescribed by your doctor (and even some that are). Some things just work against you in the end, if you understand my point.

FEMALE ORGASMIC DYSFUNCTION

Women, on the other hand, may be more apt to suffer from orgasmic dysfunction, the difficulty of achieving orgasm even with sufficient arousal. The condition affects between 11% and 41% of surveyed women in recent studies.

Women may have difficulty reaching orgasm due to contributing emotional, physical, or psychological factors may include medical conditions like diabetes, advanced aging, surgeries, or use of certain medications, especially selective serotonin reuptake inhibitors (SSRIs), which are taken for depression.

Studies found that religious or cultural beliefs, guilt, shyness, history of sexual abuse, depression or anxiety, lack of trust, stress, low self-esteem or unresolved relationship issues were most often to blame. A combination of these factors could also be likely.

Though the principal symptom is the inability to achieve an orgasm, other symptoms include unsatisfying orgasms or a prolonged period before orgasm. Even masturbation may not correct the issue.

There are actually four separate types of orgasmic dysfunction. In *primary anorgasmia*, you've never had an orgasm. *Secondary anorgasmia* is difficulty reaching a climax, even though it wouldn't be your first. The most common type is *situational anorgasmia*, when you are only orgasmic under particular situations, such as in a public place or during masturbation. The inability to climax under any circumstances, no matter how high the level of arousal or sexual stimulation, is called *general anorgasmia.*

During a scheduled doctor's appointment, you may be asked to consider a variety of questions, including questions about your sexual history. But that can be helpful, so trust your doctor and don't be shy.

Treatment will depend on the underlying cause, ranging from medication to the talking cure, depending. Couples counseling is a popular way to deal with this particular condition, and can touch on other parallel concerns at the same time. These conditions do often come in clusters.

Some people use hormone therapy, including estrogen and testosterone therapies. We recommend more organic remedies, if possible. There are over-the-counter supplements and arousal oils such as Zestra, which warm the clitoris and vastly increase stimulation. Oils such as these may be more than useful for masturbation and intercourse as well. Be careful about any interactions which might occur with anything else you're taking or using.

KINKS, PARAPHILIAS AND PARAPHILIAC DISORDER

A ***kink*** can be defined as a non-conventional sexual concept, practice, or fantasy.

Paraphilias is defined as intense sexual arousal by atypical situations, objects, or fantasies. Those who are turned on by sweaty socks, food, particularly strange roleplay fantasies are often-cited examples.

When that interest impairs a person's life, or someone else's. it's considered a *paraphilic disorder*.

Kinks are very common and most experts agree that they're generally perfectly healthy. You can't really explain them and you don't need to. Just about everybody has a fetish of some sort. And the days when these fetishes were considered anti-social or otherwise outside of the mainstream are gone.

You don't need somebody who shares your fetish, but you'd want a partner who'd be willing to try just as you'd be willing to try theirs, right? If you do find someone who shares your fetish, all the better. There are plenty of online sites for that, but always be careful on the internet.

Fetishes can be a central part of many healthy relationships. And a lot of couples try new fetishes that neither had enjoyed before. That's a good way to keep the relationship lively and it should give you something to talk about.

But it can be difficult to express your desire for such an experiment. A person is often bashful and embarrassed. That's what an intimate partner is there for, right? To listen actively without blame and judgement. So be open and welcoming and give it a fair hearing. If you're the one asking, don't be negative about it, or even bashful. Proclaim, declare, it could be a fetish which has always been of interest to your partner and they were also reticent to mention it. Make sure you are self-accepting and self-sympathetic. If you're not, your partner may not be either.

And while we're talking about declaring, if you want to try something in the bedroom, don't ask. Don't force it on anyone or do it unannounced, of course. But think about verbalizing it as a statement ("I want to try ...") instead of a request ("Can we try ...?") They can be resistant, but they can't refuse because you didn't ask. It's a way to retain power, and in this conversation, you may need all you can get. In fact, research indicates that couples who indulge in kinks also tend to communicate better outside the bedroom.

In the case of paraphilias, it may take more than trying it once. If you really don't like what they really do like, perhaps even need, that's something to seriously consider. You can't change it.

A recent Canadian illustrated that the fascination for particular behaviors is much broader than previously known. Over 35% of people surveyed, for example, were turned on by voyeurism, 26 % by fetishism in general. Almost 25% of the subjects studied enjoyed frotteurism (the rubbing of one's genitals up against someone without their knowledge or consent. Just under that same amount were fascinated with masochism, or self-suffering, and that proclivity was equally spread among men as among women.

Exhibitionism proved very popular, as did urophilia, when urine is arousing. Vorarephilia is the desire to be eaten by another being, and diaperism is the fascination of dressing like, acting like, and being treated like a baby.

It could be a gradual change from kink to disorder. It could be easy enough, for example, to enjoying bondage (a kink) to doing it all the time and need it to enjoy sex (paraphilia) to the point where it affects other parts of one's life (paraphilic disorder).

Diaperism and other age-related fantasies, can quickly dominate a person's life and become disorders. Grown women enjoy acting like infants, little girls, sassy tweens, can also become debilitating. This is because it's more than just a sexual act, but a lifestyle commitment which can affect other parts of their lives. Imagine a guy who likes to put on a leather mask and whip his partner. If he likes it, it's a kink. If he needs it, it's paraphilia. If he wears the mask to the grocery store, it's a paraphilic disorder.

But it's not so cut and dried. Some people are addicted to sex, and they do it with compulsion. These people are apt to shut over people and things out of their lives, limiting opportunities. And if you're partnered with somebody who has a paraphilic disorder, you're either in or your out.

Research indicates that paraphilias cannot be changed. But they can be understood and managed. Some use therapy, some use sex-drive reducing medication. Paraphilic disorders cannot be treated, and most who have them don't want treatment. Most are perfectly happy with their lifestyles. And nobody has a right to judge or change it. You won't be able to and you shouldn't try.

GYMNOPHOBIA

The crippling fear of nudity is a condition called gymnophobia. It certainly ranks among crippling bedroom maladies, one where things get real ... or so unreal that it may just be beyond your reach.

Gymnophobia often results from a traumatic experience, a form of post-traumatic stress disorder (PTSD). Sufferers of eating disorders and body dysmorphic disorder, a fixation on a person's own bodily imperfections, often suffer from gymnophobia.

Some people who are afraid of being naked suffer from eating disorders or body dysmorphic disorder, a mental condition where people believe they are ugly or fat or imperfect when there is little truth to it. People with this disorder often obsess over their appearance, hiding their bodies from themselves or others. Others could simply feel they do not measure up to media images of beautiful bodies and feel nervous about showing off their bodies.

Also, people with extreme forms of anxiety and obsessive-compulsive disorder (OCD) can sometimes feel uncomfortable about being naked in front of other people, due to the intrusive, compulsive thoughts that accompany the condition. Sufferers of extreme obsessive-compulsive disorder (OCD) and anxiety often suffer from this phobia.

Experts generally treat this nudity phobia as they would other phobias, encouraging gradual, safe, controlled exposure to the subject of their fear. A patient with this phobia might be encouraged to wear less and less when in the safety of the home, gradually working toward their goal.

These and other maladies could be the last line of defense. If these can't be overcome, if nothing you've tried in this book has worked out, it may be time to face the end. Let's take a look at the *how, when* and *where,* of that.

12

WHY, WHEN, WHAT, AND HOW TO END IT GRACEFULLY

You've tried everything, but the problems go on and they may even be getting worse. In that sad case, it may be time to face the facts. Not every pairing is a good one. Sometimes people really are incompatible. One or both of you may have problems which require serious treatment outside of a couple situation. It could simply be a matter of selection, not rejection. But it's important to understand this event as clearly as you can so you can handle it and yourself in the best manner possible.

Breakups can be rough, there's no doubt, sometimes very rough. So, you owe it to yourself and your partner to handle the event with grace and calm. Nobody wants to be the one who freaks out when the end comes. Nobody wants to endure that kind of emotional baggage or walk away miserable.

And, as is the beginning and the body of the relationship is key. Unfortunately, communication hasn't helped you in this case, but you can still do your best.

The first thing to avoid is self-blame. If you've used the techniques in this book, then you've done a lot more than most. You've certainly done all you can do (unless you're not being completely honest with yourself, but that's on you). But being left by an intimate partner can easily leave a person feeling doubtful, insecure, consumed by negative self-talk, and overthinking. And this can be crippling. A person may spend days, weeks, months, even years wondering what they could have said or shouldn't have said, what might have been if only they were more of this or less of that. A person may become fixed-minded and project a pattern of rejection into the future, be fatalistically certain that they're doomed to rejection. One may be prone to think they've lost their last, best chance at happiness.

This creates a downward spiral of career stagnation or even career loss, further self-loathing reinforced by the continued failure it inspires. Opportunities missed create more overthinking and the anxiety that goes along with it.

The effects of this can be crippling, even deadly, as they commonly lead to depression, poor sleeping habits and diet, substance abuse, and suicide.

It's vital to avoid this. There will be some unfortunate emotion involved, yes. And it's important not to suppress that emotion. Emotions are like food; you need them to survive. They're nourishing and necessary. But you can't carry them around forever. They have to be processed and the waste product expunged or else they will fester and become toxic and eventually they will corrode you from within. So be prepared to deal with the emotions and with the reason. But like a lot of what we've been talking about, it comes down to the *hows,* the *where,* and the *when* of how to do it.

WHEN YOU KNOW, YOU GOT TO GO

The first thing to consider is that breaking up is not always a bad thing. It's not good for anybody to waste time, energy, and money in a bad relationship. Relationships are meant to support us, make us feel more whole, more satisfied. Their place in the hierarchy of needs is fairly low, just above the basic needs. But if they're failing us, if they're preventing our self-actualization instead of helping us work toward it, then that's a good situation to get out of. In fact, being trapped in a bad relationship will prevent you from moving further up the hierarchy.

A lot of people fear being single. Autophobia is the actual fear of being alone in a room, but we're talking about people who don't want to live alone, or to die alone. But it's important to remember that the relationship which is ending is not the last relationship you'll have. Being single frees you up to be available to meet that new person, to go to new places and pursue new activities. Take another look at the things this book recommends for couples, and they'd all be great methods for individuals. Volunteer at a food bank, take some lessons or a class, take a spontaneous excursion.

Being single also gives you time to focus on yourself. Instead of thinking about what your partner is thinking or feeling, wanting or desiring, you can turn that focus on yourself. Be careful not to over-think or fall into negative self-talk, of course. Practice self-sympathy. If you can't help your partner, you can still help yourself.

As we agreed, some pairings just aren't good ones. But how do you know when the time has come to cut it loose? You don't want to be premature and live with doubts about whether you could have made it work if you'd only stuck it out a bit more. When do you know you've been hanging around too long?

Hanging around too long is a problem too. A lot of people may fore-stall leaving the other until after Christmas. But that mercy Christmas will ring sour in their memory, and it's not likely to be a very happy holiday either. They'll only wind up being miserable on Valentine's Day in six weeks anyway.

A lot of people say that there are *breakup seasons*, window of time that are better or worse for the breakup. They'd say Christmas is off-season, but the window opens just after the new year. It's open season on broken hearts until late October, when the holidays come around again. Nobody wants to be responsible for somebody's holiday suicide.

In truth, there's no good time of year to do it, so I'd say ignore all that. But there are signs you won't miss.

One of the big signs that it's time to end a relationship is that you're not acting like yourself. You might be more emotional or timid or withdrawn around your partner? That's not good. You won't be able to keep doing that, it's not healthy, and it's not honest. It's the exact opposite of clear communication, that's for sure.

Look for things like tiptoeing around or hiding things, over-monitoring yourself in your partner's company, feeling anxious and frustrated in your partner's company, worrying about being judged, avoiding eye contact, being dishonest or less than honest or if there are trust issues that just won't go away. If there are just basic differences in world views, social or political perhaps. These are deep-rooted perspectives which aren't likely to change and can be the cause of unending conflict.

If your partner is putting you down, ridiculing or humiliating you, it's time to go. That kind of abuse will only get worse, and nobody deserves that. These can be back-handed statements, sly little digs, or full-on bellowing diatribes. Enough is, at one point, enough.

And don't be fooled by the contrition which may follow. Contrition is a part of the abuse cycle; it does not reverse it, it furthers it.

We've mentioned hiding from your partner, that's bad. But it's no better when you're hiding them from your loved ones. If you're pulling back from them, it could be for any number of worrisome reasons. You might be depressed, a common reason for withdrawal. You might be ashamed at the way your partner treats you. You could be ashamed that you haven't mustered the courage to leave that person yet. Your partner may be a splitter, working to separate you one by one from your friends and family. We've looked at this and it's a treacherous play. If you're with a splitter and you've tried to correct this practice without success, it may well be time to end things.

Speaking of your family and friends, they don't like your partner, and I mean really don't like them, it might be time to reconsider. If you've been together this long and nobody's warmed up to him or her, it could be that they're seeing something from an objective viewpoint which you are missing in your subjective position. By all means don't let this be your only deciding factor, as it's your relationship and not theirs. But give it fair consideration, especially if there are other things on this list at play.

You may find that your own behavior is the problem, not theirs. And the nature of this particular behavior can be tricky. We've looked at abuses your partner may be heaping upon you, but you have to ask yourself if you haven't slipped into some abuse behaviors yourself. And it may be particular to one particular person, this particular person. If they appear weak and you have a domineering manner, you may find yourself getting frustrated and angry. And while this is a problem you should be able to solve, you may also have to admit that there are two sides to every compatibility coin, and you might not be the shiny side as much as you think. And maybe the other things about your partner may be right about you. You may simply be not that into your partner as much as you were at first or hoped you'd be. So, you may be self-sabotaging the relationship to prompt an end without having to put it quite that way.

For some newer relationships, one partner or the other may feel things are moving too quicky. Does one partner talk about marriage too soon, introduce the parents too quickly? Is one person too instantly reliant and clingy? The feelings which inspire these behaviors really should be parallel between the two partners, and if one is way off track of the other, it may be a sign that this relationship just isn't going to work out. The two are likely to react that way to virtually everything in life. It also means one may be unrealistic in their outlook, and that is a certain way to be disappointed. It may also mean the other is emotionally withdrawn and will consistently hold back and be resistant to the other's love. Through neither's fault, the failure of such a relationship seems certain.

If you're having relationship anxiety way too often, it may be time. At a certain point, you're not moving forward, you're just going around in circles. How do you know when you're at that point? Ask yourself if you're constantly questioning their behavior when they're not around. Do you suspect them of cheating or gambling or drinking? Do you seriously doubt their love for you? If you do, there could well be a reason, there probably is; and I'll bet you already know what that is. Do you constantly doubt your own value and what you're offering the relationship? Your partner may have broken down your self-image, or you may have withdrawn so deep that you know you're functionally dead in the relationship. There may be no coming back from that. Something caused the abuse or the withdrawal and those things are probably beyond your grasp by this time, at least in this context.

Along these lines, if you keep breaking up and then getting back together or taking little breaks, it's probably time to call it. There's a reason that keeps breaking you up, probably a family of related reasons. It could be insecurity, maybe a touch of autophobia, which keeps driving you back into each other's arms. Or it could be laziness or boredom or a fixed mindset, overthinking or negative self-talk. But no healthy relationship has ever been born of these things.

If you keep telling yourself things will get better, they probably won't. Time is precious and it's foolish to waste it with false hope or delusion. It's even harmful be caught in such a cycle, both mentally and physically.

If you constantly find yourself fantasizing about other partners, that's a problem. That's your subconscious mind telling you that you crave something else, perhaps not something better but certainly something other. And you may notice your partner lost in thought more and more, eyes wandering to attractive strangers or even friends and coworkers. Sometimes it's just a pretty face, but sometimes what you're looking at is the writing on the wall.

We talked about one person being too clingy too soon, but being too clingy at all can be a real problem. First of all, any couple should be the result of equal amounts of contribution. A couple is a union of strong individuals, but clingy people lack a certain personal strength. One shouldn't be relying on the other for company every minute, for constant emotional support. It' a sign of emotional stuntedness and it can create jealousy, paranoia, resentment, overthinking, negative self-talk, and can lead the sufferer into more dangerous conditions and complexes. It's a warning sign that you'll notice early on, and you may be best to avoid if you can't put a change to it quickly.

If you've lost trust, because they've cheated on you, stolen from you, or lied to you, think about ending it quick and clean. A person who behaves this way probably doesn't share your priorities at their core, and you'll never be able to make a good relationship with somebody like that. Even if they have other good qualities, and they're bound to. They'll do it again because they don't see the activity as intrinsically wrong. They may even blame you, for falling short or being fool enough. Do they even care that they hurt you, or do they simply hope to smooth things over until the next transgression? The cycle of abuse applies here, to an abuse of trust; friendly, angry, abuse, contrite. And without trust, there can't be any real love.

If you or your partner has been generally unhappy with the relationship of marriage for an extended period, years perhaps, think about calling it quits. Life is short, as we have found.

Sometimes lives diverge in different directions. New career moves may pull a partner one way. One may want children, the other not. People grow through their experiences, and they sometimes do grow in different directions until they're really nowhere near each other anymore.

So, there are real reasons a relationship may simply be doomed to the trash heap of your romantic history. But before you take the crucial steps and sit your partner down, take a moment to reconsider that not every breakup is mandated. There are times, in fact, when you want to sidestep the obvious trap of a breakup, which may seem more obvious at some times than at others. There are common situations which cause premature breakups, so beware.

There are lots of other ways you'll know your relationship is on its last legs.

If you're too agreeable, that can be a problem. You'd think the opposite, but easy agreement is often just another way of tuning out, not caring even enough to disagree. If this has been your pattern for a long time, give it some serious consideration as being symptomatic of a communication breakdown. If you can't reconnect, it's a communication crisis.

If your partner isn't the first person you share good news with, watch out! This is your most intimate relationship. You rely on and are there for your partner more than anyone else. If you're not sharing your triumphs and failures with them first, it means they're not uppermost in your mind. If you call your mother or your buddy first, that speaks to your priorities. Don't be willfully ignorant. Also, imagine how your partner would feel if they're not the first to know about that pregnancy or promotion. It can be seen as a betrayal of trust, and in a way, it is.

If you find yourself repeating things over and over, that means your partner isn't listening. If you've tried to get to the bottom of that (through the techniques in this book, for example) and failed, it may be time to cut loose. If they're not listening, it could be that they either don't want to know, are ignoring you, or that they've just tuned you out. None of those are acceptable for a long-term relationship.

If either of you refuses therapy, that's a bad sign. Even if they don't think it's necessary, if one of them does then it probably is. And a caring partner would go just in aid of the other. Refusal to do so represents a fixed mindset, somebody who is probably more fearful of judgment as a failure than they are in the final results of the sum efforts. It's not such a big sacrifice, and either partner could yet learn something valuable about themselves.

If you're staying out more often and avoid spending time at home with your partner, that's a big problem. Home is where you're supposed to feel most comfortable. You'll never be happy if you dread going home. Never.

Feelings of isolation and withdrawal are harmful, as we've seen. If you just can't beat them, it's probably because you're not with the right person. Does your behavior change around others? If so, reconsider who you're with. You owe it to yourself to consider it, at least.

If you've got kids and you spend more time with them, that's a problem. It's not to say you should put your partner above your kids, of course not. But you're not having an intimate relationship with your kids, so different rules apply. And you might be spending more time with the kids subconsciously as a way to spend less time with your partner, and that's really the problem.

The song used to say, "It's in his kiss." If the love is gone, your partner's kisses will tell you. A kiss is a very intimate expression, and it reveals much about a person's passion or lack thereof. Even a desire to kiss or an unwillingness to kiss can be very revealing about the mindset of the person behind those lips. When the kisses lose their heat, if one partner refuses to kiss at all or does it only with some begrudging quickness, that says a lot ... maybe too much.

Weight gain is a bad sign. It's symptomatic of overeating and substance abuse, bad sleeping and exercise habits. It can create depression which only feeds the cycle of misuse and increase the weight gain. This creates a downward spiral we've seen in this book before, and the results are devastating mental and physical health results which often result in premature death or suicide.

When all one partner sees (or mentions) is the other's negative qualities and none of the positive ones, perhaps they're only seeing what they want to see. If so, it's to reinforce what they want to believe, what they've already decided and only need to confirm; that the relationship is doomed.

If you've stopped talking about the future, that's a sign that one or both of the partners just aren't thinking about a future with the other anymore. In that case, there may not be one.

Hair loss is a glaring sign of anxiety and stress, and it usually comes with a very severe cause like marital distress. Don't mistake this for male pattern baldness and mistakenly blame your partner for this, though.

If you spend more time with your friends than your partner, or more time in a group than with the two of you alone, that's a big red flag. It means you're ignoring each other, and if you're still doing that after trying everything in this book, you might be through.

Digestive distress is a common sign of stress and anxiety. It could be that your gut is telling you something. Only you can answer that for sure.

BAD REASONS FOR BREAKING UP

Petty irritations are no reason to break up. Those can be dealt with. If the techniques in this book haven't helped, there are others which may. But petty annoyances are bound to pop up in any relationship, and if you don't learn to deal with them then you'll just be running from one relationship to the next.

If you're just generally happy, think first about the other things which may be making you unhappy. Ask yourself what would make you happy instead. Ask yourself a few if/then questions, reconsider what it feels like to be happy, visualize that, externalize it. It may not be the partnership which is the problem.

That usually does the trick to reignite the relationship and have some fun.

Another reason to break up is if your core principles are vastly different, or if your lives are going in different directions, but don't let the fact that you have different interests break you up. Learn about and partake in the other's interests, as you would do a couples' game night or an art class. That's something you can do together, and it just may broaden your horizons.

Even if you're both attracted to other people, that's not necessarily a reason to break up. I don't mean being attracted to all other people, or many other people, that's a problem. But a lot of healthy couple have so-called cheat lists, people each would allow the other to sleep with under certain conditions. Famous celebrities are often at the top of the list, people both partners know aren't going to wind up anywhere near them. Still, they're attracted, and that's okay if you don't let it come against you or between you.

Don't leave somebody over money, unless they're stealing from you (or spending you into the poorhouse). Money is a principle catalyst for breakups, and you're likely to have these problems with any partner you have.

Don't leave just because the honeymoon phase is over. That's when the real loving *begins*, not ends! Little annoyances you hadn't noticed earlier may rise to the fore, but they can be dealt with using any number of the techniques used in this book.

Along these lines, don't leave somebody because your partner isn't fulfilling your every dream. Your childhood dreams were probably a bit unrealistic to begin with. Unrealistic expectations are the basic building block of disappointment. And this is reality, not the dream-world. You may not be fulfilling every lofty expectation either, but it doesn't mean you're not a good partner or worth keeping.

Don't let fear of commitment keep you from further committing if that's what feels right. Fear of commitment will keep you running from one person to another for the rest of your life if you don't deal with it. And you could be missing out on great relationships in the doing.

But if it has to be, it has to be. The best thing is to accept it, learn from it, conduct yourself in a way which reflects the best you. Leave yourself with nothing to regret. You may even learn a lot about yourself if you handle the breakup right, and walk away feeling empowered and not depressed, growth-minded instead of fixed. So, let's look at how to break up with someone without destroying yourself physically, mentally, and emotionally.

BREAKING UP IS HARD TO DO

It's something a lot of people dread and probably rightfully so. It happens to everybody at some point, and yet we just don't know how to communicate during this often-traumatic event. Granted, it isn't always traumatic. Sometimes two people just agree it's time to give up the ghost.

Now that we've looked at *when,* let's look at *how.*

Breakups are as unique as the relationships they're ending, so the best we can do is lean on our new understanding and apply what we know. If you apply just a few of these tactics you're bound to have a smoother breakup and a smoother and shorter recovery as well.

Of course, there are a lot of variable factors to consider. Which end of the breakup are you on, the instigating or the receiving end? It's a lot different for the dumpee than the dumper, if you will, but each has a lot to think about when navigating these treacherous waters. Is the relationship turbulent, or have things been quiet before a final eruption?

Other questions have for forward-looking ramifications. Do you want to remain friends? Do you share a workplace or some other vortex which forces you together? How do you get over it, and what one wants to get back together? Which one that is will make a big difference.

So, let's get to the nuts and bolts of getting through a breakup.

HOW TO BREAK UP GRACEFULLY

Always do it in person. To dump somebody by email or, worse, text or message, is cowardly. You were there for the relationship, you should be there for the breakup. Also, only then can you offer the human touch that an email or other method, even a phone message, can't offer.

Be graceful. No matter which side of the breakup you're on, it's not easy. But it's harder for the person being broken up with. If that's not you, remember to begin with everything you like about your partner and don't be blameful. If you're the one being dumped, do not lose your temper or have an emotional outburst. You'll want to, but it won't help. You'll feel a lot better about yourself later if you remain calm and reasonable and then have your emotional freak-out in private.

Remember that the brain cannot be both emotional and rational at the same time. This is a time for reason, not emotion. So, fight it with all your might and maintain your dignity. It will impress your soon-to-be-ex-partner. And who knows? The future may take a turn, some people do get back together. Don't do or say anything now you may regret later (and you will).

If you happen to be in public during a breakup (which you should never be) then heed these words even more so. Throwing a fit in a public place isn't good for anyone, and it will only prove to your partner that he or she is making the right choice.

Along these lines, do not become destructive of the person's things, start throwing things into a pile in the front yard in a heap of spite and revenge. This isn't communication, it's lashing out. It's a violation of trust, because this person trusted you to not to destroy his or her things. It can have all kinds of legal ramifications, and it will obliterate any chance of getting back together. Even if that's nowhere near your intentions now, you never know. And it's just pointless destruction that will prove that you're not a good partner for your ex (or probably for anyone). Then go get serious help with your temper control issues.

While you're communicating during a breakup, try not to make the other person feel better. It's counterintuitive, because guilt and some shame will make you want to comfort your partner. It's no longer your emotional responsibility on one hand, on the other it may only make them feel worse about losing you, since you're suddenly so loving and supportive. And they'll resent later that you reserved all your grace and kindness for the end, once it was too late and it was of no use. You're showing them the best of what you are just as you deprive them of that.

Resist a final session of intercourse too, that will only complicate things emotionally and make the person feel manipulated and used, and that's probably the case. If you're not willing to just cut it off, rethink what you're doing and why you're doing it. It only forestalls the ultimate replay of the breakup scene anyway, and it'll only get worse every time.

Immediately after a breakup, you should cut ties respectfully, at least for a time. Give both parties time to adjust, to accept that it's over.

Contact may give false hope and prevent a partner from healing and moving on.

The problem is that you likely had a strong friendship with this person, though obviously not strong enough. Or other issues prevent the friendship from moving forward. Either way, you've sacrificed some of that friendship for the intimacy, and when that was lost some of if not all of that friendship may be forfeit. You can't ask somebody to remain a close friend with a broken heart and then have them watch you connect with other people. That's selfish and egotistical and hurtful to the other person. It's hard to say goodbye to one of your best friends, but that is what you're doing here. Know that.

Get advice before you do it, a friend of yours and not of your partners. That may be seen as going behind their back. You've got friends of your own, get advice from them. Then remember it when you're sitting down with your partner.

Recognize that it's a matter of incompatibility and resist blaming or shaming.

Do it quickly if you can. Don't let it drag on for hours, with the other partner begging or trying to convince you to change your mind. If you're going through with this, your mind's made up. You're not there for more constructive couples work or even therapy, you've (hopefully) tried all that. Now, just get it done. Don't be rude or frank or cold, of course, be respectful of what the other person is feeling. But you don't have to feel it with them, and you don't have to endure it. If they're getting emotional, cut it off. Advise them to calm down and to sit down again once they're rational and not emotional.

Be truthful; not blameful, truthful. The reality is more than either one of you as individuals, because the relationship was more than either of you as individuals. Recognize that, externalize the problems from the people.

Stay positive about your time together, but don't go overboard with it or you're likely to inspire an argument, a contest to your logic. And that makes sense. If the relationship was all that great, why are you ending it? Just be kind and don't let the partner feel worthless or to blame.

Don't ask for time to reconsider, because that will only forestall the inevitable. You've already given each other time to reconsider, you've been considering this yourself for some time if you're the one initiating it. But your partner may beguile and confuse you. Time to reconsider is only wasted time. And trust has already been damaged. The other partner will always be wondering how close you are to doing it again, what they're still doing wrong. They're likely to be defensive, withdrawn, inhibited. Along the same lines, you don't need a break, two weeks apart. You've probably already tried that and it didn't work. Besides, what you probably mean to say is you'd rather table the issue until it becomes moot. If you want a break, you probably have your next relationship in sight or already lined up. It may already have begun. True, it's a lot more convenient to come back two weeks later and explain you fell in love with someone else, rather than admit you were with them for weeks before the break. Things change, and isn't that convenient. Even if there's nobody else, you're probably hoping there would be, while you're letting your partner spend their energy hoping for something that's not going to happen. Your gambit may pay off, but it's more likely that it won't. Then what kind of scene will you be having, and whose fault will that be?

Just make it clear that it's over and try to move on. It won't be easy, it won't be pretty, or it wouldn't be ending. But sometimes it just has to be done.

WHERE TO DO THE DEED

Never do it in public. Some people feel this is a good way to make sure the other person doesn't throw a fit. But that's not true. They may still do that, and feel even worse that you lured them into that kind of trap. People know that gambit and they'll feel manipulated. If you fear for your safety, that will only forestall a violent confrontation later. Do it in private. If you live together, have a plan to leave them in peace for a while afterward to digest the news. Be careful though, because if they're going to trash your stuff or steal from you, this is what's going to happen.

Never do it at a family event, as this would be terrifically humiliating. Some people may reason that they have their family nearby for comfort, but that comes at a terrible price. And you'll find yourself a pariah.

This being said, sometimes a public place like a park or the beach may not be terrible ideas. They will curtail a person's possibly anti-social behavior, and that could be a concern. It could be that you'd feel more comfortable out of doors, where the tension between you won't collect in some small room. Feelings of claustrophobia can take a person in times of emotional crisis, and the ocean breeze is always a calming influence.

Another benefit to being out of doors and in public is that you probably met there. That means you can always walk away and then drive away. You're not leaving your possibly enraged partner in a house full of your valuable and vulnerable things. You're not in danger and you can control the situation.

If you live alone, do you want the person in your home or apartment? You can always ask them to leave, and it does put you in your place of comfort and power. But it also puts your partner at a severe disadvantage, lacking the home advantage. And what if they won't leave?

Meeting at their place gives them the comfort they may need, and you can always simply walk away to leave them to digest what's happened. But being in their place of power may empower them, and if they're in an emotional state, things may become more emotional.

A word about abusive people. If you're breaking up with them, you might want to take other steps. If you were or are in an abusive relationship, you were probably (hopefully) in therapy. Abusive relationships require that, if they have any hope of survival (not to mention the people *in* the relationship). So, consider meeting at your therapists and breaking up there. Your therapist will be there to moderate and ensure a peaceful resolution, if one is possible.

If you share spirituality in your relationship, a session with your spiritual leader or guide could be helpful too. These could be good approaches even outside of abusive relationships, if you're particularly worried about the emotional tumult which might ensue.

13

THE HOW, WHEN, AND WHERE OF MOVING ON FROM A BREAKUP

It wasn't easy for either one of you. But it's over now and you're going to have to deal with it and get on with your life. Hopefully, you're a growth-minded person who is ready to accept failure as a steppingstone to success. But getting dumped can rob you of that essential ability to see the positivity in certain situations and in life in general. And that creates downward spirals which may take you to the lowest times in your life, or even to the end of it.

So, the steps you take at this time will make all the difference, especially if you're the aggrieved party. Let's face it, it's a lot easier for the person doing the dumping to move on. In a lot of ways and in some very concrete instances, they may already have done so. You must do the same, to process the emotion and then let it go and move on with your life.

Still, that's a lot easier said than done.

WHEN TO KNOW IT'S TIME TO MOVE ON

Emotions will come first, as we're about to see. Then, before you apply the techniques below, you'll want to be certain that it's not just another bump in the road. Your partner could change their mind, right? *Right?*

You'll know when the time is right to get back on the horse. But keep these things in mind. Do you really want a new relationship, or to get back to the previous one? Are you ready to take the risk? Have you really left your ex behind? You don't want to bring any residual ill-will from that relationship into the new one. And you don't want a rebound, that's not fair to anybody.

But you don't want to sit around forever either. You have to push yourself beyond your comfort zone, you have to put yourself out there. Changing your behavior will have an affect on how you think and can reverse a downward spiral.

It's different for every person in every situation, so the only real advice would be to know yourself, be in touch with your feelings, and avoid the traps of overthinking, negative self-talk, isolation, substance abuse, and depression.

It's up to you!

WHAT TO DO AFTER A BREAKUP

The first thing that will result from the breakup will be the emotional fallout. Hopefully you didn't let it out during the breakup, you kept your cool and remained reasonable and rational. But you're bound to have emotions about it and you must process these emotions before you can do anything else.

A good way is to just cry it out. Have a few drinks if you need to (be very careful here) and then just let it all pour out. Nothing wrong with doing this alone. Remember that this is emotion, not reason. So, you don't need a friend to be logical with you or to talk you around. That may work once you're a bit more reasonable, but the first thing you have to do is expunge the emotion. Do it big, do it quick, and keep it up until there's no more left. Leave as little residual emotion behind to clog up your system.

Friends are a good support system after you've become a bit less emotional and a bit more reason. And don't argue with them about it, there's no argument to be had. Let them be supportive, don't plead your case. The case is closed.

Steady on, as they say in Great Britain. You may still be a bit depressed about it, but don't carry it around, don't wear your heart on your sleeve. You'll soon become a drag, and your friends may rightfully begin to avoid you (not without reason). When you change your behavior and change your language, then your feelings and perspective can change.

Do not contact your ex or any of their friends. Maintain that space at this time.

Don't wallow in your sadness too long, but don't rush into dating either. Rebound dating isn't really good for anyone and never lasts. It may even be cruel to the rebound, giving them false hope for a reliable relationship of their own with you. It's about knowing just what your needs and wants are, what their value is, and how you can get them.

If you'd hoped to be friends with your ex, wait as long as you reasonably can. Seeing them may easily cause a backslide into emotionally vulnerable territory. You want to be as strong as you can as an individual, or perhaps in a new relationship, before you revisit the old. Especially in the later case, as it could bring up feelings of jealousy and mistrust in your new relationship, and it could emotionally derail you and ruin a good, new romance.

But is it wise to stay friends? It's a nice idea to stay friends with your ex, and that surely is possible. But to call it tricky is an understatement.

Before you even think about being friends, the question comes to when it's safe to do so. Has it been long enough? I said this before but it's worth repeating. Stay away from your ex for a significant stretch of time. Come back too soon you never really got out at all.

Some people follow the *fifty-percent equation,* which states that you'll mourn a relationship for half the length of its total duration. If it was a six-year affair, you may spend as long as three years recovering from it.

Yikes! That's a lot of time.

But there's more to the decision than time. How difficult was it to move on after the breakup? Do you think you're strong enough to resist it or to go through it again? Have you really learned your lessons and advanced since the breakup? Are you ready to bring more to the relationship than you did before? Are you ready to correct whatever it was you did wrong before?

Because the initial risk of doing this is that you'll have to resist that old attraction. If your partner still does not, you're in for more pain. And though that may change, one of you would have to change significantly first.

There's also the chance of a possible mutual attraction. Unless what you want is to reignite the partnership, you don't want to sleep together at this point anymore than you do just after the breakup. It's likely to cause all manner of backsliding, overthinking, negative self-talk, doubt, presumption, assumption, false hope, and emotional complications. If you can resist it, do.

To be a friend of your ex is going to require that you change your perspective. You have to visualize, to externalize the person (your ex) from the problem (the breakup and ensuing separation). And you won't be able to act with them as if they were still your partner, no touching or flirting or presumptions of any kind. That means you'll have to find another way to deal with this person, one which is friendly despite the five-hundred-pound gorilla in the room.

If you're collected, calm, friendly, and funny, you'll be fine. Lean on your strengths and keep your distance. If anything, that will inspire admiration for your composure, and it will do wonders for your confidence.

If you're going to stay friends with your ex, make sure you always handle yourself with grace and cool. Never, never lose your cool with snotty remark, eye-rolls, huffs or sighs or other passive/aggressive displays. Your friendship won't last long, and you'll be letting your ex (and everybody else) know that a healthy friendship isn't what you really want and probably isn't really possible.

You may have grown up together. In that case, your time as a couple the first time wasn't necessarily the beginning and end of your relationship, just a significant chapter. But there was a significant chapter before it and could well be another significant chapter after it. You were friends first, and that could yet be the case again. In this case, and in others, you may succeed in becoming friends again, the friends you were before your love or the friend you were before your breakup. Those things are likely to survive, even if the romance did not.

You may even find you have a stronger friendship than before, a new and more mature friendship because you are new and more mature people.

OTHER WAYS OF COPING WITH A BREAKUP

The main thing about dealing with a breakup is communication; sharing just enough with your friends for a sounding board without becoming a pain or a sourpuss about it. Go to therapy if you need to, but first practice positive self-thought, keep a growth-oriented mindset, externalize the events from the person. Concentrate on the good and how to make things better. Set some goals and achieve them according to a timeline, with smaller goals set out in advance. Refocus on creative or productive things instead of self-pity or overthinking, which are counter-productive.

Keep yourself healthy with a good diet, limited alcohol, and physical exercise. Join a workout or self-defense course (or go back to the one you quit after three weeks when you were a couple), read a book or join a book club. Host couples' game night even if you're not in a couple, because this way you can be the gamemaster! Hey, it's *something*.

You might rethink some more personal activities, like journaling or writing a short story or novel. Chronicling your relationship could make a great story and help you work out any lingering feelings you may have. It's a tremendously cathartic exercise and you just may come up with a great novel or screenplay.

Purge everything of theirs from your life. No love letters, no pictures. It's more than just symbolic, it's important to convince yourself that you're not holding onto the past.

Make a list of your positive qualities. These are the easiest things to lose sight of but the most important things to remember. After being rejected, you may feel worthless and incapable. Take the physical steps to remind yourself that this isn't true. Keep the list where you can see it. Make copies and put it in a variety of places if you need to.

Go to three new places; drives into neighborhoods you've never seen, a city park you've never been to, a restaurant you've never tried. Avoid the places you used to go together; they'll only obstruct your progress.

Make a list of your partner's negative qualities. After your own positive qualities, these are the first things you forget but the most important to keep in mind. It's easy to remember the good stuff, but it was the bad stuff which ended the relationship, right? So, they were even more important then, apparently, and they could be of ultimate importance now.

Purge your social media life of your partner's friends, family, groups which you might have shared, your partner especially. Do not follow them on Facebook or go to their websites. Don't cyberstalk them, don't chat in IM.

It sounds counterintuitive, but you should let go of the idea of closure. Nobody really gets that. If you can't get over it on your own, no final talk will really do anything. It may even open old wounds or prevent new wounds from healing. Also, closure just isn't natural. It'd be great if we had it all the time, and we're trained to anticipate and desire it (everything from graduation to retirements to funerals are designed to give us this feeling). But graduation only begins other adventures, other studies and other, higher degrees of accomplishment. A lot of people go on to keep learning their entire lives. There's no real closure for them and that's fine. In fact, closure can be accepted by the growth-minded person who refuses perfectionism. It's the overthinking, negative self-talking perfectionist who can't get over a lack of closure, and that in itself is a lack of closure. Even if you get your closure talk, you're just as likely to feel unsatisfied, to overthink until you think of something else you could have said or would still like to say. Closure is a lost cause and a fool's errand.

If you're a spiritual person, this is the time to cling to that. There's great wisdom about love and relationships and faith and hope and doubt in all the great traditions. Be openhearted and open-minded and you may surprised at what you find there. This is also a good time for community, for some shared strength. And it'll give you something else to think about for a few hours a week, remind you that your problems are small in comparison, that you're part of something bigger, more powerful, more positive.

FINDING A NEW RELATIONSHIP

Assuming you don't want to go back but you do want to go forward, it's time to start looking for a new relationship. The *where's* and the *hows* of this are already pretty well covered in other sections of this book. Favored personal activities, workshops and workouts, lessons and classes; churches and volunteer organizations are all good places to meet new people. Friends and coworkers may have people they can set you up with. But be careful of this, as a fractious romance could divide loyalties and destroy friendships as well as romances.

And there's the internet, of course. It's chock-a-block with dating sites of every sort, chat lines and Facebook groups and clubs. Naturally you'll want to be very cautious about people you meet online. The extent of criminal activity there is beyond the imaginings of good-hearted people, who are exactly their prey of choice; lonely, heart-broken people especially. Guard your personal information, never give out your home address or phone number, request multiple photographs or a personal photo to prove you're not being catfished.

You can always arrange to meet somewhere for coffee.

No matter where you go to meet someone, a bar or a resort or our only moon Luna, it's going to come back to what you're communicating, to others and to yourself.

First of all, look to within. Whatever you need to truly make you happy has to reside inside yourself. You have to make yourself happy before you can make anyone else happy. If you're miserable, nobody can be happy for you. So, ask yourself what you want or need, visualize and actualize. Nobody can make you complete, and you can't do that for anyone else. You can only create a more complete relationship.

Live your life the way you want to. Then you'll find and attract someone who wants to live as you do, instead of somebody whose lifestyle preferences are wildly divergent to your own. You don't want to get caught up in the, *I love you, you're perfect, now change* syndrome!

If you're going to learn new things and expand your horizons that way, think about choosing those things which the people you're fond of or attracted to do. Does a person you like bowl? Learn how, it's not that hard; few things are. Along these lines, if you see qualities in others which you admire, adopt those qualities for yourself. Emulation is the way people learn from early childhood on. If somebody has a certain quality you admire, be it humor, quiet, boldness, reason, make it your own. Nobody owns these things!

Get back to the meaningful things in life. Bond with friends, reread your childhood journals, take long walks outside. Reconnect to the natural world and that will help you reconnect to yourself.

Take it slow when you do meet someone new. There's no rush. We've already seen the problems that can cause. There's no need to use a fixed mindset to presume how the relationship will go. You'll never overthink it forward, only backward. If anything, you might think about *under*thinking it. Don't assume control, but also don't be negligent. Just realize some things aren't entirely in your control, no matter how they turn out.

When you meet someone, you have a good connection with, allow that connection to develop and grow. If the person is a soul mate, he or she will also be into you, so if you both pay genuine attention to each other then something will develop.

COMMUNICATING IN A NEW RELATIONSHIP

You've been through a healthy period of grieving; you've engaged in some new or favored activities which get you out of the house. You're still wrestling with some lingering feelings, but that's okay. They'll fade with time, you're pretty sure about that. You're ready.

You've been sizing up prospective new partners and you've found one. He or she seems interested in you too, in fact they've made it clear. Now it's time to start dating again.

But keep two things in mind. On one hand, you probably haven't been on a first date or in a courtship scenario for a long time. You may not have been that great at it to begin with (some people are awkward in this stage). And you've been enduring a lot of other things, so you may well be a bit rusty at those awkward first few exchanges.

They're also crucial exchanges, ones which will set the tone for the entire relationship, if there is going to be one.

You're also coming off a breakup, so you're not exactly a blank slate. So, lets take a look at some crucial *dos* and *don'ts* of getting things off on a good foot!

First of all, do not mention your ex, not once. Don't mention any of your exes, in fact. This new person assumes you've had other partners, and hearing about them can be insulting to them, as if you'd rather be with any of them. It also sounds like you're bragging about how many partners you've had. And if you keep referencing your last partner, who broke up with you, that's a whole other sad sac of potatoes. It indicates that you're not really over it, and you're probably not. It's very offensive to compare a new date to an old partner, as the old has so much advantage over the new. It's certainly not flattering, and that's what the first few exchanges are for.

Speaking of flattery, don't let that be a one-way street. Women may be used to being flattered, but they often neglect to return the compliment. Men like and need to hear that too, and it's just selfish or thoughtless to neglect it to others. If you want a man with confidence, make him feel confident. And you're a hypocrite if you get snitty when you're not complimented if you don't share the compliments yourself.

Naturally, you'll want to stick to the standards. Don't lie, don't interrupt, listen actively, engage in eye contact with discretion. Ask them about themselves, direct attention away from yourself. Be graceful and generous in your rhetoric about others.

Don't rush things. Don't be too eager to create a life's love. If that's going to happen, it's going to happen. So, no early references to family, children, love, marriage.

Don't go too deep too soon. No confessions of past traumas on the first date. In time, but not on the first date. No emotional breakdowns. Don't be clingy. Be comfortable with yourself, live the life you want, have integrity. These things will serve you in every situation, but especially when you're making those crucial first impressions.

14

THE HOWS, WHEN, AND WHYS OF GETTING BACK TOGETHER

REUNITED AND IT FEELS SO GOOD ...?

Breakups can be rough, but they can also be handled so that things remain civil and neither party suffered needlessly. Time has gone by and you've moved on. Maybe you've had another relationship or two. You've come to grips with your feelings for your ex, you've externalized the events of your breakup and of your relationship from yourselves as individuals. And you've learned from your mistakes, become a better person for it. You've come to grips and any anger or hurt you may have had over the breakup and events leading up to it, and you have fond memories of your ex and the better times you shared.

You may even have managed to strike up a post-breakup friendship, reconnecting on some level, and that's gratifying. The parts of your friendship that were strong before and during have proven to endure, and maybe they're stronger now than ever. Or you may have made a clean break of it, for the mutual best.

But it's also possible that you retain feelings for your ex, that the notion of getting back together lingers in the back of your brain and your heart. It's not just the occasional flash, but something that keeps coming back to you.

Is it possible that you could get back with your ex? Should you? When will you know it's the right move, and how do you communicate your way through getting back together? Let's take a deeper look, beginning with when to know if getting back together is the right move.

THE FOUR RS AND THE FIVE STAGES OF REUNION

But first, it's important to note that any reunion, no matter how, when, or why it happens, is predicated on certain things, handily known as the *Four Rs.*

The four Rs, by the way, apply to both parties, no matter who broke up with who or who is coming back to who. Everybody has their portions of the Four Rs to shoulder in a situation like this.

First, there must be *remorse*. An apology, no matter how sincere, isn't going to do it. The cycle of abuse is furthered by it's fourth stage, contrition. What is required is legitimate remorse, a desire not only to correct the ill feelings but to change or eradicate the behavior which created the ill feelings to begin with. This must be more than proclaimed, it has to be evinced. It has to be honest. They have to express an understanding of your pain, and of their part in causing that pain.

There must also be *responsibility*. Real remorse requires responsibility. If you transgressed, it's not enough just to show remorse because you feel responsible, you must be responsible for your future actions. You must take responsibility and act responsibly. Don't repeat those old mistakes, don't fall back into those old patterns.

You have to demonstrate *recognition* of the other person's feelings, through calm and clear communication which avoids shaming and blaming.

And last, there must be some remedy. Making amends is one thing, but taking up a plan of action is the best way to make sure all that remorse, responsibility, and recognition goes to positive, constructive use. That could mean therapy, or just a commitment to certain techniques in this book. They're designed to keep things running smoothly and preventing communication breakdown and crises, the root of almost every relationship failure as we have seen.

Remorse, responsibility, recognition, and remedy.

There are also the Five Stages of Reunion. If you're going to get back with your ex, you must have a working knowledge of these five stages.

The first is the fantasy stage. At least one partner has likely been thinking about this reunion, fantasizing about it perhaps for years. They've visualized it, planned it, overthought it. This is the first stage of any reunion, the desire which ignites the reunion. Granted, there could be times when the ex-partners bump into each other completely by happenstance, both perfectly at peace with life yet who happen to be single and they fall back in together.

Could be.

The second stage is the re-introduction. Seeing each other on the subway or on Facebook, this spark hits the powder keg of fantasy, and a reunion may begin. Of course, it could be that you've been a coworker with your ex during the entire span between the breakup and the reunion, and you've gone through all the necessary healing steps in spite of that.

Could be.

The so-called morning after is the period after the great thrush of the re-introduction. Something's either going to happen then or not at all. This is where the real work starts and the real fun too.

You may enter a limbo stage, where trepidations arise and one partner withdraws. It's natural, and it can be dealt with if it's understood for what it is.

The fifth stage is resolution. Whatever the doubts of the limbo stage, the work of the morning after stage will help determine how things are resolved. This is the proof in the pudding, as they say.

So, realize when you are reuniting that you may be in a limbo stage, but that does not mean the resolution will go one way or the other. Be mindful that the re-introduction phase is thrilling but brief and that the morning after stage is enduring.

Now, let's move ahead and take a closer look at why you'd want to go back to your ex even after having failed with them before.

WHY GO BACK?

Make sure you're doing it for the right reasons. Are you truly longing for that ex, or are you simply lonely? Are you feeling old and lazy and sick of telling your life story to somebody new? Are you feeling like you're not getting any younger and it's time to settle for whatever you can get? You'll know if these are good motivators or not, and what your true motives are, once you employ some of the techniques in this book. Make a list of reasons to go back and reasons to stay away, prioritize the items on each list. The numbers will help you figure it out (numbers don't lie ... sort of).

Ask yourself what advice you'd give to your best friend. Ask your imaginary friend why they want to go back. Challenge them. You'll be getting to your true motivations, wants and desires. Exercise the *5 Whys* technique to discover if your motives are positive or if you're acting out of some misguided instinct.

WHEN YOU GROW BACK, YOU GOT TO GO BACK

In terms of getting back together, the *when* of it is crucial. You can't go back if you haven't been gone, right? You have to make sure that the issues have been dealt with, your issues anyway, since they're the only ones you can truly control. You have to know you've moved on. How long is that? At what point do you know you've made it over the bridge to the other side? It's going to be different for everybody. But here are a few things to consider.

It could be that the answer is never. It's pretty reasonable to think about getting back together, simply as a result of having gotten over a person. You can see the mistakes you made, the good and the bad of the relationship, the true qualities of your ex as a partner and as a friend. If you've made peace and abandoned the rancid emotional residue of the experience. And there had been a real chemistry there at one point, something most people long for, something that's increasingly hard to find, especially as one gets older and more particular in their habits and perspectives. So, it's pretty natural to be attracted to the idea of the relationship at its best, and to be convinced that it's within reach. That's the way human beings are, we're trained to try to achieve the things we imagine. And it's always possible and sometimes a positive thing.

Sometimes not.

So, make sure in your case whether you're just being nostalgic or unrealistic. Lot's of things seem like a good idea, but make sure this is really one of them.

Experts will tell you that the only time to get back together is if the issues which ended the relationship have been resolved. And that only makes good sense. It doesn't matter how much your perspective has changed if the behaviors haven't changed. Remember, whatever broke you up before is going to happen again ... unless those problems have been resolved.

And perhaps they have. These issues came up between the two individuals, but they were born from the behavior of each individual first, then in combination. So, if each individual has taken time in the post-breakup period to get back in touch with themselves, remained growth-minded, and bettered themselves, the recoupling could succeed. But the odds are against it, and it's tricky for a number of reasons.

Check these factors when the idea of getting back together pops up over and over again.

Make sure you've taken enough time to grieve. You have to process those emotions; you have to clear the residue from your system. If you're going back, you have to go back clean if you want your new relationship to be healthy. But if you've come through the grieving process and your longing endures, you might consider any possibilities which come along. Make sure there is a possibility first though, or you'll languish in that romantic limbo of longing.

Make sure you've identified your need or want and prioritize. Ask yourself some if/then questions about getting back together, visualize it. Be practical. Though they remain dear to you, were the issues you had simply matters of incompatibility? Your ex is not likely to have changed their core values or world view, and they're probably never going to; nor will you. It's possible, and it does happen, but it happens less and less as we get older (unless you're Ebenezer Scrooge).

Was this a toxic relationship? Was one partner abusive? If so, those things aren't likely to have changed, and it's just not a matter of when.

They never will change, so the answer to the question when must be never.

But if the relationship had been good for you and maybe you were the toxic element and you've learned from that and changed your ways, and your ex is still interested, it's in the realm of possibility. Make sure you really have changed and that you won't backslide into old behaviors. Some people may trigger that, and it's likely that your ex was one of them. You'd best have self-control and know how to deal with those triggers.

Strangely, some people long for exes who treated them poorly or abusively. They crave the contrition which follows the abuse, perhaps. They may have a martyr complex or a victim complex which require abuse. These conditions need serious therapy, however, and that should be engaged and the issue resolved before any serious connections can be made or healthy relationship created.

Has your ex told you that they want to get back together? That's pretty key. Everything we've just been over is predicated on the fact your ex does want you back. Even if you're friends (especially if you are) it's foolish to start planning a reunion unless you know for sure it's what your ex wants. The only way to know that is if they say it. Do not presume or assume in this case, mistaking the post-breakup friendship for more than that.

Only consider getting back together if you're sure that you both want the same thing. This is no time to go into things with different goals. If one still wants kids and the other still doesn't, that's still going to be a dealbreaker.

A word on having kids. Children are not things to be used as barter in romantic negotiations. You want to be back with your ex, but your ex wants a child; so, you decide to give her a child in exchange for a balm for your desire. That is not a reason to have a child, for so many obvious reasons.

It may not work, first of all, and then you're stuck with an ex and a child you have to pay for. I don't mean to be cold, but that ain't cheap. Do a few if/then questions to visualize what this could all look like; it's not a pretty picture. Then you may come to resent your child, which you never really wanted, and you may become psychologically abusive, or abusive in other ways. Your child may come to resent you, residual feelings from your ex. Custody battles are brutal on everyone involved.

And having children is one of the most challenging things a person can do. It brings all kinds of pressures and difficulties. Parenting has been known to destroy marriages on its own, never mind keeping them together.

Only have children if that's what you both truly want, then make sure you can pull it off comfortably. But that's another subject for another book.

Before you get back together, ask yourself how many times you broke up the first time. A lot of relationships don't simply end, as we've seen. People take breaks, or they reconsider and quickly come back. And this pattern can repeat several times before a (presumably) final break. If that was the case with this pairing, it's likely to happen again. Do you really want a relationship which is little more than a series of breakups? How likely is it that this won't be the case again? What's changed specifically to insure it won't happen again?

Have you both resolved your individual issues? If not, they'll come up again.

But if it's what both you and your ex want, and you feel the timing is right, the next thing to consider is how to do it correctly.

HOW TO COMMUNICATE THROUGH A REUNION

You and your ex have decided to give it another go. This time, you're determined to make it work. Great. But it's a difficult and treacherous time for both parties, and care must be taken when communicating through a reunion.

If you're going to begin these negotiations, and that's what they are, do it someplace casual. Unlike a breakup, this is something you can do in a café or favorite restaurant. Nobody's likely to throw a fit during this conversation.

This conversation more than most requires you use a lot of the same tactics you used when communicating through a communication breakdown.

- Be empathetic.
- Be Honest.
- Address behavior, not character.
- If you must address your partner's behavior, follow it up

quickly with a solution, which you should already have prepared in advance.

- When you move from questions to declarations, keep them about yourself.
- Avoid triggers and triggered responses and be prepared to walk away if you have to.
- When you *are* speaking, however, use collaborative language like *we, our, us.*
- Think before you speak.
- Be sober. Be kind; no personal insults. Be brief and don't repeat yourself.
- Be conscious of your body language, don't be aggressive with your gestures.
- Be diplomatic.
- Think good thoughts.
- Don't be afraid to apologize. It doesn't cost you anything, and it's probably pretty reasonable that you should.

In greater particular:

Keep it light, focus on the good memories before you move on to confronting the issues, which you'll have to do. But don't get bogged down in that, and start off on a strongly positive note.

When you're making it official and negotiating your recoupling, make sure you address old issues. Put them to bed once and for all or they will creep up and be problematic, probably sooner rather than later.

Make sure trust is secured. Clear communication can only happen when trust is strong. In fact, without trust there is no relationship to communicate about. If there were trust issues before, and that's likely after a breakup, this has to be externalized and discussed. It should be separated from the people, as in narrative therapy, and then settled. It must be agreed that trust must be established and respected, or there's little reason to move forward.

Along those lines, make sure you've truly forgiven this person for whatever's happened. If you're still carrying around emotional baggage over past events, they'll only come up again and probably recur. It also means you haven't truly gotten over it, that you're still healing. That means you haven't really reached self-actualization and you're not ready to rejoin that coupling.

As you should always do but especially during a recoupling is collect your thoughts before you raise any issues. This is a careful negotiation, after all, it requires diplomacy. Don't just wing it or you might blow it.

Share your experiences from when you were apart. You don't want any secrets at this stage in the game. And what you've done and learned surely has made you the qualified person to rejoin that relationship. Any partner would be interested in hearing about that. It may even be necessary to help instill trust and put away the old hurts, proof that you really have changed.

In general, take things slow. Moving too quickly might have been the thing which drove you apart in the first place. Let your partner be the more-excited of the two. And though you'll be excited at the notion of reuniting, there's no reason to rush. You've waited this long, and if the reunion is real it's going to last. Don't rush this.

Try seeing it as a new chapter, not a new relationship. Because that's what it is, and only when you're being realistic about who you are, who your partner is, and what you're doing, will you be able to create the relationship you could have had all along.

Make sure you're seeing things clearly, not through rose-colored glasses. That may have been fine when you were first falling in love, but you have to be clear-eyed and reasonable this time. No more unrealistic expectations which lead to disappointment, right? Right.

Know that you might not have everybody's support. Your family and friends are apt to be skeptical. But don't let them sway you if this is really what you and your ex want. It's your relationship, not theirs. But don't let it alienate you from them either. Reassure them that you appreciate their support but that you've resolved the things which could be and needed to be resolved.

Remember that you're not with a different person. This is essentially the same person you knew before. They may have improved or evolved, or your expectations may have changed, but you have to know who you're dealing with and how to deal with that person. Remember what you've learned about them and about yourself, and remember what you've learned from this book and keep those lessons in mind. Use the techniques to keep the communication open and healthy, or things are likely to go sour again.

WHEN A REUNION DOESN'T WORK OUT

You finally returned to your life's love, worked out all the issues, even employed a lot of the tips and tricks in this book to get and stay closer.

But it still isn't working out. Your friends are shaking their heads, *I-told-you-so* expressions on their faces. You may even feel foolish about undertaking such a thing, like a failure. And to a degree those things may even be true.

But the important thing, as always, is that you avoid negative self-talk. Separate your worth as an individual from the worth of the couple. Sometimes two people just aren't going to make it together, despite everybody's best efforts and intentions. There are some common reasons for that, and they should be familiar by now.

Keeping secrets is a big reason these reunions fail. Things did happen in the interval, and withholding them only creates suspicion, doubt, a downward spiral which is often fatal to a romantic reunion. Likewise, lying about what had happened or with who is a terrible idea. Lying is the opposite of clear communication, and clear communication is key to a successful relationship at any stage, this stage in particular, when guards are likely to be up.

Pushing things too hard or too fast is another big mistake. Sadly, most of these people haven't read this book! But you have and you know better. In this case, a romantic reunion is a big move and your partner may have trepidations. Rushing things only bears them out.

Ignoring the stages of reunion is a crucial mistake. Know them, discuss them, digest them, know where you are and what's coming up ahead.

Being insensitive to the changes in and feelings of the other person will kill a relationship at any stage, a reunion in particular. Lack of sensitivity is likely at the heart of the original breakup.

Ignoring the past is another reason reunions fail. People forget the lessons learned and backslide into their old habits.

Disrespect is also inappropriate, personally or of the partner's other bonds outside the relationship. This is no time to be a splitter. Those people may have been the support group who got your partner through the first breakup, their place in your partner's life need to be respected, and so do they.

Because people change over time, it could be that one person changed in ways the other simply doesn't like. Drastic lifestyle choices like veganism, for example, or radical religious conversion. People change, but not always to your taste; and the same goes for you.

It can also be that the old wounds keep opening up, that they'll never truly heal in the presence of the other. If this is the sad case, both parties should be able to recognize it. It's a sad truth that things cannot be unsaid or unheard, we can't turn back the clock. And nobody is doing anybody any good at all in refusing to face the facts.

If it works out the second time, that's great. If it doesn't, at least you gave it a good try and you'll be able to move forward certain that it just wasn't meant to be. Keep searching and you'll find what and who you're looking for. And when you find that person, you'll know just how to secure a healthier relationship through clear communication!

CONCLUSION

Well, it's been quite a trip! We've worked though the *how, why, where, and when* and *who* of beginning a relationship, helping it to flourish, avoiding its pitfalls. We've looked at different ways of getting through a breakup, of healing and growing, and even reuniting with that partner.

We've looked at your own deepest wants and needs and motivations, ways you might think and ways you might change your thinking. These truly are things you can take out of the realm of romance or intimacy and into the rest of your life. We've touched briefly on spirituality and meditation, and we can only recommend you go on to research those things further. We don't promote any in particular, but they can work in various combinations, like most of the things in this book. You'll be assembling a new library of skills and techniques to make your interactions go more smoothly and reduce conflict in every area of your life.

You've picked up a virtual education in psychology, hopefully having learned more about yourself and the world around you. That's the nature of a heathy psyche and a happy life.

No matter where you are in the romantic cycle, you've got the tools you need to put things right and make things better, to know when to walk away and when to come back.

Use this information in every corner and on every level of your relationship, and your life. You can do what seemed impossible, and you can help others do it too. And keep working. Don't resist the idea of coming back later and rereading this book. Unless you've used every technique, there are bound to be more things here you haven't tried, things you missed the first time. Think of this book and others like it as a reference manual, to be referred to whenever you need. There may be other facets of your life that could use improvement, or the lives of those you love. Keep reading, keep growing, keep learning, and keep living. Stay openhearted and open-minded. Stay healthy and be happy!

Printed in the USA
CPSIA information can be obtained
at www.ICGtesting.com
LVHW051113190324
774896LV00001B/6

9 781801 342315